J. J. Grandville

Public and private life of animals

J. J. Grandville

Public and private life of animals

ISBN/EAN: 9783337815165

Printed in Europe, USA, Canada, Australia, Japan

Cover: Foto ©ninafisch / pixelio.de

More available books at **www.hansebooks.com**

PUBLIC AND PRIVATE
LIFE OF ANIMALS.

ADAPTED FROM THE FRENCH OF
BALZAC, DROZ, JULES JANIN, E. LEMOINE, A. DE MUSSET,
GEORGES SAND, &c.

BY

J. THOMSON.

LONDON:
SAMPSON LOW, MARSTON, SEARLE, & RIVINGTON.
PHILADELPHIA: J. B. LIPPINCOTT & CO.
1877.

Contents.

PART I.

	PAGE
INTRODUCTION—	
INTERNATIONAL CONGRESS OF ANIMALS	1
RESUMÉ OF PROCEEDINGS	4
HISTORY OF A HARE	13
THE FLIGHT OF A PARISIAN BIRD IN SEARCH OF BETTER GOVERNMENT	35
LIFE AND PHILOSOPHICAL OPINIONS OF A PENGUIN	56
THE LAST WORDS OF AN EPHEMERA	75
THE SORROWS OF AN OLD TOAD	77
THE THEATRICAL CRITIC	88
THE PHILOSOPHIC RAT	98
THE SUFFERINGS OF A BEETLE	108
A FOX IN A TRAP	126
TEXT-BOOK FOR THE GUIDANCE OF ANIMALS STUDYING FOR HONOURS	138
THE INCONSISTENCIES OF A GREYHOUND	149
TOPAZ THE PORTRAIT-PAINTER	162
JOURNEY OF AN AFRICAN LION TO PARIS	175
ADVENTURES OF A BUTTERFLY	188
THE MISFORTUNES OF A CROCODILE	200
THE FUNERAL ORATION OF A SILKWORM	206

PART II.

	PAGE
DAILY BULLETIN OF EVENTS	213
HISTORY OF A WHITE BLACKBIRD	239
THE QUEEN'S HUSBAND	262
THE LOVES OF TWO INSECTS	268
THE LOVE ADVENTURES OF A FRENCH CAT	282
CELEBRATED TRIALS	296
THE BEAR; OR, A LETTER FROM THE MOUNTAINS	309
THE SEVENTH HEAVEN	318
LETTERS FROM A SWALLOW TO A CANARY	327
MEDICAL ANIMALS	344
THE GIRAFFE'S TABLETS	353
THE CROAKINGS OF A CROW	361
SOUVENIRS OF AN OLD ROOK—	
SUMMARY	367
AN OLD CASTLE	371
THE DUKE AND DUCHESS	373
AN OLD FALCON	375
WHAT ANIMATES THE HEART OF A CHAMELEON	377
HISTORY OF THE HOSTS OF THE TERRACE	380
LAST CHAPTER	384

Part First.

INTRODUCTION.

INTERNATIONAL CONGRESS OF ANIMALS.

WEARY of insult, ignominy, and the constant oppression of man, we, the so-called Lower Animals, have at last resolved to cast off the yoke of our oppressors, who, since the day of their creation, have rendered liberty and equality nothing more than empty names.

A deliberative Assembly has been constituted, with the

full sanction of the Great Animal Powers, to whom we look with confidence for that guidance and support which will enable us to carry out the measures framed for our advancement.

The Assembly has been already convoked. Its first sitting took place, on a lovely spring morning, on the green sward of the *Jardin des Plantes*. The spot was happily chosen to secure a full attendance of the animals of all nations. In justice to ourselves, let it be known that the proceedings were conducted with the harmony and good manners which the brutes have made peculiarly their own.

An Orang-outang, fired by his love of liberty, mastered the mechanism of locks, and at night, while the great world slept, opened the iron gates to the prisoners, who walked gravely out to take their seats. A large circle was formed, the Domestic Animals on the right, the Independent Wanderers on the left, and the Molluscs in the centre.

The rising sun, struggling through the gloom, fell upon a scene at once imposing, and full of great historic interest. No assembly of men that ever met on earth could possibly display a more masterly control of passion than did the non-herbivorous and carnivorous members of their powerful instincts. The Hyæna became almost musical, while the notes of the Goose were full of deep pathos.

The opening of the Congress was marked by a scene most touching. All the members embraced and kissed each other, in one or two instances with such fervour as to lead to the effusion of blood. In the interests of the Animal Kingdom, it must be recorded that a Duck was strangled by an overjoyed Fox, a Sheep by an enthusiastic Wolf, and a Horse by a delirious Tiger. As ancient feuds had existed between the families, these events were clearly referable to the power of ancestral usage, and the joy of reconciliation. A Barbary Duck chanted a solemn dirge over the body of her companion, who had fallen in the cause of freedom. Before resuming her seat, the member for Barbary made an eloquent speech, urging the Congress to overlook the accidents, and proceed with the orders of the day. At this moment an unfortunate Siamese Ambassador Elephant was about to propose the abolition of capital punishment. Being a devout Buddhist, he advocated the preservation of life in every form. Unluckily for his doctrine, he had placed his huge foot on a nest of Field-mice, killing both parents and children. A young Toad drawing his attention to the melancholy fact overwhelmed him with remorse.

In simple courtesy to the reader, we must state that the report of the proceedings was obtained from a Parroquet, whose veracity may be trusted, as he only repeats what he has heard. We crave permission to conceal his name. Like the ancient senators of Venice, he has sworn silence on State affairs. In this instance alone he has thrown off his habitual reserve.

RESUMÉ OF PROCEEDINGS.

ONE HOUR AFTER MIDNIGHT.

Nomination of President.—Questions relative to the suppression of man.—The members of the Left vote for war, the Right for arbitration.—Discussions in which the Lion, Tiger, Horse, Nightingale, Boar, and others take part.—The opinion of the Fox, and what came of it.

This publication is edited conjointly by the Ape, Parroquet, and Village Cock.

The garden paths are thronged with powerful deputies from the menageries of London, Berlin, Vienna, New York, and St. Petersburg. The Congress promises to be the most successful ever held in Paris. The death of a great French author, who devoted his pen to Natural History, has cast a gloom over the garden. The cultured animals wear crape, while the bolder spirits, proudly disdaining such symbols of grief, drop their ears and drag their tails along the ground. Here and there distinguished parties are hotly discussing the formation of the Congress, the framing of rules, and the choice of President. The Wolf sits beneath a tree, intently gazing on the Ape, whose careful attire and well-poised eye-glass proclaims man's far-off cousinship to his family.

The Chameleon considers the get-up of the Ape a graceful tribute to his human kinsman.

The Wolf suggests that "to ape is not to imitate!"

The Snake in the grass hisses.

An erudite Crow croaks from his perch, "It would be extremely dangerous to follow in the footsteps of man," and quotes the well-known line, "*Timeo Danaos et dona ferentes.*" He is loudly congratulated on the happy quotation by a German Owl, well versed in the dead languages.

The Buzzard devoutly contemplates the two scholars, while the Mocking-bird jeeringly remarks, "One way of passing for a learned biped is by talking to others of things they do not understand."

The Chameleon blushes, and then looks blue. At this moment the Marmot awoke, to pronounce life a dream. "A dream?" said the

Swallow, "nay, rather a journey." The Ephemera gasped out, "Too brief, too brief," and died.

The question of the Presidency brings the scattered groups to the centre of the garden, and to business. When all are seated and expectant, the Ass brays out silence, quite needlessly, as the only audible sound was caused by a Flea sneezing in his ear. His supporters had prepared a speech for him, and his assurance, gravity, and weight obtained him a hearing. It was whispered that the honourable member was about to move that his ancient policy of progressing backward should be steadily kept in view. The orator, so adjusting his ears as to catch the faintest murmur of applause, flourished his tail impressively, and proceeded—

"Fellow-quadrupeds, and brother brutes of all climes and conditions, the question of the Presidency of this noble Assembly is one of primary importance. In order to lift the burdens from your backs, as the lineal descendant of Balaam's ass, I offer myself as candidate for the position, hedged round as it is with difficulty and danger. It is needless to remind you of the hereditary attributes which qualify me for the office of President—firmness verging on obstinacy, patience under affliction, and a rooted determination to kick against all opposition." Here the speaker was interrupted by the Wolf, who protested against the presumption of this slave of man. Stung to the heart, the honourable Ass was about to indulge his time-honoured habit of kicking up his heels, when he was called to order by the Bear.

"Brothers," said the Bear, "let not the heat of party feeling, added to the stifling air of Paris, compel me to return to my native *climb*, the North Pole. There my suffering has been great, but in the Arctic Circle I can grin and *bear* it as becomes my nature. Here, in a circle so refined, such brawling is only fit for men whose fiery tempers dry up the fountain of their love." The Seal trembled at the sound of the dreaded voice.

The Lion roared and restored order, while the Fox unobserved slipped into the tribune, and in a brief but subtle speech so eulogised the Mule—who carried a useful appendage in the shape of a bell—that he was chosen President.

The Mule takes the chair, and the tinkling of his bell is followed by silence broken for an instant by the Watch-dog—who fancied himself at his master's door—gruffly inquiring, "Who's there?"

The Wolf casts a scornful glance at the poor confused brute.

The Parroquet and Cat, preparing quills supplied by the Goose, seat themselves at the table as Secretaries.

The Lion ascends the tribune with imposing gravity; "shaking the dewdrops from his mane," he denounces in a voice of thunder the tyranny of mankind, and continues : "There is but one way of escape open for all! Fly with me to Africa, to the sweet solitudes of boundless deserts and primeval forests, where we can hold our own against the inroads of degenerate humanity! Far from sheltering walls man is powerless against the noble animals I see around me. Cities are men's refuge, and few there are of the lion-hearted among them, if I may use the expression " [ironical cheers from the Tiger], "who would meet us face to face in our native wilds." The speaker concluded with a glowing picture of the proud independence of animal life in Africa.

The Elephant advocated emigration to Central Africa. "It is a land," said he, "where teeth and tusks are excellent passports, and where every traveller ought to carry his own trunk full of water." This latter remark was objected to by the Hippopotamus, who held that water would be more useful if left in swamps and rivers.

Hereupon the Dog protested that nothing could equal city life, and was put down by the Tiger, Wolf, and Hyæna. As for the Tiger, with a terrific howl he leaped into the tribune bellowing out, "War! blood! Nothing short of the utter extermination of man will establish the security of the Animal Kingdom. Great generals seize great occasions. Did not Rabbits undermine Tarragona? Did not liquor conquer Alexander the Great? The doom of the human race is sealed, its world-wide sway ended! The savage despots have driven us from our homes, hewn down our forests, burned our jungles, ploughed up our prairies, scooped out the solid world to build their begrimed cities, lay their railroads, warm their thin blood, roast our flesh for food. Torturing, slaying, and playing the devil right and left, men have trod the skins of my ancestors under foot, worn our claws and teeth as talismans, poisoned us, imprisoned us, dried and stuffed us, and set us to mimic our bold natures beside mummies in museums. Down with them, I say! Down with the tyrants!" Here the orator paused, he caught sight of a tear glistening in the eye of a lamb, his teeth watered, and his claws crept out at sight of this gentle tribute to his eloquence.

"Well may you weep, sweet one. He, man, robbed your mother of her fleece to clothe his guilty limbs, stole her life and devoured her, head and all. But why recall our wrongs? Is it not enough that he deprived us of our birthright? The world was ours before his advent, and he brought with him misery, confusion, death!" The Tiger concluded with an appeal to all beasts of prey to fight for liberty.

An old Race-horse, now a poor hack, begged permission to say a few words.

"Noble beasts, I must confess myself more familiar with sporting life than politics, or with the questions under discussion. I have, in my day, lived in clover; latterly the neglect and brutality of my human taskmasters have caused me much suffering. I am descended from a noble stock, the bluest blood of the turf circulates in my veins; but alas! I disappointed my first owners, and was soon sent adrift on the world. I was yoked in the last Royal Mail on the road, and earned my hay gallantly, until the accursed railways ruined my prospects. I beg humbly to move the abolition of steam traffic, and that the influential members of Congress should send me to grass, that I may end my days in the green fields, enjoying some State sinecure. Depend upon it, no one is more deserving of your sympathy and support than the reduced member of a noble family."

The President was so moved by this appeal, that he left the chair, announcing an interval of ten minutes.

CLEARING THE DRAIN FOR ACTION.

The tinkle of the bell summons the delegates to their places, which they take with a promptitude that bears witness to their zeal.

The Nightingale alights on the tribune, and in a gush of melody prays for bluer heavens and serener nights. He is called to order, as, notwithstanding the purity of his notes, he had proposed no tangible measure of reform. The Ass takes exception to the songster's low notes, as wanting in asinine richness.

A modest Camel from Mecca proposes that men should be taught to use their legs in place of the backs of higher animals. This proposal is greeted with the applause of equine animals, including the President, who, discovering that the claims of this distinguished foreigner had been overlooked, inquires as to the future of Turkish finance.

The Camel replies with much good sense, "There is one God, and Mahomet is his prophet!"

The Pig here gave it out as her opinion that trouble will never end until men are compelled to abjure the faith of Mahomet, respect Pigs, supply unlimited food and drink, and abolish sanitary law, so as to give nature free scope to expand.

An old Boar—accused by his foes of wandering about farmyards—complimented the Pig on her good taste, suggesting, at the same time, that the absence of sanitary law might tend to poison the political atmosphere. Mrs. Pig protested against insinuations calculated to mix up piggeries with politics.

The Fox, who had been taking notes, ascended the tribune and commenced—

"It is with great satisfaction that I rise to offer one or two remarks on the able speeches of the honourable members of this Congress. Before reviewing the various propositions, I take this opportunity of saying, that never throughout my diplomatic career have I witnessed harmony more perfect. Never has there been a more profound display of unanimity of sentiment than in the wagging tails of this wise assembly. The tail is the chief attribute coveted by man. ['Right you are,' growled an old Sporting-dog]. That by the way; to return to business, nothing could be nobler than the proposal of the Lion to establish and defend our animal commonwealth in Africa. It must not, however, be forgotten that that continent is distant, and inaccessible to many useful members of the Congress, industrial animals, who might succumb to savage warfare or malaria.

"The allusion of the Dog to the joys of city life is not without interest; but he is the slave of man. Mark his collar, inscribed with some barbarous name!" The subject of comment scratches his ear, and

the Mocking-bird observes that his ears must have been cropped to imitate man.

"For an instant—carried away by the tide of his eloquence—I shared the ardour of the Tiger, and almost lent my voice to the war-cry. War is very good for those who escape; but it leaves in its train orphans and widows to be provided for by the survivors. Therefore it is not an unmixed good, more especially as right does not always triumph.

"The reasoning of the Pig is both good and bad, and like that of the Boar, is more calculated to affect pork than progress.

"I take you all to witness that peace, war, and liberty are alike impossible for all. We are all agreed that evil exists somewhere, and that something must be done. [Loud cheers.] I have now the honour to propose a new, untried remedy. [Great excitement.] The only reasonable, lawful, and sacred course to follow is to struggle for knowledge. Why not take a leaf from human experience, and employ the Press to make known our wants, aspirations, customs, and usages, our public and private life.

"Naturalists imagine they have done all when they have analysed our blood, and endeavoured to find out the secret of our noble instinct from our physical organisation.

"We alone can relate our griefs, our patience under suffering, and our joys—joys so rare to creatures on which the hand of man has pressed so heavily." The speaker paused to conceal his emotion. He continued: "Yes, we must publish our wrongs.

"A word to the ladies. The circle which they most adorn is that of home, and to them must we look for information—jotted down in leisure-hours—on domestic subjects. Let them eschew politics. A lady politician is a creature to be avoided. I have further to crave the indulgence of this noble assembly in submitting the following articles—

"*Article 1st.*—It is proposed to vote unlimited funds to carry out the 'Illustrated Public and Private History of Animals,' the funds to be invested in Turkish Securities and Peruvian Bonds."

A Member of the Left proposes to take charge of the money-bag.

The Mole suggests that the funds should be sunk in certain dark mining companies, of which he is an active director.

This proposal is negatived by the Codfish, who is of opinion that they would be safer at the bottom of the sea, as molehills have hitherto proved unremunerative. A Hen came forward with her Chickens, saying, as she had a number of little bills standing open, and which must be honoured, she would take part of the coin as a temporary loan, and do her best to lay golden eggs.

This suggestion was referred to a select committee, and here the matter dropped.

"*Article* 2d.—The Journal of the Animals must combat ignorance and bad faith, the joint enemies of truth. The entire matter to be edited by competent brutes, in order to disarm criticism.

"*Article* 3d.—Men must be employed to perform the drudgery of printing.

"*Article* 4th.—The Fox must find an intelligent philanthropic publisher."

Here the Fox shook his head dolefully, and said he would try. "I have," he continued, "imposed on myself the severest task of all, as the profits of publication must, for a long time, be absorbed in corrections, discounts, and advertising."

A vote of confidence passed in favour of the speaker's integrity and ability closed the proceedings. Before the Assembly broke up, it was announced, amid loud applause, that the Ape, Parroquet, and Village Cock would enter at once on their duties as Editors in Chief of the "Public and Private Lives of Animals," and that the work would open with the "History of a Hare."

HISTORY OF A HARE.

WRITTEN FROM DICTATION BY THE MAGPIE.

CHAPTER I.

In which the Magpie begins.—Some preliminary reflections by the Author of this history.—The Hare is made prisoner.—The Hare's theory of courage.

ONE day last week, as I stood on the branch of an old tree, meditating on the closing lines of a poem I was about to dedicate to my race, my attention was arrested by a Leveret running at full speed across a field. He turned out to be a personal friend of my own, great-grandson of the hero of this tale.

"Mr. Magpie," he cried, quite out of breath, "grandfather lies yonder in a corner of the wood. He sent me to call you."

"Good child," I said, while I patted his cheek with my wing, "go your grandfather's errands, but do not run so fast, else you will come to an untimely end."

"Ah!" he replied, sadly, "love feels no fatigue. But come to one who needs your counsel. My grandfather is ill, bitten by the keeper's dog."

Repairing at once to the scene of the disaster, I found my old friend suffering intense pain from a wound in his right foot, which he carried slung in a willow-band. His head was also bandaged with soothing leaves brought by a neighbourly Deer.

Blood still flowed, affording fresh testimony of man's tyranny.

"My dear Magpie," said the venerable sufferer, whose face, although grave even to sadness, had lost nothing of its original simplicity, "our lot in this world is, at best, an unhappy one."

"Alas!" I replied, "we encounter fresh tokens of our misery every day."

"I know," he continued, "that one ought always to be on one's guard, and that the Hare is never certain to die peacefully in his form. The campaign begins badly. Here am I, perhaps blind of an eye, and certainly lamed so that a Spaniel might easily outrun me. Worse than all, I am told the shooting begins in a fortnight. I must therefore put my affairs in order, and leave the history of a short, but not uneventful life, to posterity to profit by. When mingling in the society of the world, one is constrained to observe a polite and prudent silence, and to disguise one's true sentiments. But in prospect of death, brought face to face with the last enemy, one can never hope to win his clemency by polished lying and hypocrisy. My tale will therefore be unreserved and true. Besides, in bequeathing a valuable history to posterity there is a satisfaction in feeling that one's influence will live, and prove a real power in the world long after the author's death."

I had the greatest difficulty in making him understand that I was quite of his opinion, for during his imprisonment he had become very deaf, and what rendered it still more disagreeable was that he obstinately denied being so. How many times have I not cursed the unnatural life which bereft him of hearing! I said in a loud tone, "It is a noble ambition to live one's life over again in one's works, and the history you are about to give to the world should enable you to face death calmly, as immortal fame may take the place of life. In any case, the book ought to see the light; it can do no harm." He then told me that his troubles had been great. The wound in his right foot had prevented his using the pen. He tried to dictate to his grandchildren, but they, poor little ones, had only learned how to eat and sleep. It had occurred to him to teach his eldest child to commit the story to memory, and thus hand it down from father to son. "But," he added, "oral traditions are never trustworthy; and as I have no desire to become a myth like the Great Buddha, or Saint Simon, I beg you will act as my amanuensis. My history would then, sir, reflect the lustre of your genius."

Wishing to invest this, the most important and perhaps the last act of his life, with due solemnity, he retired for a few seconds. Being a learned Hare, he thought it necessary to commence with a quotation.

> "Approchez, mes enfants, enfin l'heure est venue
> Qu'il faut que mon secret éclate à votre vue."

These two lines by Racine were splendidly rendered by the erudite speaker.

The eldest grandchild left his accustomed sport, and respectfully seated himself on his grandfather's knee. The second, who was passionately fond of stories, pricked up his ears, while the youngest sat up, prepared to divide his attention between the narrative and a cabbage-leaf he was eating. The old Hare, seeing that I was waiting, began thus—

"My secret, my dear children, is my history. May it serve you as

a lesson, for Wisdom does not come to us; we must travel by long and tortuous ways to meet her. I am ten years old—so old, indeed, that never before, in the memory of Hares, has so long a term of life been granted to a poor animal. I was born in France, of French parents, in May 1830; there, behind that oak, the finest tree in the beautiful forest of Rambouillet, on a bed of moss which my good mother had lined with her softest fur. I can still recall those beautiful nights of my infancy when simply to live was to be happy, the moonlight seemed so pure, the grass so tender, and the wild thyme and clover so fragrant. Life was to be clouded, but not without its gleams of sunshine. I was gay then, giddy and idle as you are. I had your age, your thoughtlessness, and the use of my four feet. I knew nothing of life; I was happy, yes, happy! in ignorance of the cruel fate that may at any moment overtake us. It was not long before I became aware that the days, as they followed each other, were only alike in duration; some brought with them burdens of sorrow that seemed to blot out the joy from life.

"One day, after scampering over these fields, and through the woods, I returned to sleep by my mother's side (as a child ought to do). At daybreak I was rudely awakened by two claps of thunder, followed by the most horrible clamour. . . . My mother, at two paces from me, lay dying, assassinated! . . . 'Run away,' she cried, and expired. Her last breath was for me! One second had taught me what a gun was in the cruel hands of man. Ah, my children! were there no men on earth, it would be the Hares' paradise. It is so full of riches. Its brooks are so pure, its herbs so sweet, and its mossy nooks so lovely. Who, I ask you, could be happier than a Hare, if the good God had not, for His own wise ends, permitted man to oppress us? But alas! every medal has a reverse face; evil is always side by side with good, and man by the side of the brute. Would you believe it, my dear Magpie—I have it on the best authority —that man was originally a godlike animal?"

"So it is said," I replied, "and he has himself to thank for his present condition."

"Tell me, grandfather," said the youngest; "in the field yonder were two little Hares with their sister, and a large bird that wanted to prevent them passing. Was that a man?"

"Be quiet," said her brother; "since it was a bird, how could it be a man? If you want grandfather to hear, you must scream, and that will frighten the neighbours."

"Silence!" cried the old Hare, who perceived they were not listening. He then inquired, "Where was I?"

"Your mother had just died, and you had fled."

"Yes, to be sure. My poor mother, she was right; her death was only a prelude to my own suffering. It was a royal hunt that day, and a

horrible carnage took place. The ground was strewn with the slain; blood everywhere, on the grass and underwood; branches, broken by bullets, lay scattered about; and the flowers were trodden under foot.

Five hundred victims fell on that dreadful day. One cannot understand why men should call this sport, and enjoy it as a pastime.

"My mother's death was well and speedily avenged. It was a royal hunt, but it was the last; he who held the gun, I am told, passed once more through Rambouillet, but not as a sportsman.

"I followed my mother's advice, and, for a hare only eighteen days old, ran bravely; yes, bravely! If ever, my children, you are in danger, fear nothing, flee from it. It is no disgrace to retreat before superior force. Nothing annoys me more than to hear men talk of our timidity and cowardice. They ought rather to admire and imitate the tact which prompts us to use our legs, being ignorant of the use of arms. Our weakness makes the strength of boastful men and brutes.

"I ran until I fell quite exhausted, and became insensible. When I recovered consciousness, judge of my terror! I found myself no longer in the green fields, but shut up in a narrow prison, a closed basket. My luck had deserted me, and yet it was something to know I was still living, as it is said death is the worst of all evils, being the last. But men rarely release their prisoners. My mind therefore became a prey to bitter forebodings, as I had no notion of what might become of me. I was shaken by rough jolts, when one, more severe than the others, half-opened my prison door, and enabled me to see that the man on whose arm it was suspended was not walking, yet a rapid motion carried us along. You, who as yet have seen nothing, will find it hard to believe that my captor was mounted on a horse. It was man above, and horse beneath. I could never make out why such a strong, noble creature should, like a dog, consent to become the slave of man—to carry him to and fro, and be whipped, spurred, and abused by him. If, like the Buddhists, we were to believe in transmigration after death, it would all come right at last, and we some day, as men, would have our time of torturing animals. But the doctrine, my children, is more than doubtful. I, for one, have no faith in it.

"My captor was a magnificent creature—the king's footman."

CHAPTER II.

The Revolution of July, and its fatal consequences.—Utility of the Fine Arts.

AFTER a brief but impressive pause, a shadow seeming to settle on his fine features, my old friend resumed the thread of his narrative.

"I offered no resistance. It was my fate, and I accepted it calmly. Among men, every one is more or less the servant of another, the only difference being in the kind of services rendered. Once within the pale of civilisation, I was forced to accept its degrading obligations. The king's lackey was my master.

"As good luck would have it, his little girl, who had taken me for a cat, became my friend. It was soon settled that I was to be killed. My mistress pleaded for my youth and beauty, and the pleasure which my society afforded her. Her chief delight was in pulling my ears, a familiarity which I never resented. My patience won her heart, and I felt grateful to her for her kindness to me.

"Women, my children, are infinitely superior to men; they never go hunting hares, men are their game !

"I would have suffered patiently, had I seen the faintest prospect of escape; but I dreaded the pitiless bayonet of the guard at the gate of the Louvre.

"In a small room in Paris, beneath the shade of the Tuileries, I often watered my bread with my tears. This bread of slavery seemed, oh! so bitter, and so difficult to get over, for my heart was full of the green fields and sweet herbs of freedom. No abode on earth can be more dreary than a palace when one is compelled to remain within its gilded walls. The gold and glitter soon grow dim when compared with the blue sky and free earth, the delight of God's creatures.

"I tried to while away the time by gazing out of the window, but this only rendered my bondage all the more galling. I began to hate the monotony of my new life. What would I not have given for one hour's liberty, and a bit of thyme. Often was I tempted to throw myself from the window of my prison, to take one desperate leap, and live or die for freedom. Believe me, my children, happiness seldom dwells within palace walls.

"My master, in his position as royal footman, had little to occupy his leisure; his chief duties consisted in posturing, and wearing a suit of gaudy clothes. From his lofty point of view my education seemed extremely defective; he therefore set himself the task of improving me, that is, rendering me more like himself. I was obliged to learn a number of exercises by a process of torture as ingenious as it was devilish, the lessons becoming more and more degrading. O misery! I was soon able to do the dead hare and the living hare, at the slightest sign from my master, as if I were a mere dog. My tyrant, encouraged by the success I owed to the rigour of his method, added to this series of lessons what he termed an accomplishment: he taught me the art of fiendish music. In spite of the terror I felt at the noise, I was soon able to perform a passable roll on the drum. This new talent had to be displayed every time any member of the royal family left the palace.

"One day, it was Tuesday, July 27, 1830 (I shall never forget that date) the sun was shining gloriously. I had just finished beating the roll for Monsieur the Duke of Angoulême. My nerves were always irritated by contact with the donkey's skin of the drum. All at once I heard guns going off. They seemed to be approaching the Tuileries from the side of the Palais Royal.

"Dear me! I thought, some unfortunate hares have had the imprudence to show themselves in the streets of Paris, where there are so many dogs and guns and sportsmen. But then I reflected that most of the latter were picturesque, not real sportsmen, who had never shot a hare. The dreadful recollection of the hunt at Rambouillet froze me with fright. What could hares possibly have done to man to bring down such vengeance upon them? I instinctively turned to my mistress to implore her protection, when I beheld her face filled with terror greater than my own. I was about to thank her for the pity she felt for me, when I perceived that her fear was only personal, that she was thinking very little indeed about me, and very much about herself.

"These gun-shots, each detonation of which congealed the blood in my veins, were fired by men on their fellows. I rubbed my eyes, I bit my feet till they bled, to assure myself I was not dreaming. I can only say, like Orgon—

"'—— De mes propres yeux vu
Le qu'on appelle vu.'

"The need that men have for sport is so pressing, that in the absence of other game they take to shooting each other."

"It is dreadful to think of the depravity of human nature," the Magpie replied. "I am positively obliged to hide myself towards evening, to escape the last shot of some passing sportsman, whose only reason for not firing at a magpie would be to save his gunpowder. In all probability, the wretch who might bring me down would not think even me good enough to eat."

"What is still more singular," said my friend, "is that men glory in this butchery, and a great 'bag,' filled with victims, is considered something to be proud of. I shall not weary you with the full history of the Revolution of July, although many details remain unrecorded. A Hare, although a lover of freedom, would hardly be accepted as an historian."

"What is a revolution of July?" inquired the little Hare, who, like all children, only listened now and then when any word struck him.

"Will you be quiet?" said his brother; "grandfather has just told us that it is a time when every one is frightened."

"I shall content myself by telling you that the struggle continued three whole days. My ears were torn with the mingled noise of drums, cannon, the whistle of the bullets, and the sound of fierce strife, that filled Paris like the breaking of angry waves on a rocky shore.

"While the people fought and barricaded the streets, the Court was at St. Cloud. As for ourselves, we passed a fearful night at the Tuileries. Our terror seemed to prolong the darkness. When the dawn came at last, the firing was renewed, and I heard that the Hôtel de Ville had been taken and retaken. I no doubt would have felt grieved at all this had I been able to go away like the Court, but that was not to be thought of. On the morning of the 29th a dreadful tumult was heard under the windows, followed by the booming of cannon, and dull crash of iron balls. 'It is finished, the Louvre is taken,' cried my master; and clasping the little girl in his arms, he disappeared. It was then eleven o'clock. When they had gone, I realised that I was alone and helpless, but then it occurred to me, there being no one here, I have no enemies, and my courage rose with the reflection. The men outside might kill each other, and thus expend their ammunition as fast as they chose—so much the worse for men, and the better for Hares.

"I was hidden beneath the bed, for the room was invaded by soldiers, who cried in a strange tongue, 'Long live the King.' 'Cry

away,' I said, 'it is easy to see that you are not Hares, and that the king has not been making game of you.' Soon the 'redcoats' disappeared, and a poor man—a scholar, I believe—came and sought shelter in my room. He had no taste for war; he therefore deposited himself in a cupboard, where he was soon discovered by a crowd of bloodstained ruffians, who searched everywhere, crying 'Liberty! long live Liberty!' as if they had hoped to find it in some odd corner of the Tuileries. After fixing a flag out of the window, they sung a striking song, commencing—

"'Come children of the country,
The day of glory has arrived!'

Some of them were black with powder, and must have fought as hard as if they had been paid for it. I thought that these poor begrimed creatures, as they kept continually shouting 'Liberty!' must have been imprisoned in baskets, or shut up in small rooms, and were rejoicing in their freedom. I felt carried away by their enthusiasm, and had advanced three steps to join in the cry of 'Liberty!' when my conscience arrested me with the question, 'Why should I?'

"During these three days—would you believe it, my dear magpie? —twelve hundred men were killed and buried."

"Bah!" I said, "the dead are buried, but not their ideas!"

"Hum!" he replied.

"Next day my master came back: he had not shown himself for twenty-four hours. He was changed—he had 'turned his coat,' an operation which cost him a pang, as he had made a good thing out of the king's livery. Men turn their coats as easily as the wind turns the weathercock on yonder spire. It is a mean artifice, to which we could not descend without spoiling our fair proportions.

"I learned from my master's wife that there was now no king. Charles X. had gone never to return, and the worst of all was, that they themselves were ruined. You observe, the downfall of the king was viewed selfishly, not as a national calamity, but simply as an event which blighted their own fortunes. That is the way of men. Secretly I rejoiced at the disaster, as it rendered my emancipation possible. Alas! my dear little Hares, Hares propose, and man disposes. Have no faith in the liberty born of the blood and agony of revolution. The change wrought by strife only embittered my lot. My master, who had never been taught any useful occupation, was reduced to living on his wits, which served him so badly, as to leave him often without bread. He was brought to such straits as we Hares are when the snow lies heavy on the ground. I have seen his poor child weeping for the food that men often find so difficult to procure. Be thankful, my children, that you are not men; and that you can feed on the simple herbs as nature has provided them. Although suffering from hunger, I felt many a bitter pang for my little mistress. If the rich only knew the appetite of the poor, they would be afraid of being devoured. I more times than once saw my master eye me with ferocity. A famished man has no pity; I believe he would almost eat his own children. You will readily understand, therefore, that my life was in the greatest danger. May you ever be kept from the peril of becoming a stew."

"What is a stew?" inquired the little Hare in a loud voice.

"A stew is a Hare cut up and cooked in a pan. A great man once said that our flesh is delicious, and our blood the sweetest of all animals; but he adds that we seem to be aware of our danger, as we sleep with our eyes open." At this reply the audience became so quiet, that one might have heard the grass growing.

"Nothing can ever make me believe," cried the old Hare, much moved by the recollection of that incident in his life, "that Hares were created to be cooked, and that man cannot employ himself better than by eating animals in many respects superior to him. I owe my life to the misery that reduced me to skin and bone, and to the timely word of my mistress who pleaded for my life, that I might still display my accomplishments. 'Ah!' said my master, striking his forehead and looking dramatic, as Frenchmen always do in joy or sorrow, 'I have an idea'—that was for him a sort of miracle. From that day I became a public character, and the saviour of the family."

CHAPTER III.

Public and political life.—His master becomes his charge.—Glory nothing but a wreath of smoke.

"I SOON discovered my destiny. It was not the Tuileries! My master had made a little house of four boards, which he set up in the Champs Elysées, and there, beneath the blue sky, I, a denizen of the forest of Rambouillet, was exhibited in public at the cost of my proper pride, natural modesty, and health. I well remember my master's words just before I made my *début*.

"'Bless Heaven!' he said, 'that after profiting by your more than ordinary education, you have fallen into the hands of such a master. I have trained you and fed you for nothing. The moment has now arrived for you to prove to the world your noble sense of gratitude. When I caught you, you were rustic and uninstructed. The airs and graces which you have acquired were taught you for your amusement. Now they will enable us to enter upon a glorious and lucrative career. It has always been understood that men, sooner or later, reap the fruits of their disinterestedness. Remember that from this day our interests become one. You are about to appear before a people, the most polished, proud, and difficult to please, and all that is required of you is to please everybody. Be careful never to mention King Charles, and all will go well, as crime and injustice have been abolished. Do your part, and I will relieve you of the task of receiving the money. We shall never make millions; but the poor manage to live upon less.'

"'Ah me!' I said to myself, 'what a modest speech! My master is a bold tyrant; to hear him, one would think that I had voluntarily relinquished my liberty, and besought him to snatch me away from all that was dear to me in life.' For all that, my *début* was a most brilliant affair; I became the rage of Paris. During three years I beat the roll-call for the Ecole Polytechnique, Louis Phillipe, La Fayette, Lafitte, for nineteen ministers, and for Napoleon the Great. I learned—go on writing, my dear Magpie—to fire cannon.

"For a long time, by great good luck, I never mistook one name for another, and never once abused the trust of those depending on me. My master praised my probity, and declared me incorruptible.

"During my public career I paid some attention to politics. In the Oriental question I felt deeply interested. It was at last settled by

diplomatic subtlety, to the satisfaction of the Hares of all nations. In the East the Hare has been an object of great political importance. It may be as well here to record my conviction that there is no reason to dread the immediate development of the power of the Ottoman Empire, or to give credence to the report that a cure has been discovered for the moral and physical obliquity of Mongolian eyes.

"To continue my narrative. Once, at the close of a long fatiguing day, I had just finished the fiftieth representation, and obtained numerous cheers and coppers. The two candles were nearly burned out, when my master insisted on my firing a number of guns. I felt fagged and stupid. At the words, 'A salute for Wellington,' I ought to have refused to fire; but bang went the gun. I was accused of treachery by the crowd, who hurled my master, show and all, into the middle of the road. As for myself, I fell pell-mell with money, candles, and theatre. St. Augustine and Mirabeau were right when they said, each in his own way, 'That glory is nothing but a wreath of smoke,' or like a candle that may be extinguished by the slightest breath of adversity. Happily, fear gave me courage. Amid the tumult I sought safety in flight. Hardly fifty feet from the scene of my fame, I still heard the clamour of the angry crowd. About to cross the road at a single bound, I was caught between the legs of some one, who, like myself, seemed to be fleeing from the fray. My speed was so rapid, and the shock so violent, that I rolled into the ditch, carrying the owner of the legs with me. My doom was sealed, I thought. Men are far too proud not to resent being brought low by a poor Hare. My life will be sacrificed!"

CHAPTER IV.

"Birds of a feather flock together."—Our hero secures the friendship of a subaltern Government Clerk.—An unfortunate death.— Good-bye to Paris.

"I COULD hardly believe my eyes—this man, of whom I was in the greatest dread, was himself as frightened as if the devil had got between his legs. Good, I said, my lucky star has not left me. This old gentleman seems to have adopted my theory of courage. Both being naturally timid, we will constantly agree. 'Sir,' I whispered, in my softest and most reassuring tones, 'I am unused to addressing your fellow-men, but I make bold to speak to you, as, if we are not blood relations, we are at least brothers by sentiment. You are afraid, you cannot deny it! and your emotion renders you all the more worthy in my eyes.'

"At that moment a carriage passed, and by its light I perceived that the stranger I had brought down was the wise man who hid himself in the cupboard in the Tuileries, and who had been one of the most attentive of my audience. He had a man's body, it is true, but from his honesty, and the gentle expression of his face, I felt certain that his ancestors had belonged to our race. His joy was great when, regaining his habitual calm, he recognised in me his favourite actor. 'The fear,' he said, 'that seized upon me is infinitely worse than its cause.' These words seemed to me to sound the very depths of profundity. I felt, for the first time, a true attachment, and permitted my new friend to carry me away. I soon discovered that he was extremely humble and poor, being employed as a sub-Government clerk. He was bent less by age than by his constant habit of saluting every one, by his care to keep his head lower than his superiors, and by his duty, which consisted in doing the work of those above him, as well as his own. Next to his son, who bore a close resemblance to him, he loved what he called his garden, a small box of earth at the window, and a few flowers, which opened with the sun. They were the little censers of his worship, whose fragrance ascended to heaven with his morning prayers."

"'My dear sir,' said one of our neighbours, an actor more successful in life than my master, 'you are far too modest; you do not make enough of yourself. I was once modest like you, but I cured myself of that grave defect. Do as I did—compel the world to accept you at your own value. Speak louder; bluster about; give yourself full voice and swagger. It is wonderful how it tells, although the voice owes its depth to the emptiness within, and the swagger to the fact that without it your natural endowments would never lift you from the gutter.'

"The world is always liberal with advice to the poor; but my master preferred his humble position to all the riches and fame that might be acquired by becoming an impostor, whose energies would always be strained to enable him to crow lustily from his own dunghill.

"Our life was a very regular one. The father left early for his office, and his son for school. I was left alone in charge of our room, and should have felt dull had not the quiet and rest their peculiar charm after the fatigues of my life in the Champs Élysées. After the day's work we were all united at our evening meal, a most frugal one. I was, indeed, often afraid of being hungry. They would have shared their last crust with me. It is always so with the poor. I felt nearer God in this little room than I had done since I left the green fields; I noticed so many acts of self-denying love.

"One day my master came home very much agitated, and burying his head in his hands, exclaimed, 'My God! they talk of another change of Ministry; if I lose my place, what will become of us? We have no money!' 'My poor father,' said the son, 'I will work for you. I am big, and can make money.' 'No, my boy, you are still young, and know nothing of the world.' 'But, father,' he continued, 'why not go to the king, and ask him for money?' My master said, 'They are only beggars who live upon their miseries; and besides, the king has his own poor relations to provide for.'

"Since the rich have always their poor relations, why have not the poor their rich ones?"

"Tell me," said the little Hare, who had slipped behind her grandfather, so as to shout into his ear; "You talk of king and ministers— who are they?"

"Be quiet," replied the old Hare, "it cannot be of any consequence to you who or what the king is. It is not yet certain whether he is a person or a thing. As to the ministers, they are the gentlemen who cause others to lose their places, until they have lost their own."

"Ah me!" said the little one, much satisfied with his explanation; "never let it be said that it is useless to speak seriously to children."

"The fatal day came at last. My master lost his place by a change of Ministry, and soon after died of a broken heart. His poor son was not long in following him to the grave. I was left alone in the empty room, as everything was taken and sold to meet the funeral expenses. I should myself have been sacrificed had I not escaped after nightfall, and sped through the streets of Paris, scarcely halting to take breath until beyond the Arc de l'Étoile. There I paused for a moment, casting a look of compassion on the great city wrapped in slumber beneath a dark cloud, that shut out heaven from its view."

CHAPTER V.

Return to the fields.—The worthlessness of men and other animals.—A Cock, accustomed to the ring, provokes our hero.—Duel with pistols.

"I SOON reached a wood, and felt my chest expand with the pure air. It was so long since I beheld the full extent of the sky, that I seemed to look upon it for the first time. The moonlight was bright, and the night-breeze laden with a banquet of fresh odours that it had caught up about the fields and hedgerows. Endowed by nature with an acute sense of smell, nothing could be more delicious to a weary Hare than the fresh fragrance of grass and thyme. Each breath I inhaled filled me with the fond memories of my childhood, which passed into my dreams as I slept in the open air. Early next morning I was roused by the clang of steel. Two gentlemen were fighting with swords, and appeared to me determined to kill each other; however, when they were tired of fencing, they walked off quietly arm-in-arm. Other combatants followed, but not one fell, and no blood was spilt in these affairs of honour, after nights of gambling and debauchery.

"Journeying onward until within sight of a village, I fell in with a Cock. As I had been cooped up in a town, and seen nothing but men and women for so long, this bird interested me greatly. He was a fine fellow, high on his legs, and carried his head as if he could not bend his neck. He had quite a martial bearing, reminding one of a French soldier.

"'By my comb!' he exclaimed, 'I hope you will know me again. I never came across a Hare with such a stock of assurance.'

"'What!' I replied, 'may I not admire your fine proportions. I have been so long in Paris, I have quite forgotten the grandeur of nature.'

"Would you believe it? Although my answer was so soft and simple, yet the fellow was offended, crowed like to split my ears, and cried, 'I am the Cock of the village, and it shall never be said that a miserable Hare can insult me with impunity.'

"'You astonish me,' I continued, 'I never intended to insult you.'

"'I have nothing to do with your intentions. Every insult ought to be wiped out with blood. I am rather badly off for a fight, and I shall have much pleasure in giving you a lesson in good manners. Choose your arms.'

"'I would rather die than fight. Let me pass—I am going to Rambouillet to rejoin some old friends.'

"'Fight you must, else I will put a ball through you. Here are an Ox and a Dog, who will serve as seconds. Follow me, and do not attempt to escape.'

"What could I do? flight was impossible—I obeyed. Then addressing the seconds, I said, 'Sirs, this Cock is a professed duellist. Will you stand by and see me assassinated? I have never fought, and my blood will be on your heads.'

"'Bah!' said the Dog, 'that is a trifle. Everything must have a beginning. Your simple candour interests me. I will stand by you. Now that I am certain of you, it concerns my honour that you should fight.'

"'You are extremely polite, and I am touched with your goodness; but I would rather deny myself the pleasure of having you witness my death.'

"'Hear him, my dear Ox,' cried my adversary. 'In what times do we live? Has it positively come to this, that cowardice, impudence, and low-bred nature are to triumph over all that is chivalrous and noble in the world?'

"The pitiless Ox bellowed with rage. The Dog, taking me aside, said in a soothing tone, 'It makes little odds in the end how one dies; and between us two, I don't half like this Cock. Believe me, I heartily wish you success. Were I a sporting Dog, you might doubt my sincerity, but I have settled down to a country life, that would be quiet were it not for the early crowing of your foe, who permits no one in the village to sleep after daybreak.'

"'I shall never be able to get through it,' I replied, half dead.

"'You have the choice of weapons. Choose pistols, and I will load them.'

"'In the name of all that is canine and good,' I said, 'try and arrange this affair.'

"'Come, make haste,' cried the Cock. 'Enter this copse! One of us will never leave it!' he added.

"At these words I felt a cold chill run through me. As a last resource, I reminded the Ox and Dog of the law against duelling.

"'Those laws are made by cowards,' they replied.

"I endeavoured to work upon the tenderest feelings of my adversary's nature by inquiring what would become of his poor hens should he fall. All was in vain. Twenty-five paces were marked off; the pistols were loaded, and we took our places.

"'Are you used to this arm?' said the Dog.
"'Alas! yes; but I have neither aimed at nor wounded any one.' As good luck would have it, I had to fire first.

"'Take good aim,' said the Dog, 'I detest this fellow.'
"'Why on earth, then, don't you take my place? Are you still at enmity with me,' I said to my foe. 'Let us kiss and forget all.'
"'Fire!' he replied, cursing fearfully.
"This roused me. The Ox retired and gave the signal; I pressed the trigger, and we both fell—I, from emotion, and the Cock from the ball that pierced his heart."
"'Hurrah!' cried the Dog.
"'Silence, gentlemen,' I said, 'this is no time for rejoicing.' But he was a jolly dog, and light-hearted.
"'Bravo!' said the Ox, 'you have rendered a public service. I shall be glad if you will dine with me this evening. The grass is particularly tender in this neighbourhood.'
"I declined the invitation and said, 'May the blood of this miserable bully be upon your heads. Gentlemen, good morning.'
"My journey to Rambouillet was, as you may be certain, a sad one. It was long before the dread image of my dead enemy vanished from my eyes. The freshness and beauty of nature at last acted as a balm to my spirits; and ere I reached the forest, with all its souvenirs of my youth, my troubles were forgotten. Some months after my return, I had the pleasure of becoming a father, and soon after a grandfather. You know the rest, my dear children, so now you are at liberty."
At these words his audience awoke.
"Since my return, my dear Magpie, I have had leisure for reflection, and have come to the conclusion that true happiness is not to be found in this world. If it does exist at all, it is most difficult to attain, and the most fleeting possession of our animal nature. Philosophic men without number have wasted their lives in vainly attempting to discover some clue to the mystery, and all to no purpose. Some of them would fain have us believe that they had nearly created a heaven for themselves where self-love had only set up its own image as its god. Other men demand happiness of heaven as if it were a debt owed them by its Divine Ruler, and probably the wisest section settle down to enjoy the pleasures which life undoubtedly affords, and to make the best of 'the ills that flesh is heir to.'
"I believe, on the whole, that our lives, although they have their disadvantages, are pleasanter than the lives of men, for this reason. The present is to us everything. We live for to-day. Men live for to-morrow. The to-morrow that is to be brimful of joy. Alas! thus

human hope is carried on through all the days of life ; but the joy is never realised, and the hope goes with men beyond the grave."

THE FLIGHT OF A PARISIAN BIRD

IN SEARCH OF BETTER GOVERNMENT.

PARISIAN Sparrows have long been recognised as the boldest of the feathered tribe. Thoroughly French, they have their follies, and their virtues to atone for them; but above all, they have been for many generations objects of envy to the birds of foreign climes. This latter reflection is sufficient to account for all the calumnies heaped upon them by their enemies. They who dwell amid the splendour of the capital, are a happy tribe. As for myself I am one of the number of distinguished metropolitan birds. Of a naturally gay disposition, an unusually liberal education has lent gravity to my appearance. I have been fed on crumbs of philosophy; having built my nest in the spout of an illustrious writer's dwelling. Thence I fly to the windows of the Tuileries, and compare the anxieties of the palace and the fading grandeur of kings, with the immortal roses, budding in the simple abode of my master, which will one day wreathe his brow with an undying glory.

By picking up the crumbs that have fallen from this great man's table, I myself have become illustrious among the birds of my feather, who, after mature deliberation, have appointed me to select the form of government calculated to promote the welfare of sparrows. The task implied is a difficult one, as my constituents never remain long on one perch, chattering incessantly when their liberty is threatened, and fighting among themselves almost without cause.

The birds of Paris, ever on the wing, have many of them settled down to thinking, and are now giving their attention to such subjects as religion, morality, and philosophy.

Before residing in the spout—in the Rue de Rivoli—I made my escape from a cage in which I had been imprisoned for two years. Every time I felt thirsty, I had to draw water to amuse my master, one of those bearded animals who would have us believe they are the lords of creation. As soon as I regained my liberty, I related my sad story to some friends in the Faubourg St. Antoine, who treated me with great kindness. It was then, for the first time, I observed the habits of the bird-world, and discovered that the joy of life does not consist in simply eating and drinking. I was led to believe that even the life of the sparrow has higher ends, and to form convictions which have added greatly to my fame.

Many a time have I sat on the head of one of the statues of the Palais Royal, where I might be seen with my plumes ruffled, my head between my shoulders, and, with one eye closed on the world, reflecting on our rights, our duties, and our future. Grave questions forced themselves upon me. Where do sparrows come from? Where do they go to? Why can't they weep? Why don't they form themselves into societies like crows? Why don't French sparrows settle everything by arbitration, since they enjoy such a sublime language?

Great changes were taking place around; houses were supplanting gardens, and depriving birds of the insects and grubs found in the shrubs and soil. The result, as might have been expected, was to draw the line still more markedly between the rich and poor, and to set up "caste" as it exists among certain types of the human race. The sparrows in the densely-populated quarters were reduced to living on offal, while the aristocracy fed daintily, and perched as near heaven as the trees of the Champs d'Elysées would allow them.

This defective constitution could not last long; one half of the feathered tribe chirping joyously in the fulness of their stomachs, surrounded by superb families, and the other half brawling and clamouring for filthy refuse. The latter, driven to desperation, determined indeed to use, if need be, their horny beaks to improve their social condition.

With this laudable object in view, a deputation waited on a bird who had lived in the Faubourg St. Antoine, and assisted at the taking of the Bastille. This bird was appointed to the command of the sufferers, who organised themselves into a body, each one feeling the necessity of implicit obedience.

Judge of the surprise of the Parisians who beheld thousands of small birds ranged on the roofs of the houses in the Rue de Rivoli; the right wing towards the Hôtel de Ville, the left on the Madeleine, and the centre on the Tuileries. The aristocratic birds, seized with panic-fear at sight of this demonstration, and dreading the loss of their power and position, despatched a fledgling of their number to address the rioters in these words:—"Is it not well that we should reason together and not fight?"

The rioters turned their eyes upon me. Ah! that was one of the proudest moments of my life: I was elected by my fellow-citizens to draw up a charter to conciliate all, and settle differences among the most renowned sparrows in the world, sparrows who for a moment were divided on the question "how to live," the eternal backbone of political discussions.

Those birds in possession of the enchanting abodes of the capital, had they any absolute right to their property? Why and how had caste become established? Could it last? Were perfect equality established among Parisian sparrows, what form would the new government assume? Such were the questions asked by both parties. "But," said the hedge-Sparrows, "the earth and all its riches should be equally divided." "That is an error," said the privileged ones; "we live in a city, and are subject to the restraints, as well as to the refinement, of society; whereas you in your condition enjoy greater freedom, and ought to content yourselves with the hedgerows and fields, and all that satisfies untutored nature."

Thereupon a general twittering threatened to lead to hostilities, but the popular tumult with sparrows, as with man, is the labour-pangs of national deliverance, and brings forth good. A proposition was carried, to send an intelligent bird to examine the different forms of government. I had the honour of being selected for the post, and at once started on my mission. What would one not sacrifice for his country? To tell the truth, the position was one which conferred both dignity and emolument. Let me now lay the report of my travels as an humble offering on the altar of my country.

The Ants' Form of Government.

After traversing the sea, not without difficulty and danger, and experiencing many of those adventures which take the place of genuine information in modern books of travel, I arrived at an island called Old Frivolity. Why it should be termed old I could never make out, as it is said that the world was created all at once. A Carrion-Crow, whom I met, pointed out the government of the ants as a suitable model, so you may understand how eager I was to study their system, and discover their secrets. On my way I fell in with scores of ants travelling for pleasure. They were all of them black and glossy, as if newly varnished, but utterly devoid of individuality, being all alike. After, indeed, one has seen a single ant, one knows all the others. They travel coated with a liquid which keeps them clean. Should one meet an ant in his mountains, on the water, or in his city-dwelling, his get-up is irreproachable. Care is even bestowed on the cleanliness of his feet and mandibles. This affectation of outward purity lowered them in my estimation. I inquired of the first ant I met, "What would happen to you were you for an instant to forget your careful habits?" He made no answer; I discovered, indeed, that they never exchange a word with any one to whom they have not been formally introduced. I fell in with an intelligent Coralline of the Polynesian Ocean, who informed me that she had been arrested by the fishes when engaged in raising the coral-foundation on which a new continent was to repose. She mentioned a curious fact relating to the government of the ants, namely, that they confer the right upon their subjects to annex all new lands as soon as they appear above sea-level. I now found out that Old Frivolity was so named to distinguish it from New Coral-reef Island. I may mention in passing, that these are private confidences, and caution my noble constituents not to abuse them.

As soon as I set foot on the island, I was assailed by a troop of strange animals—government servants—charged with introducing you to the pleasures of freedom, by preventing you carrying certain contraband objects you had set your heart upon. They surrounded me, compelled me to open my beak in order that they might look down my throat in case I should be carrying prohibited wares inland. As I proved to be empty, I was permitted to make my way to the seat of the government, whose liberty had been so lauded by my friend the Crow.

THE FLIGHT OF A PARISIAN BIRD. 39

Nothing surprised me more than the extraordinary activity of the people. Everywhere were ants coming and going; loading and unloading provisions. Palaces and warehouses were being built; the earth,

indeed, was yielding up all its finest materials to aid them in the construction of their edifices. Workmen were boring underground, making tunnels to relieve the traffic on the surface of the island. So much taken up, indeed, was every one with his own business, that my presence was not noticed. On all sides, ships were leaving laden with ants for the colonies, or with merchandise destined for foreign shores; vessels were crowding into the ports, bearing produce from distant parts of the world; messages were flashing from agents abroad, telling merchants of the abundance of products that might almost be had for the lifting. So clever are these ants in everything connected with commerce, that whenever they receive a message, they send off their vessels, laden with cheap wares which they sell to weak races at the highest market prices. Some semi-savage nations assert that the strong drink the ants export is too potent, and that the narcotic they extract from a certain plant, which is watered by the sweat of a servile race, affords a powerful stimulant to national decay,—is, in fact, a physical and moral poison. To this, diplomatists reply that the trade is lucrative, that there is a demand for the narcotic, and that so long as the demand lasts the ants must supply it at their own price. There are those among them who abhor this traffic, and condemn it as a moral slave-trade, in so far as the effect of the narcotic on its consumers is to render them its bondsmen for life. These ants, curiously enough, profess the Christian religion, and send propagandists to all parts of the world. For all that, I soon found out that many of them are idolaters, worshipping gods made of gold by themselves, and set up in shrines called banks; other idols, called "consolidated funds," railway stocks, and generally sound investments, yield their owners a temporal good, and enable them to "live in clover." Other idols, again, when sunk in foreign loans and spurious companies, rebel and bring down all sorts of calamities on the widows and orphans of the most industrious ants of the island. There are those among them, whose avocation it is to make these images out of clay with such attractive ingenuity that, when set up to public gaze, worshippers flock to the shrines and take their glitter for pure gold; these gods are for "raising the wind," but they sometimes bring down a storm and are overthrown, crushing in their fall thousands of poor devotees.

In the midst of the general activity I noticed some winged ants; and, singling out one, inquired of the guard, "Who is that ant standing unemployed while all the others are labouring?"

"Oh," he replied, "that is a noble lord. We have many such as he, patricians of our empire."

"What is a patrician?" I asked.

"They are the glory of the land,—fellows with four wings who fly about in the sun, and are at their wits' end to know how to pass the time most pleasantly."

"Can you yourself ever hope to become a patrician if you work hard?"

"Well, no; not exactly. The wings of patricians are natural; they

run in the families, so to speak. But artificial wings may be ingrafted by the sword of the sovereign for distinguished service; these, however, are never strong enough to enable the wearer to soar clear of his plebeian fellows into the high heaven of aristocracy. I must tell you that some of the four-winged order are almost indispensable to the state; they nurse the national honour, and plan our campaigns."

The noble ant who had caused my inquiries was coming towards us. The common ants made way for him; these working ants of the lower order are extremely poor, possessing absolutely nothing. The patricians, on the other hand, are rich, having palaces in the ant-hills, and parks, where flies are reared for their food and sport.

The ants display the tenderest regard for their offspring; and to the care bestowed upon the training of the young they attribute their national greatness. It is astonishing to see the neuters watching over the young. In place of sending—as some of our Parisian sparrows do— their callow-brood to be nursed by birds of prey, they themselves tend the orphans. They, indeed, live for them, sheltering them from the cold winds that sweep their island, watching for the fitful gleams of sunshine to lead them out. These ant-neuters watch with pride the growth of the young lives, and the development of the instinct for war and conquest in the young brood; not alone the conquest of lands and races, but the mastery over the elements of nature that informs them how to brave the worst storms, and build their wonderful ant-hills. These nurses, although tender-hearted, are proud, and will unflinchingly buckle the swords on to their favourites, and send them away to fight for fame, or die for their country. From the point of view of a philosophical French sparrow, all this seemed to me strangely conflicting, and on the whole a sign of defective national character. At this moment the patrician ascended one of the city fortifications and said a few words to his subordinates, who at once dispersed through the ant-hill; and in less time than I take to write I noticed detachments issuing from the stronghold, and embarking on straw, leaves, and bits of wood. I soon learned that news of a defeat had arrived from abroad, and they were sending out reinforcements. During the preparations, I overheard the following conversation between two officers:—

"Have you heard the news, my lord, of the massacre of the innocents by the savages of Pulo Anto?"

"Yes; we shall have to annex the territory of these painted devils, and teach them the usages of civilisation."

"I suppose it must be so; our fellows will have some rough

work in the jungle, and the expedition to punish a handful of barbarians will cost no end of money, and some good lives."

"As pioneers of progress, we must be prepared to sacrifice something for the common good, and our men are in want of active service. Besides, Pulo Anto is a rich island, and will yield a good revenue."

This last remark was very much to the point, so conclusive, indeed, as to satisfactorily terminate the dialogue. Will it pay? is the final question which settles all the transactions of this military and mercantile race. I imagined that the noble lord spoke of the "common good" in the sarcastic tone peculiar to his nation. This phrase meant the immediate benefit of the Ant kingdom, and the ultimate disappearance from the face of the earth of a weak neighbour. The ants carry the process of civilising a savage nation to such a degree of refinement, that the subliming and re-subliming influences of contact gradually cause the destruction of the dross of savagedom and the annihilation of race. It seemed to me that what the ants happen to like they look upon as their own, and make it their own if it suits their convenience. They extend their empire, and carry warfare and commerce into the ant-hills of their weaker neighbours. They wax stronger and richer year by year, while the nations with which they trade, many of them, grow weaker and poorer.

I remarked to an officer that the aggressive policy of his government was much to be reprobated.

"Well," he replied, "there may be truth in what you say, but we must obey the popular voice, open new fields for our commerce, and keep our army and navy employed."

"You, sir, call this fulfilling a divine mission; a foreign war is a sort of god-send to keep the fighting ants employed. You go on the principle of the surgeon who cuts up his patients to keep his hand in, and his purse full. Such work ought to be left to the butcher."

"Oh no; you labour under a great mistake. I own we do something in the way of vivisection, just as would the skilful surgeon to increase his knowledge, and enable him to heal the festering sores of humanity. When we find pig-headed ants or deaths-head moths"——

"What are pig-headed ants?"

"A species of insect devoid alike of reason and all the nobler qualities which we ourselves possess. I say, when we find them, it becomes our duty to use strong measures to raise their condition, or remove them out of our way."

"Just as a physician who fails to effect a cure would feel justified in killing his patient?"

"Again, sir, you misapprehend my meaning. It is the custom of Parisian sparrows, when they clamour for liberty, equality, and fraternity, to kill each other, in order to purify the government. Having no real grievances at home, we find it convenient to redress our wrongs and seek for sweets abroad. Thus we preserve our independence, and confer a benefit on the world at large. My time is precious—good morning!"

My noble constituents will readily understand how I stood petrified at the audacity of this fighting ant, who stoutly maintained that might alone was right, and that his corrupt form of government ought, forsooth, to be set up as a model.

I had it in my mind to tell him that the chief successes of his foreign policy were effected by the subtile diplomacy of maintaining intestine divisions in foreign states. In this way the time of their enemies is fully occupied, and their strength weakened.

But he retreated before superior force, well knowing that his arguments must be crushed by the criticism of a Philosophical French Sparrow.

I afterwards learned that the officer had retired to his property in the country, "there," as the ants would say, "to practise those virtues God has imposed upon our race."

The only good points about the government of Old Frivolity lie in the protection extended to the meanest subjects, and the way they manage the working neuters, in making them pull together to effect great ends. This latter would prove a great element of danger were it introduced among ingenious Parisian sparrows.

I started much impressed with a sense of the perfection of this oligarchy, and the boldness of its selfish measures, and left regretting that in governments, as in individuals, close scrutiny reveals many defects.

Monarchy of the Bees.

Profiting by what I had seen in the Ants' empire, I resolved in future to observe more closely the habits of the tribes, before trusting myself to princes or nobles. On reaching this new dominion I stumbled against a bee bearing a bowl of honey.

"Alas!" he exclaimed, "I am lost."

"Why?" I asked.

"Do you not see I have spilt the queen's soup, happily the cup-bearer, the Duchess of Violets, will attend to her immediate wants. I should die of grief if I thought my faults would not be repaired."

"How came you to worship your queen so devoutly? I come from a country where kings and queens and all such human institutions are held in light esteem."

"Human!" cried the Bee; "know, bold Sparrow, that our queen and our government are divine institutions. Our queen rules by divine prerogative. Without her wise rule we could not exist as a hive. She unceasingly occupies herself with our affairs. We are careful to feed her, as we are born into the world to adore, serve, and defend her. She has her sons and daughters for whom we rear private palaces. The latter are, too frequently, wedded to hungry, petty princes, who thus claim our service and support."

"Who is this remarkable queen?"

"She is," said the Bee, "Tithymalia XVII., a woman endowed with rare wisdom; she can scent a storm afar off, and is careful to lay in stores for severe winters. It is said also that she has treasures in foreign lands."

Here a young foreign prince came forward, and cautiously inquired if we thought any of the young ladies of royal blood likely to want a husband.

"Prince," said the working Bee, "have you not heard of the ceremonies and preparations for departure? If you wish to court any daughter of Tithymalia you had better make haste. You are well enough in your appearance, although you could do with a new coat."

I beheld a splendid spectacle. One of the princesses was about to be married. The pageant on which I gazed must have a powerful effect on the vulgar imagination, and wed the people to the memories and superstitions which are about the only links uniting the higher with the lower orders of society.

Eight drummers in yellow and black jackets left the old city called Sadrach—from the name of the first Bee who preached social order; these were followed by fifty musicians, all of them so brilliant that one might have said they were living gems. Next came the body-guards armed with terrible stings. They were two hundred strong. Each battalion was headed by a captain, wearing on his breast the

order of Sadrach—a small star of beeswax. Behind them came the queen's dusters, headed by the grand duster, then the grand tooth-pick-bearer, cup-bearer, eight little cup-bearers, and the mistress of the Royal House, with twelve train-bearers, and lastly, the young queen, beautiful in her maidenly grace, her true modesty. The wings which shone with great splendour had never yet served for flight. The queen-mother accompanied her, robed in velvet, aglow with diamond-dust. Musicians followed humming a hymn of praise composed for the occasion. After the band came twelve other old drones, who seemed to me to be a sort of national clergy. They were all alike one to the other, and buzzed uniformly and monotonously. About ten or twelve thousand bees marched from the hive, upon the edge of which stood Tithymalia, and addressed these memorable words to the multitude :—

"It is always with a new pleasure that I witness your flight, as it secures the tranquillity of my people, and that "——She was here interrupted by an old drone who was afraid of the queen using unparliamentary language — at least so I thought. Her Majesty continued—" I am certain that, trained by our habits of thrift and industry, you will serve God and spread the glory of His name on the earth which He has so enriched with honey-yielding flowers. May you never forget the honour due to your queen, and to the sacred principles of our government. Think that without loyalty there is anarchy, that obedience is the virtue of good bees, that the strength of the state depends upon your fidelity. Know that to die for your queen and the church is to give life to your land. I give you my daughter Thalabath as queen. Love her well ! "

This eloquent speech was followed by loud buzzing.

As soon as the young people had left with the queen, the poor prince I had noticed buzzed around them, saying, "Oh most noble Tithymalia, unkind fate has bereft me of the power of making honey, but I am versed in economics, so if you have another daughter with a modest dowry, I "——

"Do you know, prince," said the grand mistress of the Royal House· " that with us the queen's husband is always unfortunate. He is looked upon as a sort of necessary evil, and treated accordingly. We do not suffer him to meddle with the government, or live beyond a certain age."

But the queen heard his voice and said, "I will befriend you, you can serve me; you have a true heart, you shall wed my daughter, and lend your pious aid to the work of our kingdom."

This cunning prince, one of no mean power, had fallen in love with one of the fair princesses.

There is one remark I have to make which has nothing to do with government, and that is, that love is the same everywhere. Here was a fellow who had winged his flight from a foreign land to bask in the sunshine of his true love, follow her from flower to flower, sip the nectar from the same cups; to worship even her shadow as it flitted across the pale lily, or kiss her footprints on the dew-spangled rose. Ah me! these thoughts send a tide of fond memories throbbing through my old heart. There is one thing certain, on my return, I must have a commission appointed to inquire into the nature of this passion among men and bees.

My constituents will be pleased to learn that my fame gained me a reception in the palace. I had despatched a bee to inform Her Majesty that a stranger of distinction from Paris desired to be presented to her.

Before being led into the audience-chamber, several magnificent bees examined me to make certain that I carried no dangerous odour or foreign matter about my person to soil the palace. Soon the old queen came and placed herself on a peach blossom. "Great Queen," I said, "you see before you a member of the Order of Philosophical Sparrows, an ambassador sent to study the governments and organisation of the animal kingdoms."

"Great ambassador, wisest of birds, my life would be a dull one were it not for the cares of government and the events that compel me to seek retirement twice every year. Do not call me Queen or Majesty, address me simply as Princess, if you wish to please me."

"Princess," I replied, "it seems to me that the machine you call the people excludes all liberty. Your workers do always the same thing, and you live, I see, according to the Egyptian customs."

"That is true; but order is the highest public virtue. Order is our motto, and we practise it, while, if men strive to follow our example, they content themselves with stamping the motto on the buttons of their national guards. Our monarchy is order, and order is absolute."

"Order is to your profit, Princess. The bees on your civil list are all workers, and only think of you."

"What else would you have? I am the State; without me the State would perish. In other realms order is freely canvassed, and each one follows it according to his own idea, and as there are as many orders as opinions, constant disorder prevails. Here one lives happily, because the order is always the same. It is much better that these intelligent bees should have a queen instead of hundreds of nobles as in the Ants' kingdom. The Bee world has so many times felt the danger of innovation, that it no longer seeks for radical change."

"It is unfortunate," I said, "that well-being can only be obtained by a cruel division of castes. My bird's instinct revolts at the notion of such inequality."

"Adieu," said the queen; "may God enlighten you! From God proceeds instinct; let us obey Him. If it were possible that equality should be proclaimed, should it not be first among us whose duties serve a great end. Our affections are ruled by laws the most mathematical. But for all that, the hive and our various occupations can only be maintained by our wise system of government."

"For whom do you make your honey? for man!" said I. "Oh, liberty!"

"It is true that I am not free," said the queen; "I am even more bound than my subjects. Leave my State, Parisian Philosopher, else you may yet turn some weak heads."

"Some strong heads," I replied. But she flew away. When the queen was gone, I scratched my head, and made a peculiar sort of Flea fall out of it. Being a perfectly cosmopolitan bird, I was about to enter into conversation with this bloodthirsty intruder, but he had leaped for dear life. Gaining confidence, he returned and said :—

"O Philosopher of Paris, I am only a poor Flea, who has made a long journey on the back of a Wolf. I have listened with profound interest to your remarks, and felt honoured while I sat upon your learned pate. If you desire to find a government modelled on your own principles, go through Germany, cross Poland, and make your way to Ukraine, where you will find, in the administration of the Wolves, the noble independence you require, and which you pointed out to that old twaddler of a queen. The Wolf, Sir Bird, is the most harshly-judged-of animals. Naturalists quite ignore his purely republican principles, for he devours those of them who may cross his path; but he cannot kill a bird, so you may safely trust yourself to his hospitality, and perch on the back of the proudest of them."

THE WOLVES' REPUBLIC.

Parisian Sparrows, birds of every clime, animals of the whole world, and ye petrified relics of antediluvian reptiles and monsters, admiration would seize on you as it did on me, could you behold the noble Wolves' Republic—the only one in which hunger is conquered—This is what elevates the animal spirits.

When I reached the magnificent steppes which stretch from the Ukraine to Tartary, the weather was already cold, and I felt convinced that the privileges of the subjects must be great to compensate for living in such a land.

I was met by a Wolf on guard. "Wolf," I said, "the cold is chilling my blood. I shall die; and let me tell you, my death will be a loss to the world at large. I am a traveller of renown!"

"Get upon my back," said the Wolf.

"Pardon me, citizen, I prefer to cultivate your acquaintance afar off. Perchance you wish to whet your appetite with such a dainty morsel as a Parisian Sparrow."

"What manner of good would you do me, stranger? Should I eat you, I should be neither more nor less hungry. You are evidently a studious Sparrow. You have burned the midnight oil, and offered up every drop of your blood on the shrine of science or literature. Skin, bone, and feathers. Ugh! you would only trouble me in my empty stomach, and there study out at leisure the various odds and ends of my organisation. No, no! get up; give my mouth a wide berth; sit on my tail, if you like the fur."

Concealing my dread of his hungry fangs, I perched lightly on the tail, where I was not unfrequently disturbed by the tremor of his emotions.

Fellow Sparrows, the tail of a beast of prey is the safest perch, and it affords a true index of the play of passion in the brute.

"What are you doing here?" I said, to renew the conversation.

"Well," said he, "we are awaiting some visitors at yonder castle, and intend to devour them, horses, coachmen, and all." Here the tail whisked so briskly that I had difficulty in keeping my feet.

"That would be an extraordinary proceeding. Men, to be sure, are our foes, and you, no doubt, perform a useful function in keeping down their numbers. As they are Russians, you won't eat their heads," said I.

"Why?"

"It is said they have none."

"What a pity! That will be a loss to us, but that won't be the only one."

"How so?"

"Alas!" said the Wolf, "many of ours will fall in the attack, but it will be in our country's cause. There are only six men, a few horses, and some provisions. Too few! too few! They won't serve for a meal to the right wing of our army. Bird, believe me, we are nearly famished!"

He turned and showed his fangs so hungrily that I almost fainted with fright. "We have had nothing to eat."

"Nothing," I said, "not even a Russian?"

"No; not even a Tartar. Those rogues of Tartars scent us two miles off."

"Well, then, how do you manage?"

"The young and strong among us are bound to fight on an empty stomach. She-wolves, cubs, and veterans must feed first."

"That is a fine point in the character of your Republic."

"Fine!" he said; "why, it is only fair. We know no distinction other than that of age and sex; all are equal."

"Why," said I, "how can that be?"

"Because we are all of us the same in the sight of God."

"And yet you are only a sentinel."

"Yes, it is my turn to be on guard."

"But, General," said I—here the fellow pricked up his ears, and seemed immensely pleased with even the shadow of distinction carried in a name—"to-morrow it may be your turn to command."

"Exactly, that's how we square. Your intelligence, Sir Sparrow, does your nation credit. It is something like this. When in danger we meet together, and elect a leader, who, after the peril is passed, falls again into the ranks."

"Under what peculiar circumstances do you meet?"

"When there is, say, a famine, to forage for the common good. In time of great distress we share and share alike. But do you know we are driven to the direst straits, when, as frequently happens, the snow lies ten feet deep on the ground; when the houses are covered, and no food is to be had for months. Strange! our stomachs grow

smaller and we crowd together for warmth. We pull together wonderfully. Since the Republic was formed, the wolves have abstained from devouring or destroying each other. This ought to make men blush. The wolves are each and every one sovereign. They govern themselves."

"Do you know, General, that men say sovereigns are wolves, and prey upon their people? You will have no need of punishment in your land."

"Yes, we have; when a wolf commits a crime he is punished. Should he not scent his game in time, or fail to secure it, he is beaten. But he never loses caste on that account."

"I have heard tell that some of your wolves in office are secretly ravenous, devouring the substance of the country, and given to dividing the good things of government among their friends."

"Hush! Gently, please. These are matters of which we do not speak. The natural tendency of wolves is to feed on carrion, and when the body politic becomes corrupt, they perform the healthful function of licking the sores. It is only wolf-nature to seek such office and profit by it. One good feature in the Republic is, that a wolf is free to hunt down his own game, and when required, he may rely on the community."

"This is indeed excellent," I replied, "to live and govern one's self. You have indeed solved a great problem." Yet I thought to myself that the Parisian Sparrows will not be simple enough to adopt such a system.

"Hurrah!" cried my friend, whisking me from his tail into the air. All at once from a thousand to twelve hundred wolves with superb fur, and agility wonderful to behold, arrived on the scene. I saw two carriages drawn by horses, and defended by masters and servants. In spite of the sword-blows that fell on all sides, and the wheels that crushed the assailants, the wolves fixing their fangs into the horses soon overpowered the caravans. The prey was portioned out. One skin fell to the sentinel, who devoured it greedily. Other valiant wolves were allotted the coats and buttons, and soon only six human skulls remained that proved far too thick and hard for the profane fangs of the destroyers. The corpses of the slain wolves were respected and became the objects of a strange usage. Hungry wolves lay concealed beneath them until such time as a flock of birds of prey had settled on them. These they deftly caught and devoured. This was a touching example of thrift, recalling the various modes by which men take a profit out of their dead. I am told they set up tombstones over them, as baits for the world's applause. A man will inscribe on the stone which covers the remains of some poor wife sentiments of deep regret and undying affection, while his carnal eyes are bent on some pretty bird fluttering over him and sympathising with his grief.

One thing struck me about the Republic, and that was the seemingly perfect equality of the people which arose, not so much from the nature of their government, as from the fact that by nature they are endowed with equal strength and instinct. The failure of human Republics arises out of the unequal intellectual and physical capacities of men. A more perfect system of education and a higher moral code, strictly observed by all, may one day bring man and man to the same level. Hereditary defects of character will then disappear, and all men will regain something of the perfect image of the God that created them. In the Wolves' Republic the weak ones go to the wall, die off, as the struggle for existence is severe, so severe indeed that only the strong survive. The young wolf is educated in warfare and suffering. Indolence and want of pluck are punished by starvation, as all must work, and it becomes a habit to toil, and to toil ungrudgingly. Ah me! I almost despair of the task of reforming a country spoilt by luxury. Parisian birds, some of you are daintily fed on grubs and grain in golden cages, others, alas, have to pick up a precarious living on the streets. How shall we raise the poor to the level of the rich? Raise them from their lowly perch and place them in palaces? The wolves obey each other quite as heartily as the bees obey their queen, or the ants their laws. Liberty makes duty a slave. The ants are fettered by habit, and so are the bees. The Wolves' Republic possesses many advantages, for if one must be a slave to anything, it is better to obey public reason than to become the votary of pleasure, or the football of fate.

I must own, whether to my shame or glory, as I approached Paris my admiration for wolfish freedom gradually diminished in the presence of refinement; and while I thought of the priceless boon of a cultivated mind, the proud Republic of the Wolves no longer satisfied me. Is it not, after all, a sad condition, to live on rapine alone? If the equality of wolves is one of the sublimest triumphs of animal instinct, the war they wage against man, birds of prey, and horses, is a violation of animal right.

The rude virtues of a Republic thus constituted depend alone on war. Is it possible that the best form of government can be sustained by ceaseless warfare, by continuing to push one's conquests into the territory of weaker, simpler, and perchance more virtuous foes? This, my philosophic companions, is the policy of the great country of the wolves. Better rather to die of hunger, while we, by our self-denial, add a single green leaf to the laurel-crown that decks the brows of our country. We are placed here on God's earth, not to destroy, but to build up His glorious works. Take this to heart, ye visionaries who seek to establish the edifice of peace on a foundation of vice and blood. However humble our lot, let us rather—like the coral insects who, by their toil, build up the loveliest islands of the world—seek to do our duty in our allotted spheres, that we may leave behind us an unsullied fame.

Life and Philosophical Opinions of a Penguin.

"Must one seek for happiness?" I inquired of the Hare. "Search," replied he, but with fear and trembling.—*The Anonymous Bird.*

I.

HAD I not been born in the extreme South, beneath the rays of a burning sun, which helped to liberate me from my shell, and was quite as much to me as the brave Penguin which abandoned me to fate, I might have proved a happier bird ; but being, as I said, hatched under a tropic sun rather than a lucky star, I became an unhappy bird. I had a hard struggle to get into the world, as my shell was an uncommonly thick one. When at last I had found my way into the light, I stood for some time gazing at my prison with feelings not unmingled with surprise at the event which had introduced me to freedom. One, of course, has only a confused remembrance of those early days, and can hardly be expected to give a full account of the sudden change implied in birth. I have heard it said that men when they are born—some of them—smile blandly on the prospects that life presents to them ; while others, and they the majority, begin life with a wail of regret, the prophetic note of a sorrowful existence. Be that as it may, I remember, as soon as I was able to reflect, thinking how uncomfortable I must have felt, doubled up in a shell too contracted to admit of motion. The change was truly appalling. There lay the shell, to me a world which I had first filled and then broken, to find myself a mean tenant of immeasurable space. The prospect puzzled and hardly pleased me; I had exchanged my little egg for one boundless in its infinity. Far from being modest, on finding myself in the world my first notion was that all I saw belonged to me, and that the sole purpose of the earth was to contribute to my support.

Forgive the infantile pride of a poor Penguin, who, as the years rolled on, has been taught humility. As soon as I discovered the use of my eyes, I found myself alone in what proved to be the hollow of a great rock overlooking the sea. The rocks, the stones, the water; a boundless horizon around, immensity, indeed, and myself, in the midst of it all, nothing more than an atom! I vainly inquired, "Why is the universe so large?" and the echo from my empty shell answered "Why?" The question had been asked before, and, as I afterwards learned, had never been more conclusively answered. A little world, quite a small one, filled by those alone who are devoted to each other's welfare, would have been more to my liking than this great gulf in which all seems lost, and hopeless confusion reigns,—in which there is space enough and to spare, not only for those creatures who detest each other, but for nations whose conflicting interests cause endless strife, and allow full scope to the play of crime and passion. Penguins in general, and you my personal friends, would not a world framed for ourselves have been better? a world with one low mountain bathed in sunlight,—a tiny, leafy plain bordering the sea, carpeted with flowers, and shaded by fruit-bearing trees, in which a score of social birds might build their nests—birds decked with gay plumage and bursting with song, unlike the poor Penguin whose lines you are now reading?

These are vain imaginings, there is no such paradise for Penguins or any other creatures. There are fields and flowers, foliages and fruit-bearing trees, birds with bright plumage, and others with song; but, alas! the wide world shares their charms—flowers here and fruit there, all so scattered and dispersed as to minister alone to the sport and pleasure of mankind. Yes, man alone has the power of making nature his slave, of bringing all these elements together, of rendering his mansions musical with the nightingale, his lawns gay with flowers, and his orchards glorious with varied fruits.

Again I crave pardon, dear reader. The habit of dwelling alone has rendered me gloomy, and I forget myself, forget that I have no right to forget my humble lot and obscure destiny.

II.

I ought to say that my early isolation and ignorance tempted me to brood over the unattainable. Nevertheless, I claim credit for self-denial in pruning my introduction, as I might have dived deep into the miseries of solitude—the solitude of my early days. The theme was a prolific one, which I should not have allowed thus to escape. It is so soothing to complain; so comforting, indeed, as to pass for real happiness.

I had not been alive a day before I learned what heat and cold were. The sun disappeared, leaving my rock as cold as an iceberg. Having nothing to do, I began to move, and felt about my shoulders something I conceived must be intended for use. Stretching forth these little arms or wings with which Nature had endowed me (she has lived too long on her reputation of being a good mother, loving equally all her children), after prolonged efforts I at last succeeded in rolling from the top of my rock. Thus my first experience in life was, as you see, a fall, which I speedily resented by digging my beak into the unsympathetic soil. This only increased my pain, and led to reflection. "It is evident," I said, "one ought to be careful about one's first step in life, and to reflect well before moving." I then inwardly pondered over my destiny as a Penguin, not that I had the faintest pretension to philosophy, only when one is forced to live, and one is not accustomed to do so, one must find out some rules of life.

" What is good ? "
" What is evil ? "
" What is life ? "
" What is a Penguin ? "

Before I could solve these questions, my eyelids closed in sleep.

III.

Hunger rudely awoke me! Forgetting my resolutions, strange as it may seem, I did not wait to inquire, " What is hunger ? " but immediately proceeded to satisfy the craving by eating some shell-fish that were yawning before me. I ought to have first indulged in a dissertation on the possible danger of following this ancient custom. My inexperience was punished, for by dint of eating too fast, I was nearly choked. I have no notion how I learned to eat, to drink, to walk, and move to right or left, measure distances with my eye, to know that all one sees is not one's own; to come down and ascend, to swim, to fish, to sleep standing, to content myself with little or nothing, &c. It is sufficient to say that each and all of those studies caused me countless troubles, fabulous misadventures, and unheard-of trials.

IV.

What are our duties in the world? What will ultimately become of Penguins? Where do we go to after death? Why were some birds created without feathers, some fish without fins, or animals without feet?

My worldly experience often tempted me to wish to return to my egg. One day, after profound reflection, I fell asleep, and during my repose heard a noise, which was neither that of the waves nor any sound to which I was accustomed. "Wake up!" said the active part of my being, that which never seems to slumber, and is ever on the alert like a guardian angel to ward off danger. "Wake up, and you will behold something to rouse your curiosity." "Certainly not," said that other most excellent part of ourselves which requires sleep. "I am not curious, and have no desire to see anything. I have already seen too much." Still the other insisted, and I continued: "It would be wrong to break my slumber for anything spurious; besides you deceive me, the sound has gone. It is a dream; let me sleep! let me sleep!" I really wished to sleep, stubbornly closed my eyes as best I might, and folded and fondled myself to repose with all those little cares common to sleepers. But, alas! all was of no avail; I woke up. What shall I come to? I, who vainly thought myself the most considerable creature living, the only bird in creation. I sank into utter insignificance before the sight that met my gaze. There, before me, I beheld at least a dozen most charming creatures, some with expanded wings floating in mid-air, others diving into the waves, and again rising to display their snow-white plumage in the morning sun. Surely, I thought, these are the inhabitants of a happier and more perfect world. Had they descended from the sun or moon? What unknown caprice had brought them to my rock?

They were endowed with a sublime mastery over the elements, skimming the waves as if to laugh at their fury, resting for an instant on the solid earth, and, as if disdaining its support, again cleaving the air with their glorious wings. So wrapt was I in admiring the grace and perfection of their movements, that jealousy never clouded my mind. At last, carried away by the ardour of youth, and the emotion with which the beautiful fills the breast, I rushed into their midst, exclaiming: "Celestial birds, fairies of the air!" Here I had to pause for want of breath.

"A Penguin!" cried one of them.

"A Penguin!" repeated the whole band; and as they all laughed on seeing me, I concluded that my presence gave them pleasure, and so I boldly introduced myself in the following words:—"Ladies and gentlemen, you are right, I am a Penguin, and you are the fairest forms I have gazed upon since the hour I left my shell. I am proud of your acquaintance, and should like to join in your sport."

"Penguin," said my lady friend who had first addressed me, and who appeared to be the queen, but who, I afterwards learned, was only a laughing Gull. "You do not know what you are asking, you may, however, profit by experience. It shall never be said that such an elegant Penguin received a denial." She then gave me a flip with her wing which sent me reeling into the midst of the group, another did the same, and they all followed suit, flipping me about, first to one side, then to another. This was sport!

As soon as I could get the words out, I shouted, "Stop! you are killing me."

"Bah!" said they, "we are only beginning, hah! hah! Keep him warm. Keep the ball rolling." The sport began anew, and with such vigour that I soon fell to the ground thoroughly humbled and exhausted. The Gull who had first called me Penguin, and who had taken the lead in maltreating me, noticing my prostration, reproached herself for her conduct.

"Forgive us, my poor Penguin. You do not seem to relish our rollicking style, yet it is our nature, so pray do not blame us if you are hurt." She then came forward and bent over me with such a tender look, that, in spite of what she had just done, she seemed for the moment perfectly beautiful and good.

But pity often comes of self-love, and is nothing more than regret for harshness. What I mistook for the dawn of affection was only

LIFE AND PHILOSOPHICAL OPINIONS OF A PENGUIN. 61

sorrow for having done wrong. Thus, as soon as she saw me comforted, away she flew with her companions.

This sudden flight so startled me, that it was impossible to find a

single word or gesture to prevent it, and again I was alone. From that moment solitude seemed insupportable.

IV.

To tell the truth, I was blindly in love, and savage at having done nothing to win a bride so beautiful. Why did I not exercise my blandishments? While pondering these things I wandered to the edge of a pool of water. It was placid and clear, reflecting only the blue heaven, until, bending down to dip and cool my fevered beak, I beheld my own image, and nearly choked as the picture of my unsightly proportions flashed on my mind. I left the mirror, and soon by reason of vanity forgot what manner of bird I was. Sleepless nights and miserable days became my portion. Eagerly I listened to the whisperings of the wind, thinking that I heard the gentle sound of that lovely spirit of the air descending to soothe my troubled heart. Vain thought! she never came, and worse luck, my appetite had gone with her. My only solace was the sea. There was something in the mournful voice of its waves, as they broke on the great rocks, that soothed me in my saddest hours. There was something in its immeasurable depth typical of the grief which overwhelmed me.

The reader may feel inclined to smile at my vulgar and unpoetic proportions, nevertheless, let me remind him that God has so framed the world, that in the rudest and most unlikely forms among men and beasts repose the sublimest attributes. Thus human genius is seldom found mated with bodies of herculean type. So the sentiment of a lovesick Penguin can never be estimated by the appearance of its too solid body.

V.

"Suspense becomes intolerable, I can no longer bear it," I said, and cast myself into the sea to drown my sorrow in its mournful waves.

VI.

Unfortunately, I discovered how to swim, so my history does not end here.

VII.

When I rose to the surface—one always rises two or three times before drowning—yielding to my passion for soliloquies, I inquired what right had I thus to seek to destroy myself; if the world would not be just one Penguin worse off, had I met my end, &c. My soliloquy was long. I was drifting many leagues straight ahead; now and again diving with the dire resolve of going to the bottom and remaining there. But for some reason I always found myself coming to the surface, and, to tell the truth, the air seemed all the more refreshing after each dip. Just as my seventh attempt at suicide had miscarried, I rose to find myself side by side with a creature whose simple unaffectedness won my heart at first sight.

"What were you after below there, Mr. Penguin? and where are you going?" he inquired, bowing profoundly.

"I hardly know," I replied.

"Well," said he, "suppose we go together."

I willingly agreed, and on the way related my misfortunes to him. When I had finished, he asked me if I had formed any plans for the future. "No," I said, "not any, still I have half a mind to travel in search of my lady-love, the Gull."

"How came you to love a Gull? You look a large solid bird enough. Why don't you devote your affections to one of your own decent stay-at-home kind? Depend upon it, the Gull, could you wed her, would only bring grief. She is puffed out with feathers, and ever on the wing; she would soon desert you for one of her own kind."

This seemed severe, and I replied testily, "There's no accounting either for tastes or for love. It came upon me like a sunbeam from heaven."

"From heaven!" said my companion. "Lovers' language! A

strong light, this light of love ; and it has left a shadow of pitchy darkness somewhere, has it not ? "

"Ah ! sir," I said, "you look dejected. My story, perchance, stirred up old memories." He said nothing, but wrapped in profound melancholy ascended a rock left dry by the tide, and I followed. There was such an air of profundity about him that I inquired what he was thinking about.

" Nothing," he replied.

"But who are you, whose silence is so eloquent ? "

"I am of the Palmiped family, and my name is Fool."

"You, Fool ! " I cried. "Come ! "

" Yes," he replied, "I am so named in the world from my habit of minding other people's affairs and neglecting my own ; so sinking myself, what can I do for you ? Listen, my friend," said this sublime bird ; "not far from here is an island called the 'Isle of Penguins.' It is only inhabited by birds of your tribe. They are all of them equally ugly; go there, and who knows, you may even be thought handsome."

" Am I then so unsightly ? " said I.

"Yes," he said, "you are as unlike the gull as the grub is unlike the butterfly."

VIII.

During our voyage, encountering a severe storm, we rode it tranquilly on the breast of the billows, while great ships, freighted with the wealth of the world, were wrecked and lost before our eyes. It was pitiful to hear the shrieks of the perishing sounding above the tempest, men and women who had braved the dangers of the deep, some to seek happier climes, others, the riches they were doomed never to enjoy.

At last through many dangers we reached the shores of the "Happy Island."

"Let us pause here," said my sage companion, "and note the native mode of seeking what I hold to be a myth—earthly happiness."

Shaking ourselves dry, my friend, who had studied geography, elevated his beak, and casting his eye along its line, took our position from the sun. The result was curious and instructive to navigators, and even to mankind generally, not to mention birds. According to our calculations, we had been availing ourselves of every slant of wind to push ahead, and, strange to say, reached land a hundred miles astern of the point we started from. Had we been men, pioneers of civilisation, gifted with a sublime belief in our own powers, we should have no doubt proved to our own satisfaction that we had made unheard-of progress. Men and mules, without knowing it, go as often backwards as forwards.

My friend here remarked that the island was unknown, had never, in fact, found its place in any map. Our observations, therefore, cannot fail to prove useful.

"Let us go inland. If you don't object?"

"With all my heart;" and in my youthful ardour was about to kiss the happy soil.

"There, calm yourself," said the Sage. "This is neither Peru nor the Penguins' Paradise. The name alone misleads you. This land, 'Happy Island,' is so named because its inhabitants (all of them) inherit a furious desire for happiness, not because they are happy; they spend their lives chasing a phantom, and when it seems nearest, they are swallowed up in the grave. These islanders cannot be brought to understand that wrong must exist, and that happiness may be obtained by redressing wrongs and grievances, and that the most one can do is to snatch moments of bliss from one's days and years of toil and sorrow. I have heard that men, after trying all sorts of new-fashioned receipts for happiness, fall back on the oldest plans, imagining they have discovered in them a new panacea for all earthly woes.

"These curious islanders make self their god. They make it a rule each one to seek his own personal gratification, this plan is most ancient: love, sympathy, self-sacrifice, devotion, virtue, duty, are with them nothing more than words whose meaning has been long forgotten. Another rule is to avoid doing anything that will in any way mar one's enjoyment, or spoil one's ease. It will be seen that only the rich among them are able to carry out their principles to the full extent. Let us note how they manage affairs. Do you see the mansion over there? is it not beautiful? In it the disciples of pleasure carry on their amusements. Let us look in; we may learn something. Over the doorway we read in Latin, 'Here we are, four hundred of us, all happy'; followed by a text from their sacred classics, 'Neutralise the influence of parents upon children, and all will go well.'"

In the first room we came across a charming illustration of the text —a number of showily-dressed, attractive-looking mothers, who refused to sit on their eggs. Some of them had strolled into the garden to spend their time more usefully in flirting with dangerous-looking

male friends. Somehow the poor little ones were hatched. "You unwelcome rubbish!" said the mothers; "now that we have

had all the trouble of bringing you into the world, some one must nurse you—we are otherwise engaged. We will return and spoil you later on, if we think of it." Guardians are found. A Weasel displayed the deepest interest in the eggs, an Adder watched them tenderly as they were about to break, while Wolves feasted on the young to keep them out of harm's way.

By far the most telling scene was met with in the schoolroom. There we saw bloated-looking Boars prosecuting their studies by lying on their bellies, or rolling over on their backs. Oxen, that had abandoned the plough, and Camels striving to make their neighbours carry their humps.

Those who were not asleep were yawning, or going to yawn, or had yawned. All of them seemed profoundly dull. Near the centre sat a Monkey nursing his knee, who, with his head thrown back, seemed to be absorbed in his reflections.

"Sir," I said, addressing him, "are these dejected-looking creatures around you happy?"

"I fear not," was his reply; "although their sole pursuit is happiness, some of them are miserable enough. As for myself, I feel supremely uncomfortable on this confounded stool, but as governor I must keep awake."

On our way we passed in front of the shop of a blacksmith, who was fitting a pair of carpet slippers to a tender-footed horse. Suddenly I said to my travelling companion, "I have had quite enough of this 'Happy Island,' let us continue our voyage."

IX.

PENGUIN ISLAND.

Two days later we reached Penguin Island. "What does that mean?" I said, on perceiving some two hundred individuals of my kind ranged as if in battle-array along the shore. "Are these troops intended to do us honour, or to prevent our landing?"

"Fear nothing," said my friend, "these Penguins are our friends. It is the custom of their country to parade the shores in flocks."

We were received with much kindness, and conducted with great ceremony towards an old *Sphemiscus*, the King of the island. This good King was seated on a stone, which served as a throne, and surrounded by his subjects, who seemed to be all known to him.

"Illustrious strangers," he exclaimed, as soon as he perceived us approaching, "we are delighted to make your acquaintance," and as the crowd around him barred our way, he continued: "My children,

range yourselves on one side, and allow the strangers to pass." The ladies stood on his right, and the gentlemen on his left. "You, sirs, are welcome to enjoy the freedom of our kingdom."

I ventured to say, "Sire, your renown is the talk of the whole world, and the hope of seeing you alone sustained us through the perils of our journey."

"Good!" whispered my friend; "you are a courtly liar for one so young; but be careful, else you may die a diplomatist."

My speech so pleased the King, that he cast off his Phrygian cap, descended from his perch, and clasped me to his breast, saying, "You are, for one so young, a bird most fair and honest. Remain with me to aid me in my old age."

"Noble sir," I replied, "your knowledge of Penguin character is truly worthy of your fame. I will gladly accept your generous offer, trusting that my youth and inexperience may excuse my many shortcomings."

"Stay, are you married?"

"No, your Majesty, I am a bachelor."

"He is a bachelor!" cried the King, turning towards the ladies, who at once, and for the first time, overwhelmed me with their fond gaze.

"A bachelor! a bachelor!" cried a chorus of voices, "what a dreadful creature!"

"Hush!" said the King, "we have cured worse maladies. There is my daughter."

"But, Sire," I protested, "my heart is lost to another."

"The remark is worthy of your modesty. You shall wed my daughter; the notion suits me; it is a question of privilege, not of heart."

I so little expected this proposal, that I remained mute with amazement.

"He who says nothing, consents," said the King. Before I had time to decide, my eyes met those of the princess. It was but for a moment. The god of love had kindled a perfect conflagration in her breast. Everything was arranged before I could say no, so engrossed was I with my own reflections. That momentary glance had evidently sealed my fate. So far as one's after-life is concerned, it had more effect in neutralising my happiness than if I had, from my earliest infancy, set myself the task of inventing the best means of blighting my peace.

"Well," said the monarch, "look at your future wife. Are you not delighted? too happy to find words to express your joy? Is she not lovely?" The poor old potentate looked tenderly on his daughter, and with tears in his eyes, continued—" You cannot know what I am offering, she is a good child, a good child! and will make a dear wife. Not a single subject in my realm boasts smaller eyes, yellower beak, rounder form, or larger feet. She is indeed beautiful!"

The wedding was arranged, and we were married in great state. My wife's father paid all the expenses; for in Penguin land kings as well as subjects have enough to marry and dower their daughters. This was how I became the King's son, and how foolish marriages are made. My real troubles date from the close of the ceremony, as my wife was neither very handsome nor very good.

X.

I might finish here, but as I have gone so far, I may as well relate the bitter end.

I dreamt one night that I beheld my first love, and that she beckoned to me to follow her. The whole scene was so vivid that when I awoke, I felt I could recognise the spot if it existed in any part of the earth. In a weak moment I resolved to start in search of this heaven and its goddess. At last, I left the Penguin shore, ostensibly on a diplomatic mission. For two whole years I searched the world over; but in vain, until, just as I was giving up hope, I discovered the object of my solicitude on a sandbank, stooping over the filthy remains of a stranded Whale, in the society of a ragged, vicious-looking Cormorant, the meanest of birds. This then was the Gull of my dreams! the spirit of the air! the ideal of beauty, the Peri, the sylph, whose seductive image had cursed my life. My eyes opened, but too late to discover how the fool mistakes the glitter of the basest metal for the lustre of pure gold. What would I not have given to crush the memory of my folly out of my heart; to begin life anew, and ponder well the first false steps. Yet I reflected, all may be well, better far the bitterest truth than the sweetest falsehood.

Setting sail for Penguin Island, I resolved never again to quit it shore, and to become a good husband, father, and prince.

XI.

On landing, I first visited the people, who were well, next, my father-in-law, who, thank God, was better than the people. I then

began to look for my dear wife and child, and—good heavens! I found my family had increased to four. My wife, poor soul, had taken another husband, thinking I had deserted her.

I at once repaired to my old friend and travelling companion, whose ability the King had sought to reward by making him Prime Minister; but he refused to add to his cares that of office, and retired to live as a hermit on the top of a rock. He had chosen the highest rock in the realm, whence, far above the turmoil of the state, he bent his philosophic gaze on the lower world which he had abandoned to its fate. I felt much in need of sympathy and advice. After recounting my woes, the answer of the recluse sent a thrill of despair through my heart.

"Bah!" he said, "I am sick of all the affairs of life. Each hour wounds, but happily, the last kills us. Forget your troubles. Arm your heart against the malignant influences that mar the peace of brutes and men. Why the devil should *you* be happy? (he was a profane bird). What have you done to merit happiness? How fared you in your journey? Have you seen enough of the world—sinned too much? Hah! hah! Is your punishment greater than you can bear? Poor deluded Penguin! you have been the football of our old enemy, fate. It must have been great fun for the old rascal, to mark your abortive attempts at heavenward flight with these half-formed wings. Hah! hah! what a capital joke!"

"You seem merry, my friend," said I, "your levity wounds me deeply."

"Listen, my child," he replied. "You have spent the best of your days in vain pursuit of the unattainable. Depend upon it, the nearest approach to happiness is found in paths obscure and humble. Paths of duty along which kind Providence will ever act as our guide."

"You puzzle me," I remarked, "your language is as changeable as English weather. At one moment you are a wicked bird, at another a moral philosopher."

"Nay, friend," he said, "these are but the passing moods of the mind. I am told that men as well as birds have their moods. Even some most religious men, they tell me, wear a sombre cloak to conceal the sinful thoughts that are always present with them. They resemble the shells they employ in warfare; harmless enough, until thrown to the ground by some sudden shock of passion which fires the fuse and destroys them. It seems to me, in order to succeed in the pursuit of happiness you must prefer clouds to sunshine, rain to fair weather, grief to joy. You must possess nothing, and yet find yourself too rich, take all that is done as well done, all that is said as well said, believe nothing, and yet know everything. Dream while you are living, live in your dreams. After all when you feel really happy, have patience, and time will surely destroy the illusion."

Here the philosopher paused for breath.

Reader, if you are unhappy, let me counsel you to take warning from the life of a poor Penguin, who blighted his hopes by worshipping at the shrine of a false goddess.

The Last Words of an Ephemera.

It was the opinion of the savants of our race who lived in ancient times, many minutes, indeed, before we came into being, that this vast world would dissolve and disappear within eighteen hours. That this hypothesis is not without foundation, and at the same time worthy of the erudition of the ancients, I hope to be able to prove. The great luminary travelling through space has, during my own time, sensibly declined towards the ocean which bounds the earth on all sides. If, therefore, we base our calculation on the space traversed by the sun per second, it will be found that, before eighteen hours have elapsed, his fire will be quenched in the ocean, and the world given up to darkness and death. He has already passed the zenith. For all that, the moment when the bright disc will dip beneath the waves seems distant as eternity, when measured by the span of our lives. I myself have enjoyed several moments of existence, and feel age creeping on apace. I see children and grandchildren around me dancing in the joyous light. I may live a few seconds longer, and witness many changes; yet my life has been so full of sad experiences, as to convince me that, in the course of nature, I must soon follow those who have gone before. In reviewing my past existence, while clearly discerning its failures and follies, I venture to hope that it has not been altogether misspent. My researches have contributed not a little to solve some of the problems connected with the most curious phenomena of hedge-rows and ditches, keeping altogether out of account the facts which I have established connected with the duration of the earth. I have applied the most refined analysis to discover the true constituents of the atmosphere, and the meteorological conditions which promote or destroy insect life. I could reveal secrets to mankind, to which their microscopes and spectroscopes can never afford the faintest clue. These are certain elements necessary to our existence only known to ourselves, as also the important functions we perform in carrying out the wise economy of nature.

Men are blind to everything that does not, as they conceive, bear

76   PUBLIC AND PRIVATE LIFE OF ANIMALS.

directly or indirectly on their own interest, and in their folly they imagine that our lives are worse than useless. They cannot perceive that we are ministering spirits of the air, sent by an all-wise Creator to correct abuses of which they themselves are the authors. But life is short; all too short for the labour it implies. Alas! my end draws near, and my friends console me by saying that I have done enough to earn lasting fame, and to promote the happiness of my race, until the eighteenth hour witnesses their destruction, and the wreck of this great plain which men call the earth.

The Sorrows of an Old Toad.

My father was already well up in years and corpulence, when the joys of paternity came upon him for the last time. Alas! his happiness was of short duration. My poor mother's strength was overtaxed with a dreadful laying of eggs, and, in spite of the tenderest nursing, she at last succumbed to the effort of bringing me to the light. I was brought forth in sorrow, and to this fact I attribute the deep shade of melancholy which has clouded my existence. I was always of a dreamy, contemplative nature. This, indeed, formed the basis of my character. The early days of my Tadpole life are wrapped in gloom, so dense as to render them void of incident. I can just dimly recollect my father, squatted beneath a broad leaf on the bank of a stream, smiling benignly as he watched my progress. He had always a soft, liquid eye, in whose depths I could read the love of his tender heart. His eyes were of a greenish hue, and protruded. This, taken together with his noble proportions, his enemies attributed to high living. He was in reality a contemplative Toad, whose greatest success lay in the cultivation of philosophic leisure. He carefully avoided the water, and, little by little, withdrew himself from the scene of my exploits. I am ashamed to say that his absence never caused me to shed a tear. I had two or three brothers about my own age, with whom I giddily threw myself into all the pleasures of life. It was a joyous time! What would I not give to recall those fleeting hours of my youth, with all their happy experiences. Where is now the lovely stream, over whose dewy banks the reeds and grasses bent to watch the play of sunlight on its smiling face? Where the crystal pools, the scenes of my adventures in an enchanted world? the dark-bearded stones, 'neath which we followed many a giddy course, our hearts throbbed with fright as we came face to face with some motionless Eel, or touched the silver scales of a dreamy Carp? I can recall the great fish, troubled in his sleep, viewing us with a quick, angry glance, until, perceiving our shame and confusion, he smiled, and we renewed our game.

It is impossible to describe the pleasure of being rocked, caressed and fondled by the current as it pursues its tranquil course. Every ray of sunlight that found its way through the willows revealed new wonders. The dull, dead sand was glorified by the light until it shone like a bed of jewels. Myriads of creatures seemed to spring into life. The weeds flashed with a thousand hues, the hard-hearted pebbles flung back the rays with a brightness that pierced the deep recesses of the stony bed.

Delirious with joy, how often have I not dived to mingle with the light, to catch something of the fleeting charms it scattered so lavishly around. At such times I completely lost my head. (Pardon me, dear reader, should I seem to exaggerate; a Tadpole who has lost his head must make the most of his *tail*, as he has nothing more left to him.) We then thought ourselves indomitable, pursuing shoals of microscopic fish that sought and found shelter beneath the stones. But the huge Spiders, walking on the water and devouring all they came across, afforded rare sport. Gliding cautiously up behind, we used to lick the soles of their feet, and dart off, amazed at our own audacity, to seek cover beneath the shade of lily leaves. I have passed whole days under those leaves, examining with the profound admiration of youth, the delicacy and beauty of their configuration. In each one of their pores I discovered little lungs, and such a marvellous organisation, that I dared not touch them, so much was I moved by the notion that, like ourselves, they must have feeling as well as vitality. These reflections intensified my curiosity to such a degree, that I made my way among the roots to try and find out the secrets of plant life, and see for myself the source of so much beauty. It seemed to me that the water-lily was a perfect type of goodness. It ungrudgingly displayed its charms to the gaze of the world, at the same time sheltering with its broad leaves the tenderest forms of life. Flower, leaves, and root alike refused to yield up their secrets, and yet though silent, every detail of their form was eloquent with the praise of their Creator. Thoughts of the good fellowship subsisting between plants and animals brought tears to my eyes, which I suppose I must have shed and thus swollen the stream beneath which I was submerged. All those things made a permanent impression on my mind, although I have had my days of scepticism, when it appeared to me that disorder and misery were the ruling powers of the world. As my age advanced, my powers made corresponding progress; strange longings for a higher state of development filled my head, while my tail shortened and responded more and more tardily to its office of oar and rudder. Sharp pains shot through my posterior, ending in the growth of feet and lungs. In truth, I was becoming a Toad! The transformation is not without its moral significance. New members brought with them obligations to which I was a stranger, hardly knowing how to use the attributes Providence had placed at my disposal.

One day, I descried on the bank of the stream a Goose and her family about to take their daily bath. The scene was not new to me, but the emotions which filled my breast differed from anything I had experienced. The Goslings were lying all of a heap on a tuft of fine grass, and from my point of view, presented a confused mass of down, gilded by the sun. Here and there a little yellow beak might be seen. But the immobility of their position, and the utter abandonment of their postures informed me of their perfect contentment and tranquillity. The young brood was steeped in sleep, while the mother, bending a tender, watchful eye over them, uttered a sound so touching to their hearts, that every eye blinked, and every beak opened with a joyous quack.

"Good morning, mother," they seemed to say, "Is it time for our bath?"

"Yes, lazy little ones. Do you not hear the music of the stream, or feel the heat of the mid-day sun? Your heads are exposed to its scorching rays."

"O mother! don't disturb our rest," they replied. "You have no notion of our comfort. The drowsy humming of the bees, the languid nodding of the harebell, and the scent of the new-mown hay are soothing us to sleep."

"Hush your silly prattle and wake. A little courage, a little self-denial, my dears, and up with you."

This was too much for the Goslings who slowly separated, presenting a confusion of pink feet, plushy wings, and golden beaks most interesting to behold. Some rolled over and over in their attempts to gain their legs. At length they succeeded, and went waddling, and wagging their stumpy tails streamwards. When they reached the water's edge, after many hesitations, strivings, and chatterings, they at last stretched their necks and entered boldly to float with the current.

"Strike out, my dears," said the dame. "Heads erect, mind. It is supremely vulgar, my children, to bend the head unless to pick up something to your advantage. Kick the water bravely; it is made to serve you."

It was a beautiful sight, and I was about to ask permission to make one of their number, when the mother, in passing, haughtily tossed her beak in the air, saying, "Avoid slimy toads, and all such creatures—their presence is defiling!"

Judge, dear reader, of my pain and surprise. I dived into a dark pool to drown my wounded pride. When I again came to the surface, the interval had transformed me into a truly melancholy toad. A large spider, with whom I had become acquainted, passed over my head, smiling kindly at me; but he won no responsive smile. Feeling need of breath, I mechanically sought the bank, and was startled by a hoarse voice shouting—

"Confound you, reptile!" I turned, and perceived a gay personage decked in blue and gold—a Kingfisher. "What are you doing there, stupid? You with the four superfluous feet, body, head, and eyes. You slimy scoundrel! Don't you know your vile presence poisons the stream? Get out, else I will swallow you like a gudgeon. Ugh!" I thought he was going to be sick. "Make off, you frighten my clients." He was a fine-looking fellow, the colour of heaven itself; but with a voice like a lawyer, or the devil. To tell the truth, I was so afraid of him that I made for the bank. When fairly out of the water, I leant over its surface to return thanks for all the pleasure it had afforded me. To my horror, I beheld at my feet a strange misshapen thing, bearing some likeness to my father. I moved my head, it did the same; I raised my feet, it imitated the motion.

"Hah! hah!" shrieked the Kingfisher, "you lovely coquette! what do you think of your beautiful proportions?"

"What!" I said, "is that my image?"

"Yes, my treasure; are you not proud of the picture?"

It was all too true. There I was, and the willows above me as a frame, and the blue heaven as a background to my poor image. Well, after all, I thought the pure mirror of the stream was perhaps my truest friend, as it taught me to know myself. Bidding adieu to my former haunts, I turned my back upon the stream, and soon felt humbled and forsaken. My departure was quite unnoticed. The river went on its way as before, not a single blade of grass, not an insect moved to wish me a happy journey. Could I then be so completely dispensed with, I who at first had thought the world all my own? I felt so ashamed of giving offence that I asked pardon of the Kingfisher, who replied—

"Go to ———!" I dare not repeat his answer, it was of such a nature as to convince me that he was a bird of the world. Day began to decline, and feeling fatigued, I sat down to rest. Being of a dreamy disposition, I found pleasure in contemplating nature. In front was a forest wrapped in a veil of purple mist, behind which the sun was setting and shooting its rays like fiery arrows through the leaves. Above, the calm sky was of a pale green hue, so soft, so full of tenderness, it filled my breast with the feeling that after all I was not forsaken, and gave me courage to live on. Pray do not set me down as a foolish toad, living on the pleasures of imagination. It is in such follies as these that I have found the chief joys of my life. The disinherited ones of earth must gather consolation where they can. The air was hushed, the flowers and grasses sparkled with dewy gems, the birds had sought their evening perches, and were singing each other to sleep. All around were crowds of little beings, pushing on to their homes, tired of the business of the day and covered with dust. Some one, doubtless, was waiting and watching for the return of each insect wanderer. Such thoughts as these again weighed down my heart with a feeling of utter loneliness and despair. Happily, not far from where I stood, I perceived a hole between two roots, which I prudently approached, and timidly feeling the walls, I entered. Surely, I thought, this will prove a quiet resting-place, when I heard a regular monotonous noise resembling some one snoring.

"Who is there?" cried a gruff voice; at the same moment I felt a sharp prick in my hind-quarters.

"I am a young toad, sir, not long out of the water."

"Oh, horrors!" continued the voice.

"Forgive my intrusion, I will leave your house." My eyes had become accustomed to the darkness, and I made out my adversary to be a jagged ball—a porcupine, would you believe it? This redoubtable personage was rather good to me. The stab with his quills, which had nearly killed me, still causes great suffering in damp weather. On my assurance that I did not snore, he allowed me to pass the night in his quarters. After he had a fair view of me, he cried—

"You are ugly! and that is drawing it mild. You are ugly, feeble, clumsy, impotent, silly!"

"Yes," I murmured, for I felt he spoke the truth.

"You little affected monster, do not add to your ridiculous appearance by simulating wisdom and modesty. You are neither rich enough nor independent enough to indulge in such vanities. You are doomed to be hated, strive to hate in return, it will give you strength, and when one is strong, one is joyful. Should any one approach you, spit at him! Resent even a look by your noxious spittle. Show your spots, your wounds, your slimy horrors. Make men flee and dogs bark at your hideousness. May the hatred of others be a shield to you. You, if you are not a fool, will find joy in hating. Be proud of your horrible envelope, as I am of my quills, and above all, do as I do—love no one."

"If you do not love me a little"—here he burst out laughing—"just a very little, why do you give me such good advice?"

"Why, my simple friend," he said, "I do not love you. You amuse me, since the rôle you are about to play resembles my own. My enemies will be yours also. Don't you see that the prospect of wounding their superfine feelings through such an ugly medium affords me a new pleasure? Let us be mutually accommodating, a joint-stock thorough nuisance to all who affect to loathe what God has made for some good end. I hardly know what I am made for, and next to erecting my quills offensively, like the bayonets on which some thrones are built, my chief happiness consists in doing nothing."

These maxims seemed odious to me. I had no hand in making myself, otherwise my mouth should have been more contracted, and my stomach less capacious. Had I been consulted, I hardly think I would have chosen a "fretful porcupine" as my model, nor yet my father, poor old toad! who lived a contented sober life, and died regretting that his paunch had reached its fullest rotundity. It was no fault of mine that I inspired horror. If ugly and deformed, I was endowed with a profound love of the beautiful, which compensated in some measure for my awkward appearance, and, if I may use the expression, with a merciful provision of vanity, which enabled me ever to admire and cherish my own body. If my body was all too solid to respond to my every wish, yet my dreams and imaginings were unfettered as the wind. The reader, if he cares to study the habits of such an humble creature as the toad, will discover much truth in what I say; moreover, if he be an ill-favoured person, he may find comfort in my philosophic view of life.

A love-sick toad may be deemed by some an object worthy of ridicule; nevertheless, as my romantic experiences form one of the most eventful pages in my history, I am bound to take the reader into my confidence.

I had reached that period of development when, rejoicing in the strength of youth and the full maturity of my faculties, I leaped from place to place, not without aim, as many might suppose, but in the pursuit of knowledge, frolic, or recreation. The sun shone brightly, grass and flowers were in full bloom around, breathing an intoxicating perfume into the midday air, when I first beheld the object of my dreams. My enemies may think me a plagiarist, and that I have lifted my sentiment from some modern novel. All I can say is that my book is nature, which I recommend to the study of writers of fiction, many of whose works would poison the morals of toads, for these prefer unadorned truth to the gaudy tinsel of the literary showman.

My love was bewitching in her dress of pale green. Oh how fondly I followed her with my eyes as she leaped from leaf to leaf, until at last I beheld her against the sky, her silken wings spread out to their fullest, descending lightly on to a blade of grass, which bending, swayed to and fro in the breeze! Flying in the air, toying with the flowers, making them quiver on their stems without soiling a single petal, skimming the placid water, admiring her own image on the wing, this fair creature won my heart. Vainly I strove to court her glance, forgetful that a vile toad in love is no more pleasing to the eye than a toad in grief or any other mood. At last she turned towards me, and in that weak moment I tried to smile, thinking I should look less repulsive. Alas! I discovered that my capacious mouth, bloated-looking eyes, and unyielding physiognomy, were powerless to respond to the sentiment of my heart. Besides, my pretty grasshopper failed to see me, or mistook my form for a clod of earth. Soon a deep shadow fell across me, and turning, I perceived a chubby boy advancing slowly, cautiously, armed with a huge net at the end of a long stick. I had already frequently observed him trying to catch butterflies and winged insects. When one of these poor, pretty, perfect little things escaped him, he lost his temper with his coveted prize, and savagely continued pursuit, crushing the first victim that fell to his net. I said to myself, "This is horrible! To this boy it appears a crime for an insect to strive to escape death. What have they done to warrant such a fate? They have not even the misfortune to be ugly." This cruelty had such an effect on me, that one night I dreamed I saw large toads become light and mobile, catching men-children in their nets, and pinning them to the trunks of trees. I accepted the dream as a bad omen, and rightly, for not long after I descried the child coming towards the grasshopper, and divined that he was bent on capturing my lady-love. Not a moment was to be lost. I saw the danger, calculated my distance, and leaped just to the spot where the boy's foot fell; he slipped on my back and rolled to the ground.

My love escaped from the snare! But I suffered greatly, having one of my hind-feet crushed and broken; yet, in spite of my agony, it was the sweetest moment of my life. The child got up crying, and seeing the cause of his fall, ran off in terror, only stopping in his flight to cast a stone at me. Happily he was as unskilful as wicked, and I was left with only a few scratches. My heroine, who had taken in the whole situation, came towards me accompanied by many friends. I should have preferred her being alone. Her companions were daintily dressed, perfumed with the fine essence of flowers, and seemed to be led towards me more by curiosity than compassion. When they had gathered around, I raised my eyes in hope of the happiness that I thought awaited me.

"Is it this poor wretch, did you say, my darling, who was crushed?" murmured a grasshopper in the tone of one about to perform a very disagreeable duty. "Oh! ah! This is really disgusting. Mark the creature's wounds—how horrible! If one were not sustained by elevated sentiments, one would feel inclined to quit the scene. Oh, the hideous monster! Is it not strange that heroism should appear in such ignoble guise?"

Here this heartless drivelling fool stroked his chin with his foot and looked as if he had said rather a good thing. My grasshopper-goddess laughed affectedly, and I think made a sign to them to fetch her the strongest perfume to stifle the odour of my bleeding body. Addressing me, she said, "Say, my good fellow, why did you render me this service? Do you know that yours was a fine action?"

The moment had arrived for me to cast myself at her feet and proclaim my love, and I stammered out, "Willingly would I have sacrificed my life to save you, my love! my treasure! my"——

Sad to relate, my voice was drowned in the coarse laughter of the lady and her foolish friends.

"Upon my honour," said one, "this is a gay toad!" "Hah! hah! a mangled toad in love!" roared another. "Isn't he a romantic-looking creature?" inquired a third. "Come, ladies, one of you waltz with him. Nay, don't go too near, I think he has teeth."

They then walked round and examined me with their glasses in the most insulting manner.

"I find him less hideous than grotesque," murmured the queen. "It is his head that is unique. Why, his face is enough to make the daisies yellow, and freeze the swamps with fright! Have you all seen his eye?"

"Yes! yes! his eye," they replied, "is very strange! very strange!"

Could anything be more galling to my pride to be thus made the butt of these hateful fools? Had they stabbed me to the heart, I think I should have survived in spite of them, but their jeers and laughter made me die a thousand deaths. Under the dominion of proud sentiment (of which I am now heartily ashamed), I raised myself on my bleeding foot and addressed the grasshoppers.

"I ask you for neither pity nor recompense. You yourselves witnessed"——

"Listen!" said one; "he speaks well, although thick, like a person in liquor."

"This is horribly interesting."

"You witnessed," I continued, almost fainting, "an act of devotion. I loved"—— The hilarity burst forth anew, and the grasshoppers, no longer able to control themselves, joined hands and danced round me like a troop of green devils, singing—

"Hail, lover, hail! joy to your tender heart."

They certainly enjoyed themselves thoroughly that day. After all, they had only obeyed their nature, and I had mistaken my own.

I had fully proved my own vanity and stupidity—at least, that was the opinion of my friend the Porcupine, who that night drove me out of his den.

From that time I felt myself an outcast, and sought humbly to win the favour of my own kind by making myself useful in my own proper sphere. I became almost a creature of the night, and lost sight of much of the beautiful that had charmed me, for the world is full of beautiful things to those who can look out of and beyond themselves. It boasts also fortunate beings whose lives would be all the more happy if they would only consent, now and then, to yield up one of their joyous hours to gladden the hearts of the poor. I ask you, dear reader, is it not so? You may be a creature, charming in person, refined in manner, and successful. Their attributes, as you use them, may make you either a god-like ministering spirit in the world, or a fascinating fiend. Your strong sympathy and timely help may lighten the burden of the poor, may cause a deformed brother to forget his deformity and delight in your beauty as much as if it were his own. There would be no plain-looking or even ugly creatures to curse the day of their birth, were there no cruel, well-favoured observers to wound them with their looks and gestures. But I am forgetting the lesson which I myself learned late in life. I had put myself in the way of finding out by experience that a poor toad could never have wings, nor, though everything is fair in love and war, could he hope to win the heart of a grasshopper.

I am now full of years and philosophy; my wife, like myself, is a contemplative full-bodied toad, in whose eyes I am perfectly beautiful. I must own my appearance has greatly improved. The like compliment cannot be honestly paid to my mother-in-law, who has caused me no small trouble. She increases in age and infirmities. The reader will pardon my repeating, that notwithstanding my rotundity, I am no longer ugly. Should he have any doubt on this point, let him ask my wife!

The Theatrical Critic.

My dear Master,

YOU must feel alarmed during this hot weather at seeing the walls inscribed with "Death to poodle-dogs," having yesterday, with your own hand, sent me adrift without either muzzle or collar. You knew that I wanted my liberty; I was indeed constrained to beg of you to let me go by what you would term "some subtle indescribable impulse." To tell the truth, the conversation you carried on with your friends about Boileau, Aristotle, Smith's last book, and the "five unities," proved dull. I listened to you as long as I could, then yawned, and barked as if I heard some one at the door. Nothing would for one instant draw your attention from scientific discussion.

You even pushed me off your knee just as you had clinched an argument by pointing out that the ancients were always the ancients.

It was truly unkind of you to persist in remaining indoors when duty and inclination called me abroad. At last you let me go. I had found on the table an order for a stage-box in the Theatre of the Animals, a glorious place where they were only waiting for you and me. For two reasons I will refrain from writing down a full review of the play: first, because I am only a novice in the art; and secondly, because you, my master, gain your bread by descriptive writing. How could you cram your paper daily if you had not at hand all the stock phrases of dramatic criticism? As for myself, I feel rich in the mine of poesy that prompts every wag of my shaggy tail.

I should be an ungrateful dog if I robbed you of your capital. Your imagination I have nothing to find fault with, seeing that your greatest successes, as a dramatic critic, were penned on plays you never took the trouble to witness.

I made my way to the theatre on foot, for the weather was fine. I came across some agreeable acquaintances on the way, all going with their noses to the wind. The bulldog at the door respectfully inclined his head as I entered the box and threw myself carelessly into a chair, my right foot on the velvet cushion in front, and my legs resting on a couch. This graceful attitude you yourself assume when preparing to sit out, or sleep out, a five-act play.

I had hardly been seated two minutes when the orchestra was invaded by musicians. These personages were the gayest to behold. The flute was played by a goose, while a donkey struck the harp—*asinus ad lyram*, wrote some erudite poet. A turkey clacked in E flat. The

symphony began, and resembled those of which you speak so enthusiastically every winter. The curtain then rose, and my troubles as a critic commenced.

It was a very solemn drama, written by a sort of greyhound, or half-greyhound and half-bulldog, a half-English half-German animal, who had entered the Dogs' Institute of Paris.

This great dramatic poet, whose name is Fanor, has a way of manufacturing dramas as ingenious as it is simple. He first goes to Mr. Puff's Pug and demands a subject, next he makes his way to Mr. Scribe's Poodle and engages him to write it. When the play is put on the stage, he employs six pariahs to applaud it, brutes they are who bark savagely. He is a wonderful fellow. Fanor wears his coat well brushed and most artistically curled, altogether he is just the sort of cur to wait upon rank and bow it into the boxes.

The play was said to be new. Let us skip the first scene. It is always the same—servants and confidants explaining the nature of the crimes, griefs, intrigues, virtues, or ambitions of their masters.

Do you know, my master, it was perhaps a great mistake to remove the muzzles of our poets. The traffic in the sublime has been left to an unmuzzled race of poodle-dog poetasters. It was not so with the ancients who wore the bands of art, and who dwelt far from the common crowd within the temple of the Muses. As well-fed watchdogs, they were thus restrained from poking their noses into the accumulated filth of history.

There is more in the muzzle than one would think. It is a safeguard against the spread of the hydrophobia of literature, so prevalent in our own times, and requiring all the bullets of cold-blooded critics to keep it in check. Evils other than the unnatural howlings and riot of modern tragedy are caused by liberty. There is an unearthing of old bones, which are scraped, polished, and displayed as the product of that modern genius the nineteenth-century dramatist, who with tragic instinct consigns the memory of their real owners to eternal death and oblivion.

The tendency of some grovelling dogs thus to become resurrectionists is too well known to require further comment at my hands. Death to those who before us said what we will to say, "*Pereant qui ante nos nostra dixerunt!*"

Little by little the plot expanded. When the pugs had revealed all their masters' secrets and hidden thoughts, the masters themselves appeared, and in their turn gave us the paraphrase of what had preceded, together with the culmination of their passions. If you only knew how many odious persons I beheld. Imagine two old foxes in mourning for their tails: these with a couple of superannuated wolves, recumbent, and gazing vacantly around; a pair of badly-licked dancing bears, waltzing to soft music; weasels with frayed ears and gloved hands, made up a staff of threadbare comedians, all professing their loves and passions on the stage. Yet I am told that outside the theatre door they would tear each other's eyes out for a leg of mutton or horse's ham. But I had for the moment forgotten that the secrets of public life should be carefully walled around, so I dutifully returned to my analysis, in, I own, a roundabout sort of way. The language was not very intelligible. It was all about the sorrows of unfortunate Queen Zemire and her lover Azor. You have no notion of the singular and unaccountable stuff crowded into this hybrid composition.

The beautiful Zemire is a Queen of Spain, descended from a noble stock, counting among her ancestors a jolly dog named Cæsar.

In the back-kitchen of the castle, and in the noble *rôle* of turnspit, a mangey animal, but withal a worthy fellow, named Azor, turned the queen's spit (while Queen Zemire had turned his head). He says—

> " Belle Zemire, O vous, blanche comme l'hermine,
> O mon bel ange à l'œil si doux
> Quand donc à fin prendrez-vous
> En pitié mon amour, au fond de la cuisine," &c. &c.

These verses, improvised by the pale light of the lamp, were found admirable. The friends of the poet exclaimed, "Ah! sublime! They are perfumed with the profoundest sentiment!" In vain the linguists —curs, griffins, and boars—sought to criticise. "Why," said they, " should kitchen and cookery in a high-class composition be mixed up with flowers and sentiment? What was there in a turnspit and its associations—the devouring appetite of the queen, &c.—to fan the flame of passion?" These expressions, let fall at random, nearly cost them their seats.

The verses were forcibly rendered by Azor, who scratched himself at intervals, either to relieve his feelings or lend piquancy to his love. At last the lover subsided into his daily barking prose.

"Zemire! Zemire! Oh how I long to kiss the ground beneath thy feet!" (in carrying out this ardent desire he would have encountered no reasonable difficulty, as the full-bodied lady left her footprints wherever she trod—this by the way). Azor howls in his agony of heart, when the kitchen-boy all at once throws some hot cinders into his eyes to remind him of his neglected duties at the spit.

I must tell you that in the castle there is a nasty dog, a Dane named

Du Sylva, an intimate friend of the Count's horses, with whom, for his own pleasure, he goes hunting. He is, as you shall see, a cur fierce, jealous, implacable, and desperately wicked. He is hopelessly enamoured of the beautiful Zemire, who treats the attentions of this northern boor with scorn. What does the Dane do? He, of course, dissembles with such craft one would imagine he had forgotten the insults heaped upon him. Alas! the traitor is only biding his time. One day he finds Azor in the castle moat, looking fondly towards his lady's nest. "Azor, follow me," says the Dane. He obeyed, and followed with his tail hung pensively between his legs. What does the Dane then do? He led Azor to a neighbouring pool, and ordered him to plunge and remain there for an hour. Azor obeys gladly. The cool water soothes his skin, and carries off the taint of cooking. It imparts lustre to his disordered fur, grace to his sickly body, vivacity to his eyes, which have been dimmed by the light of the fire. Leaving the pool, Azor rolls with delight on the sweet-smelling grass, impregnating his coat with the odour of flowers. He completes his toilet by whitening his teeth against the lichen of an old tree. That done, he feels the return of youth. The warm blood throbs through his heart, and his pensive tail wags briskly with the sense of new life. The whole world seems to open before him. There is nothing to which he may not aspire, not even the paw of Zemire. At sight of these extraordinary transports the Dane laughed in his sleeve, like the crafty rascal he was. He seemed to mutter, "Curses fall upon you, fool! You shall pay dearly for my fellowship!"

I ought to tell you, master, that this scene was played with great success by the celebrated Laridon. He is perhaps rather stout and old for his rôle, nevertheless, as they say in the papers, his energy and chic carry all before them.

Perhaps the finest scene was laid in the forest of Aranjuez, when the queen-dog walked pensively along with ears cast down, and a poodle held her graceful tail. Suddenly, at the bend of a path, she encounters Azor—Azor renewed, resplendent—the Azor of her dreams. Is it really he? Oh mystery! oh terror! oh joy!! Their eyes meet, and, eloquent with passion, tell their tale of love. Everything was forgotten in those moments of bliss. Had any one reminded Zemire that she filled one of the proudest thrones in the world, she would have replied, "What of that, so long as one loves?" Had Azor been informed of his humble position, he would simply have shown his teeth. Oh delights, miseries, joys of love! and also, to conclude my exclamations, oh vanity of vanities! know that

every door has a hinge, every lock a key, on the rose is a grub, in the kennel a dog, and to every lamp, for the most cogent reason, there belongs a wick, and so in the forest of Aranjuez there lurks a terrible Dane who views our friends' behaviour from afar.

"Ah! oh! so you love each other, do you? Tremble! tremble! for your fate." While speaking thus, when Zemire had quitted the scene, the Dane approached Azor. "So! so!" said he, "Zemire thinks you angelic in your borrowed beauty. You must now assume the skin of a porcupine, and with quills erect, dirty, hideous, smeared with sand and ashes, show yourself to Zemire, and break the spell that binds her!" Thus howled the Dane, giving full vent to his passion in foaming rage. Poor Azor obeyed, and appeared before his mistress. Standing beneath a frightful long-beaked heron, he bowed to the queen, declaring that he had played her false, as he was only an obscure turnspit, and

begging her forgiveness. Then he remained motionless, prepared for his doom. Zemire cast herself at his feet, "Ah!" she said, "let me share your sorrows. I love you still, even in your vile condition. There! I give you my paw in the face of all the world."

During this touching scene the whole house was moved to tears, and at the close came down with thunders of applause. Every one, beasts and birds—even to a flea on the tip of my nose—seemed delirious with excitement. With great presence of mind I bit the tail of an impulsive cock, arresting his flight to the stage to challenge the Dane. In a few soothing words I assured him that the villain was really a very decent fellow in his own house. At the same time I reminded him that, as the village cock, he might be missed in the morning from his dunghill, where he performed the useful office of heralding the dawn.

The curtain fell on the fourth act. As to the fifth, I do not intend to usurp your place as critic, but will conclude by saying that in this act the dogs had become tigers—a natural metamorphosis of which good authors avail themselves. The tiger, with equal consistency, killed his wife by mistake, and consoled himself by slaughtering his

friends. It seems, when fairly married, Zemire became a tigress. This, I have heard, is one of those unaccountable changes which not unfrequently occur in real life. Be that as it may, the curtain at last fell on scenes of crime, murder, and confusion.

After the close of the drama, attendants handed round refreshments. As for me, I followed your example. As it was the first night of representation, I left the box at once with the air of one burdened with thought; and making my way to the green-room, joined a group of theatrical critics walking about with a supercilious pedantic air. One had the sting of the wasp, another the beak of the vulture, a third the cunning of the fox. Beasts of prey were there, hungering for helpless victims. Lions proudly showing their teeth. Of mischievous animals of all sorts, it was a goodly company. I ought to inform you, as soon as it became known that you belonged to me I was permitted to go behind the scenes, and to cultivate the acquaintance of the actors. But I must now conclude this rambling review, a friendly greyhound is waiting to join me at supper.

THE PHILOSOPHIC RAT.

PERSONAGES.

GNAWER, *Rat with grey beard.*
TROTTER, *A young rat, pupil of Gnawer.*
BABOLIN, *Dispenser of holy water.*
TOINON, *Daughter of Babolin.*
A VOICE.

SCENE I.

A DINING-ROOM MODESTLY FURNISHED.

GNAWER *alone, coming and going, seemingly much preoccupied.*

My pupil Trotter is coming to share my dinner. I hope he may find no cause to regret his old master's invitation [*smelling an old piece of cheese he found under the table*]. There now is a bit of cheddar whose delicious perfume would make a dead rat come to life! We shall hear what my pupil thinks of it. The rats of the rising generation are so strange they seem to care for nothing. Nothing pleases them, or dispels the frown they constantly wear. In my young days we were less fastidious, we took things as they came. One day we dined off corn, another off wood—wood or corn, it was all the same to us. Now, alas! all is changed. There is no contentment. If my pupils have bacon and nuts, they lament the absence of cheese. What is the world coming to? Trotter is late, I wonder if anything has happened to him.

SCENE II.

THE OLD RAT AND HIS YOUNG PUPIL.

Trotter. [*Looking in at the window.*] Master, may I come in?

Gnawer. What! by the window? can't you find the door? But I forgot, you rats of the modern school never do as others do. Come, let us dine, the things have been waiting long enough.

Trotter. Master, it is no fault of mine if, instead of crawling under the door, I was obliged to make a long journey round and come over the roof.

Gnawer. [*Laughing.*] Nor mine that I know of. [*He helps himself.*] Try a little of this grilled nut; it is delicious!

Trotter. [*Gloomily.*] I suppose it is my fate.

Gnawer. Again prating about fate. Can't you leave fate alone?

Trotter. Master, fate is never tired of persecuting us. Is it not fate that has filled the hole you cut with such labour at the bottom of the door? so that your friends and neighbours might find no difficulty in visiting you.

Gnawer. And you really think that fate filled up the hole?

Trotter. What else could it be, tutor?

Gnawer. It was Toinon. [*He helps him.*] This lard is delicious. There is no one save Toinon has such good lard.

Trotter. But who is Toinon, tutor?

Gnawer. The mistress of the house, daughter of Babolin. The most charming woman, oh! and such a worker. She toils at sewing from morning till night.

Trotter. And pray what interest can she have in stopping up holes?

Gnawer. What interest? [*Laughing.*] Taste this cheddar. Why, her legs to be sure; Toinon hates draughts. Besides, she is a charming girl, who makes crumbs when eating, and always leaves the cupboard door open. She will make an excellent wife. I wish I could marry her.

Trotter. [*With bitterness.*] You?

Gnawer. [*Good-naturedly.*] Yes, I wish I could marry her—to a youth she loves. It would give me the greatest pleasure to make two such beings happy. Who can prevent me?

Trotter. Reflect, master; you are but a miserable rat, and yet you speak of rendering human beings happy. We are of a despised race. There is nothing so mean in the eyes of men as rats. "Poor as a rat" is a common phrase with them.

Gnawer. Your temper is soured, my boy. Let us walk to aid digestion. The fresh air may clear your mind of these notions. Did you ever come across the songs of Béranger? He says that the poor, or rats, if you prefer it, have for their portion probity, wisdom, and happiness. A celebrated Scotch poet has even spoken of mice and men in the same line—

"The best-laid schemes o' mice and men
    Gang aft a-gley."

That line recalls some incidents that have come under my personal notice, where the wisdom of the rat proved superior to the schemes of men.

Trotter. Yes; it is all very well talking, nevertheless, the fact remains. We are a doomed race. Romantic ideas, however well expressed, will never feed the poor, or rats, when dying from hunger.

Gnawer. Yes; who is in the habit of dying from hunger? Are you? Did you die yesterday? Are you dying to-day?

Trotter. [*Aside in a mysterious tone.*] Who knows? [*Aloud.*] If I do not die, others do. Have you forgotten Ratapon and his numerous family? They suffered for several days from hunger: taking heart, they asked their neighbours for help; but the first they came to, a big fat porker, whose sty was full of corn and vegetables——

Gnawer. Well, I know what happened to them as well as you do. Roused by their cries, Mr. Pig looked over the wall, and addressing them in a surly tone, said, "What is all this noise? What do you vagrants want?" "Your charity, my lord." "Be off instantly. How dare you interrupt me in the middle of my dinner?"

Trotter. That was all that came of it; only, next morning the bodies of Ratapon and his family were found scattered over the country. Want and despair had killed them.

Gnawer. Want and despair! You are drawing on your imagination, my boy. It was simply poison—some balls of lard-and-arsenic which they greedily swallowed without waiting to send them to the parish analyst.

Trotter. What more simple, more soothing than death? Is it not our lot? Are we not menaced with cats, poison, and traps every day of our lives?

Gnawer. Yet we—some of us—reach a happy and honoured old age.

Trotter. Yes; nevertheless, it seems to me that every hour of our life is full of misery.

Gnawer. A thousand evils and misfortunes overcome are preferable to the event that deprives one of life.

Trotter. Better for fools, but the courageous rat has no love for a life full of torments, and casts it from him.

Gnawer. Ah, so you contemplate suicide? and would withal be accounted a wise and courageous rat. It is a gay thought to toss lightly away the life you lack the courage to defend and protect.

Trotter. This is no time for jesting; I am sick of life, and I give it up.

Gnawer. Believe me, you are wrong. Life is not a bad thing. It has its hours of joy and hours of sorrow. I myself have more than once seen our last foe face to face, and yet I live. The traps made by man are not so cleverly constructed that one may not escape from them, and the cat's claws are not always fatal. If my poor father were living, he would tell you how by patience and perseverance a rat may draw himself out of even the most perilous situations. I was still very young when one day the smell of a nice piece of bacon led him into one of those traps, vulgarly called rat-traps. We all met around his prison, and imitating our poor mother, wept and clamoured for his release. My father, calm, dignified, and self-possessed even in misfortunes, said, "Stop your crying and work, every mother's son of you. The enemy may be hidden only a few steps off. Those traps invented by the perversity of man are simple enough. The door hangs on a lever" (my father had finished his education by devouring a dry scientific encyclopædia; he therefore knew a little of everything). "It is said that a lever and a weight might lift the world. If by applying weight to this lever you can give me back my liberty, you shall have achieved a nobler work. All of you climb to the top of my prison and hang on to the long end of the lever." Executing his orders promptly, we succeeded in raising the door and saving my father. Suddenly, with a terrible spring, a furious Tom cat leaped upon us. "Fly!" cried my father, whose courage remained unshaken—"fly! I alone will face the enemy." A fierce struggle ensued, in which my father, severely wounded, lost his tail, but not his life. Soon after he regained our domestic hole, and while we licked the blood from his wounds, he smilingly said to us, "You see, my children, danger is like drifting wood—portentous in the distance, paltry when it has drifted past."

Trotter. [*Coolly.*] That is just my sentiment; I have no dread of danger, I could face anything.

At this moment a noise is heard like a pebble on the window, Trotter is about to flee, Gnawer prevents him

Gnawer. Ah, my friend, where is your boasted courage? You

begin to face danger by running away. Calm yourself, I know this signal. It is Toinon's lover throwing stones at the window. We may remain here. Lovers are dangerous to no one, they only think of themselves.

SCENE III.

THE SAME.

Toinon has softly opened the door and crossed the room on tiptoe; she approaches the window and whispers, "Is that you, Paul? How very imprudent! Oh! if my father were to come in."

A Voice. It is now two whole days since I saw you. I could wait no longer. Is your father still opposed to me?

Toinon. More than ever, love! He means to go to law.

Paul. What? to law about my cousin Michonnet's house?

Toinon. Exactly.

Paul. Seeing that it was left to me lawfully, it is mine.

Toinon. My father has a will which, he says, renders yours invalid.

Paul. He is wrong. Besides, if he would only consent to our union the house would be his as well as mine.

Toinon. He says he hates you, and it would be better I should die an old maid than marry a scamp.

Paul. [*Piteously.*] Do you also, my darling, share his opinion?

Toinon. Alas!

Gnawer. [*Aside.*] That alas goes to my heart. It says more than enough.

Paul. Heavens! your father is coming down the street! I am off.

Toinon. [*Retreating from the window.*] If only he escapes unobserved. If he does not, what shall I do? [*She enters her room.*]

SCENE IV.

THE SAME.

Trotter. Hah! hah! Old Babolin will spoil your matrimonial scheme, my master!

Gnawer. I have decided that this marriage shall take place.

Trotter. That of course alters the matter. If you have pledged your word, Babolin must fall.

Gnawer. Yes, certainly!

Trotter. Is Babolin a weather-cock, that you can turn him at will?

Gnawer. No; he is anything but a weather-cock. It would almost take a surgical operation to get a notion out of his rat's head when it is once there.

Trotter. [*Astonished.*] Is the parent of this fair girl a rat?

Gnawer. No, not exactly. He is what men call a Church Rat. He dispenses holy water at the door of Notre Dame, and sells candles to the faithful, which they piously light in honour of God and the saints.

Trotter. I know. The candles which are lit on the shrine when their owners are present, and carefully extinguished and saved when they have gone, by order of the thrifty saints perhaps. So men in their pious thrift exact a heavy percentage of profit out of holy things.

Gnawer. Come! come! You may grow indignant at your leisure. I hear Babolin approaching. Let us leave him a clear field; he might tread on us.

SCENE V.

Enter BABOLIN.

So, so! In spite of my express wishes he meets my daughter. Comes like a thief to the window under cover of night. I shall show them what I am. [*Calls Toinon; Toinon enters.*] Where are my rights as a father? where are they? It is Mr. Paul who mocks me! [*As if struck with an idea, he pauses.*] What if I said nothing about my mischances? If I acted the clement loving father. Paul loves my daughter. My daughter loves Paul. If, like the really kind-hearted man that I am, I yield to their wishes? That would do me honour, and make me appear before the world a model of virtue and forbearance. [*Approaching his daughter.*] Say, my little Toinon, does it grieve you very much not to wed your Paul? [*Toinon, whose heart is too full for speech, bursts into tears.*] Toinon, if instead of going to the lawyer we go to the notary?

Toinon. [*Smiling like the sun through a rain-cloud.*] To the notary, my father?

Babolin. Yes, my darling, that he may hasten to draw up your marriage contract.

Toinon. With whom, my dear papa?

Babolin. With Paul.

Toinon. [*Throwing her arms round his neck.*] O my dear father! how good! how kind of you! I dared not speak openly to you for fear of giving you pain; yet without Paul I should have died.

Babolin. Confound it! no. You must not dream of dying. Come to the notary.

SCENE VI.
STITCH-GNAWER AND LITTLE TROTTER.

Gnawer. Well, what do you say to all this, my little pupil?

Trotter. I say you are a sorcerer. As to the will of the late Mr. Michonnet, what has become of it? have you hidden it?

Gnawer. I inherit my father's love of books and curious documents. He was a learned rat, having devoured some of the oldest and dryest works in his master's library. It will not surprise you, therefore, to learn that this morning I gratified my natural taste, and at the same time served my young friends, by breakfasting off the will of the deceased Michonnet. Thus, thanks to my timely aid, a lawsuit—one of the greatest evils of this lying age—has been nipped in the bud, and a wedding concluded. You see, my dear pupil, that notwithstanding our miserable condition, we, if we do not neglect our opportunity, can render the greatest service to humanity. But what ails you that you caress your tail so pensively?

Trotter. Oh, I was only thinking that we would neglect our opportunities were we not present after the wedding breakfast. There will be no end of good things going.

Gnawer. Very good. You have wisely abandoned the idea of suicide?

Trotter. I should rather think I have. The world has many traps; but it has also its tit bits of old cheese, for which sudden death would spoil one's appetite.

Gnawer. These are sage reflections, but pray bear in mind the lesson of the lost will. The destruction of this instrument, so small in itself, happily turned the tide of events for generations to come. The wise householder sets his foot on the spark that would have consumed his whole substance. The loving heart crushes the first cruel word that would wreck his happiness. The mariner marks the little cloud on the horizon, furls his sails, and his trusty bark rides out the tempest. Your humble servant has gnawed through the lines by which an unworthy father left an inheritance of misery to his children.

The Sufferings of a Beetle.

VIOLET, who is the most amiable and sensible dove in the world, wore, the other day, a very pretty pin in her collar. A lettered antiquarian owl told her it was perfectly charming.

"Indeed," said Violet, "it is a present from my godmother, and represents an insect on a peony leaf. By means of this talisman common sense is secured, enabling one to see all things in their true light, not through the illusive medium of passion."

The owl approached to examine the jewel, but the dove, perceiving that her white neck against which it rested interfered with his minute inspection, took it off and gave it to him.

"I will return it to-morrow," said the bird of night. "During my nocturnal studies the insect may disclose its history, then will I know the secret of your wisdom and beauty."

As soon as the owl reached home, seeking the retirement of his study, he placed the pin on the table. Directly he had done so, the beetle walked about on the leaf. The insect was green, and its whole demeanour spoke of a worthy and candid nature. Passing a polished foot over its eyes, stretching out first one wing then the other, it directed its pointed proboscis to the owl, and with a mingled air of modesty and intelligence proceeded to relate its story in the following words :—

"I was born on the banks of the Seine, in a garden named after a temple of the goddess Isis. My parents had been consigned to their last resting-place by weevils, when I woke to the consciousness of existence beneath the shade of a *Mimosa pigra*, the sensitive idler, whose juice was my first aliment. The wife of an excellent gardener had taken me in, but while she was absent at market I expanded my wings and flew away. My companions were simply beasts, so I found my sweetest associates in wild flowers, and poppies became my special favourites. I was already well grown, and amused myself by looking for bushy roses, and chasing the busy bees who stopped for a moment to joke with me. Alas! these joyous days passed like a dream. A craving for the unknown gradually forced itself upon me and rendered my simple habits contemptible. I at length decided to raise the veil of the future, and have my fortune told by a weird capricorn beetle who passed for a soothsayer, and who spent her days in a lonely part of the garden.

"She wore a long robe covered with cabalistic signs. Setting out for her cave, the crone received me graciously, and after describing certain mystic circles with her horns, she examined my foot, saying, 'Thou art one of a noble line. The horns of thy forefathers have been proudly exalted, and as woefully depressed by fate. Whence comest thou to this lonely place? I had deemed thy race long extinct, had I not seen thee. The armour of thy ancestors can alone be found in the collections of entomologists. Happiness may never be thine!'

"'Now then, old woman,' I said, 'my ancestors are dead and no manner of good to me. Tell me, once for all, am I likely to play an important part in the world, or am I not? I feel fit for anything.'

"'Hear him, ye powers invisible!' cried the witch. 'Thou wouldst willingly be a Don Juan! consent to drink the nectar of the gods! feast with the immortals, and cancel the debt of thine imprudence by suffering the tortures of Tantalus. Like Prometheus, thou wouldst steal the celestial fire at the risk of being torn by vultures. Alas! thou wilt need no prompting to find misery enough and to spare. I will endow thee with the vile instinct of common sense, remove the mask from all that glitters and is not gold; dissolve the fair form of things, and reveal the ghastly skeletons they conceal.'

"I left this cave and its hideous old witch, feeling discomfited by her strange prognostics. For all that, I still burned with the desire to cast myself into the garden of Isis, where thousands of insects swarmed, rejoicing in its intoxicating air. One day, while taking a morning walk through a kitchen-garden, I fell in with a rhinoceros beetle meditating beneath the shade of a lettuce. Trusting to his wisdom, I humbly besought him to favour me with some of those flowery and precious counsels which Mentor bestowed upon Telemachus.

PUBLIC AND PRIVATE LIFE OF ANIMALS.

"'It will afford me the greatest pleasure in life,' he replied. 'Your appearance recalls some famous old pictures in Lord Diamond's collection. You evidently come of a brilliant line of beetles. Do you see the bloom of luxury in yonder garden? Your horns and credentials will at once gain you an introduction there into our set—the finest society in the world. The life will be new to you, but the jargon is easy. You must make some polite contortions before the mistress of the house, and when you have listened attentively to all the current nonsense of the day, you will be regaled with a little hot water, after which you can amuse yourself with the dragon-flies. Take care to listen patiently to all the unkind things whispered about intimate friends. You are not required to make remarks. Judicious silence will better establish your claims to sentiment, poetic feeling, and profundity, than any remarks you could hope to offer. Your acquirements will be gauged by your power of appreciating the wit or wisdom of those who address you. Above all, be careful to whom you give your heart, as you are almost certain to be deceived. These will make up the list of your pleasures, while your duties will be light and easily performed. Five or six times a year military dress must be worn and tactics studied, when you shall be required to obey implicitly the orders of the hornets.'

"'Five or six times!' I exclaimed. 'What a frightful task!'

"'The country requires it. Go now and enjoy your privileges. You are warned.'

"This gloomy picture of my prospective joys and privileges would have scared any beetle less green and less intrepid than myself. The impetuosity of youth carried me on, and I looked upon the rhinoceros as an old croaker, who had seen too much of the world and of this particular garden.

"'Come with me,' said he at last, 'society waits our appearance.'

"I formed a close intimacy with a May bug, who one day said, 'I shall take you to the theatre, and other places of amusement, where we may spend a pleasant evening.'

"My new friend asked if I was a lover of music. 'Yes,' I replied; 'in the garden of my nativity we had some very fine tom-tits.'

"'We have something much better than that to offer you. I shall introduce you to the Academy, where we shall listen to the sublime in art.'

"My companion, before entering, readjusted his feelers and collar.

He then procured tickets from a wood-louse stationed at the entrance of a large acanthus flower. The concert-hall was filled by one of the most brilliant assemblages of the season. Certain well-known members of the insect aristocracy thronged the private boxes, gazing around with that air of superfine insolence which freezes the muscles of the face into an expression of languid-icy indifference. Slender-waisted wasps and dragon-flies formed charming groups; while a crowd of restless fleas filled the upper gallery. Flies in solemn black —as if mourning for the frivolity of the hour—were seated in the pit, patiently waiting to regale their ears with the music.

"'This gathering,' I said, 'conveys a pleasing impression to my mind. It is astonishing to see youth and beauty so thoroughly engrossed with the prospect of listening to good music.'

"'Do not deceive yourself, my friend,' replied the May bug. 'It is not the art of the musician that is the chief attraction. These are, most of them, slaves of fashion, who know little and care less about music. Chut! here is the first harvest-fly about to open the concert with her celebrated song.'

"The singer, decked in resplendent wings, sang something thoroughly dramatic. Her notes, sometimes loud, sometimes low, deep, high, long, short, were hurled into the hall in a manner so utterly perplexing that I whispered to my friend, 'Do you think she is all right?'

"'Right?' he replied. 'My uninitiated friend, you are listening to a prima donna, the finest soprano on the stage. The rendering of the cantata is sublime. Mark the modulations of the voice, the syncopation of the passages, the—so to speak—rhythmical delivery, the volume of sound filling every corner of the room, the'——

"'But after all,' said I, interrupting him, 'as a mere display of the variety of sounds contained in the voice, the performance is perhaps very fine, yet I would rather listen to the heart-song of a linnet than all the throat-melodies of the world.'

"'Believe me, you must be mistaken,' said the Bug. 'She is a universal favourite; and, moreover, anything so popular must be in itself good.'

"The fly was followed by a band of a hundred cathedral crickets who intoned a chorus. They seemed to be so nervously affected each one about his notes that the fall of the curtain afforded me great relief.

"The interval was filled by the evolutions of a grasshopper ballet corps, who exercised their feet and legs quite as much as the others had their lungs. It seems—so my companion says—they express in their gestures and steps many of the most subtle feelings of the heart. As for myself, I failed to perceive anything beyond the rather indecent gambols of a band of immodestly-dressed female grasshoppers. The display, although utterly devoid of the refinement which each male member of the assembly claimed as his special attribute, seemed to afford uumixed delight. To tell the truth, I myself was beginning to take some interest in the spectacle, when the whole band disappeared, and the din of instruments began louder than ever. Oh my poor head! how it ached! I was compelled to seek the fresh air.

"'Is this what you promised me?' I said to the May-bug. 'I asked for songs, and in place of them you have taken me to listen to a troop of liberated fiends, who play all manner of tricks with divine harmony! Take me, I pray you, where one may listen to music unaccompanied by swords, torches, and operatic tinsel.'

"'Come, then,' said my friend, 'we will go to a place where music is heard in all its purity. There you will be enchanted by the rich voice of a trumpeter beetle of world-wide fame.'

"We winged our way to a fine red tulip that marked the entrance of the hall. As soon as we had seated ourselves, the trumpeter appeared and sang the finest air in a masterpiece. This time I was delighted; his rich deep voice reminded one of the boom of distant thunder, the roll of the sea, or the noise of a steam-power mill. The song was short, and followed by the croaking chorus of miserable crickets. The contrast was so marked as to be revolting. Here my friend explained that each musical star is always attended by a constellation of minor luminaries, whose feeble light is borrowed from the centre round which they revolve. Theatrical managers profit by their study of natural phenomena. They say, 'As there is only one sun in heaven gladdening the earth, so in the theatre we should have one star at a time, so managed as to make the most of its refulgence.' Two stars cannot be allowed to cross each other's track on the stage. Such an irregularity would result in the total eclipse of the one, and in theatrical chaos.

"'Come, let us go elsewhere. Like a boy with sweets, I have kept the best to the last. You must tighten the drum of your ear, adjust your sense of hearing to its finest pitch, in order to appreciate the delicate strains that should touch your heart.'

THE SUFFERINGS OF A BEETLE.

"'I hope,' I replied, 'to tune my tympanum so as to gather up the finest chords.'

"'I am by no means certain about that,' said my Mentor. 'Even I myself, who am thoroughly initiated, lose some of the finest phrases. One must know by a sort of intuition how to discover the sentiments of the composer, just as a gourmet selects the carp's tongue, while a vulgar person polishes the bones. Wherein do you think consists the charm of instrumental music ?'

"'In the selection of a choice melody,' I replied, 'and the happy association of such harmony as shall lend it force and beauty; just as in a picture the true artist so marshals his lights and colours as to give power of expression to his composition.'

"'You are quite wrong,' said he; 'such notions are at least a century old. Nowadays the charm of music consists in the agility of the performer's hands, in the shaggy vegetable-looking growth of the insect who manipulates the sonorous tool. It is undeniable that the harmony and sweetness of instrumental music lies in the nervous appearance of the animal who wakes the articulation of his instrument, in the colour of his skin, roll of his eyes, and the curious manner in which he curves his spine round the violoncello. We are about to listen to one of those profound artists who give a mystic, and at the same time lucid, rendering of the vague harmony that breathes in the moods and passions of life.'

"'Oh, bother !' I said, 'such fine affairs will be far beyond my dull comprehension. No matter, lead on, my curiosity exceeds my discretion.'

"May-bug introduced me into the open calyx of a *Datura fastuosa*, richly decorated for an instrumental concert, to which one could only gain admittance by paying a very high price. The assembly was even more brilliant than that of the Academy. A number of insects were ranged round an instrument with a very long tail, from which were to be drawn prodigies of harmony by the feet of a famous centipede.

"After waiting two hours the artists at last arrived; the Centipede seated himself before his instrument, and looking calmly round at all present, a profound silence was at once established. The piece opened with a succession of thunder peals rolling on from the lowest to the highest notes on the board. The performer then addressed himself, though I thought regretfully, to some of the medium keys, after which commenced a vague slow adagio of an undistinguishable measure, rendered still more confusing by graces of manipulation. The air was poor, but what matters the poorness of the stuff when it is so covered with embroidering as to become invisible ?' This was only a prelude to give a foretaste of the piece. As there were many thunderings and preliminary canterings over the keys—reminding one of a horse getting into form for a great leap—I fancied that something grand would follow; yet it was quite the contrary. The dark foreboding cloud of the introduction cleared away, and was succeeded by a popular ballet-tune, a brisk lively air, which seemed to dance gaily over the green turf.

"This spurious air, which had sprung up like a jack-in-the-box, had been danced to for at least ten years; one had had enough of it in every possible form, but the audience seemed to recognise in the air a delightful old friend.

" At the close of this inspired theme and its endless chain of varieties the performer played the tune with one foot on the base keys, while the remaining ninety-nine feet were producing a furious running accompaniment on the treble, ascending and descending in interminable runs of demi-semiquavers.

"These were repeated over and over to the infinitely growing delight of the assembly. All at once the clamour ceased and the virtuoso counted time with the treble, like the slow tolling of the bell of doom that seemed to say, 'Tremble! tremble! thy death is at hand!' The artist-executioner then seized the doomed air as a Turk would a Christian, tore off its limbs one by one, cut up its simple face, twisted its fingers, and dashed its common metre into the splinters of six-eight time. Here, in a frenzy of rage, he tossed the disjointed members on to the hot anvil of his key-board and pounded them into dust, blinding and stifling one's senses.

"The Centipede continued to hammer louder and louder, faster and faster, keeping the dust of the pulverised air floating in a tempest around, and his audience in a tumult of excitement. The measure was left to look out for itself amid the din and confusion. The insects, seized with the contagion of the musical slaughter, kept time with the fluctuating measure until their bodies shook as if with palsy.

" Composedly retiring within myself, I escaped the excitement, while the piece concluded with prolonged banging of chords, by which one discovered the true genius of the Centipede.

"'Oh, the power of music!' said a moth to her neighbour. 'My soul has been wafted to the luminous spheres of the firmament, ah me!' and she fainted away. Another exclaimed, 'How wonderful! In these few minutes I have climbed to the last rung of the ladder of passion, love, jealousy, despair, fury—I have experienced all these in the twinkling of an eye. For pity's sake, some air—open a window!' 'Oh!' cried a third, 'I have become the slave of harmony. Why can it not leave my imagination to slumber in peace? I have seen white ants devouring their young; bees stinging each other; mosquitoes drawing blood from stones; centipedes committing suicide; charming butterflies metamorphosed into death's-head moths.'

"'Alas!' said an old Cantharis, 'what delight, what bliss to possess such genius! This centipede is truly wonderful! wonderful!!'

"I turned towards a large gadfly who appeared to have some common sense, and inquired timidly if it were not my ignorance which rendered me unable to appreciate the marvels which are being applauded.

"'Imprudent fellow!' replied he, drawing me into a corner. 'If you were heard letting fall such remarks you would be torn to pieces by the Cantharis. You had better go with the herd; say it's no end of soul-stirring, you know, and all that kind of thing. It is fashion, my boy. The Centipede is all the rage.'

"'Thanks for your warning, but is one compelled to come and listen to these torments of h-harmony?'

"'No, not exactly compelled, and yet we cannot escape it. It's supposed to be the correct thing to do.'

"The emotion had now subsided, and we had to listen to a distinguished earwig violinist, who followed so closely in the strain of his predecessor that I will dismiss him without further comment.

"Before leaving the hall I was introduced to the Centipede, and congratulated him on his power over his instrument. The fellow turned away indignantly, saying, 'You take me, then, for a sort of musical machine. A day is coming in which I shall prove to the universe that my own compositions are alone worthy of my genius as a performer. Good-evening, Mr. Beetle.' A slight touch of vanity this, but the faintest trace of it! Ugh!

"The May-bug approached me with a triumphant air, 'I told you we should have a splendid evening.'

"'So very splendid,' I replied, 'I should like at once to sleep off its effect.'

"Next day my guide led me to understand that it was expedient to go and visit some death's-head moths who view nature from their own ideal standpoint and endeavour to imitate its forms and colours.

"The majority of these unfortunates had nothing more left than mere stumps of their once ample wings; they had lost them in ambitious flight while yet too young. The first moth we visited spoke very highly of his craft.

"'Nothing good can ever be achieved,' he said, 'without art, and there is no art without its rules. The precepts of the masters must be followed. No composition can possibly be worth the canvas on which it is painted unless it will bear the tests of law. To produce a good picture, it is necessary to select from nature's storehouse; but to select only such elements as are pleasing to the eye and taste, and to reject all that are offensive. I have striven to carry out and embody all the rules of art in the composition I am about to show you.'

"The Moth then unveiled a large canvas, representing a battle of the animalcules, seen by the microscope in a drop of water. He could not have hit upon a happier subject to display not alone his knowledge of art, but of the fierce passions which characterise even the lowest living organisms. The distinct genera and species were treated with masterly skill. The complicities of structure in the Rotifera lent force and dignity to the action; while the breadth of expression in some of the mouths, the dangerous attitude of the heads, the curves of the tails and antennæ, all contributed to render this one of the most striking productions of modern art.

"In the next studio we visited, the Moth had met with an accident; he had singed his wings by venturing too near his light (candle-light). For all that, we found him a most enthusiastic limner, who discoursed like a lunatic on the subtle fire of genius. His speciality was portrait-painting, about which he had his own notions.

"'It is necessary,' he said, 'in order to idealise the subject, to carefully study the habits of plant life, and impart something of its grace and tenderness to the outlines of the insect who is sitting for a portrait. It is wonderful to observe the effect produced by peculiar habits of life, and most necessary for the artist to note their influences in the treatment of a subject. One requires to make one's self master of the life and thoughts of the sitter, so as to give a poetic rendering to his idiosyncrasy. Thus the low-life vulgar habits of a patron which impress their stamp on his physiognomy must be studiously concealed beneath a virtuous mask of paint and outline. In this way

we depict what the insect under happier influences might have been, in place of what he really is.'

"'In other words,' I said, 'you portray your client as the insect

God made him before he himself wrecked the fair image by giving himself up to the works of the devil. In this way I suppose you serve God and Mammon at the same time. After all, truth is truth, whether on canvas or in conversation, and it seems to me that you prostitute your sublime art by handing down painted lies to posterity.'
We had to leave this studio, as the new light I had thrown on this moth's studies singed his wings afresh.

"My Mentor next led me to a brilliant group of the *Coccus cacti*, or cochineal insects, from the forests of the 'Far East,' who were awkwardly colouring dead leaves.

"'Strangers,' said one of them, 'there has been only one great epoch for the fine arts.'

"I was about to suggest that there had been four great epochs, and to concede that one of the four had perhaps been the greatest of all.

"'The ancients!'

"'That will do,' said one of the painters. 'The ancients were children, chrysalides groping in darkness.'

"'Perhaps you deem the Augustine epoch the greatest?'

"'The age of Augustus! What of that? We know nothing about it.'

"'Perhaps, then, the period of the Renaissance?'

"'The Renaissance! A period of beggarly decadence!'

"'Ah, then, to revive signifies to decline.'

"'Decidedly; so far as the Renaissance goes.'

"'The only period remaining is the seventeenth century.' My voice was here stifled by groans.

"'Who is this Coleopterous? Have you lived in a hole? Learn, Sir Beetle, that which is known and sanctioned now-a-days we utterly condemn and ignore, while all that is obscure, lost in the dust of oblivion, we bring to light and restore with the varnish of our enthusiasm. Depend upon it, there has never been but one really grand epoch, which lasted twenty years and three months. This was in the twelfth century, during the time of Averroes. The Saracens brought art to the highest pitch of perfection.'

"'Let us leave these driveling fools,' I whispered to my companion.

"'Willingly.'

"Our next flight was across the garden to a spot I had never seen before. Its name was taken from an ancient causeway on which it had been erected. We entered a rich tulip where a number of insects were assembled.

"'Here you see,' said my companion, 'the whole entomological race—peacock-butterflies, admirals, generals, princes, counts, satyrs, even Vulcan and Argus.' You are aware the beetles are descended from an Egyptian race of insects accustomed to translate hieroglyphics of the physiognomy, and thus read the secrets of the heart.

"I therefore understood at a glance that all the females of this vast assembly were ranged in a ring for no better purpose than criticising each other's appearance and dress. They were indeed, without a single exception, secretly employed in picking each other's robes, jewels, and looks to pieces. The males stood at some distance. I remarked to my friend that this chosen society appeared to me dull and miserable. Not wishing to judge hastily, I determined to listen to the conversation.

"A group of sporting spiders were wholly engrossed with talk about hunting, dining, and betting, and how their blandishments had done for some gay thoughtless flies who had been decoyed into their chambers in pursuit of pleasure, and rewarded with death. Two fine females were whispering behind their fans. I slipped quietly up to them to listen. Imagine my surprise when I heard them using the slang of the lowest vermin living.

"Their chief theme was the best means of draining their husbands' purses to enable them to pursue their selfish pleasure, while I found out that their devoted partners were nearly driven to despair to make ends meet. My horns stood up on my head with horror. Addressing my companion, I said, 'Is this what you call the pleasures of the world? In the modest field where I was born, it was not so. When a simple insect puts on her best dress, she wears her sweetest smiles all for her fond husband.'

"'Well,' said my Mentor, 'what can one do? Fashion is king here, and he is a hard task-master. All these are his slaves in every detail of life, dress, and language.'

"'But,' I said, 'if one thinks only of personal adornment, putting on one's back all one's worldly possessions, how fares the household?'

"'The household!' replied he; 'who ever thinks of that? Domestic bliss belonged to our grandmothers.'

"'And the budget? those two famous ends of the year which it is so important to join together decently.'

"'That does not matter either to you or to me.'

"Two rather unsightly insects were putting their heads together in a corner. 'Who are those two creatures?' I inquired.

"'They are ant-lions of finance. Their habits are droll. They meet together in the morning in a temple consecrated to their operations. There they plan how best they may undermine the finest structures of their neighbours. Their form of worship is perhaps the most dangerous in the world, as they sacrifice many victims, simple and innocent ones. When one of these ant-lions has done a good day's work, sucked the life's blood from some widow or orphan, he is the pleasantest evening companion imaginable. That bejewelled female with the dirty diamond-ringed neck and fingers is one of their wives.'

"I soon left the husbands to talk over their pitfalls, and listened to the gossip of their wives.

"'My dear friend,' said one of them, 'you have a musical cousin always about you of whom we may talk undisturbed.'

"'Bah! we do not get on; he grumbles so if I eat sweets while rendering *sonatas* or *quatuors* of Haydn or Mozart.'

"The sad counsels of the old Rhinoceros came to my mind, and I began to understand that he had been at least truthful. My reflections were here interrupted by an altercation between two insects. The questions discussed were taken up by all the others. I afterwards learned the nature of the questions, and the decisions were the following:—

"1st, Green tea is more destructive to the nerves than black tea.

"2d, Self-love is the motive of all action in insects.

"3d, The hill of St. Denis is about as steep as that of Clichy.

"4th, It is cheaper to live in France than in England.

"5th, It is better to be rich than poor.

"6th, Friendship is a sentiment weaker than love.

"This last question was given up as insoluble at the request of the ephemera present. An Alpine hermit made a note of it, so as to be able to meditate on the subject at leisure in the solitude of his cell. I then, taking my friend by the arm, inquired, 'Is there no spot in this large garden where one could find an insect that would converse without pretending to be interesting?'

"'Yes,' he replied, scratching his pate with an air of embarrassment; 'follow me.'

"We flew away into the dark night, but my guide made so many circuits that I perceived he was quite at a loss where to go.

"'I do not think,' he said, 'it would be worth while to take you into that vast swamp where one lives in isolation like a water-rat. Let us cross the river. On its bank yonder are lilies to whom I might introduce you. They live in peace and silence, fearing to defile themselves by unkind sentiments.'

"'Is there any gaiety there?'

"'In the land of lilies one is sadder than elsewhere, but the reason of that is too long to enter upon here.'

"Tired of these flights, I profited by the darkness to leave my companion. A bright star, as if by chance, directed me to the third floor of a climbing rose, and there at last I found the object of my search, a good honest family of lady-birds established in a simple and commodious dwelling. Most amiable creatures, living without show or ostentation. Our conversation was animated by a genial gaiety, and we sat down to a simple supper. My place was between two hostesses who proved most agreeable companions."

Here the Beetle relapsed into silence.

"Mr. Beetle," said the Owl, "I feel certain your history does not end here."

"That is true, Mr. Philosopher," said the insect; "I had reserved a portion. From the happy moment that separated me from my Mentor I have only once felt pain. A certain day, at a certain hour, I was summoned to put on my military dress and mount guard at a place pointed out to me. I had to obey under pain of death, in common with many other insects of peace, who were compelled to imitate wasps and hornets in order to secure the safety of the country, which was in no real danger. After a day and a night of this warlike parade, I again obtained my liberty. I had caught cold and toothache, but seeing a poppy on my way, I plunged into it and swallowed some opium, which brought on profound sleep. At last I was roused by the voice of a magpie, who had seized me round the waist with his iron beak. He was an old collector, and, more than that, a sorcerer. 'Here,' said my captor, 'I have found a pretty beetle, which I shall place in the middle of a peony leaf, and give to my godchild as a jewel and talisman to protect her against the sway of fashion.'

"I permitted myself to be placed on the leaf and attached to the dove Violet's neck, where I have determined to remain, as the situation suits me, and I hope to make her lucky."

"Sir," said the Owl, "it seems to me that you are studiously concealing the most interesting part of your narrative. A beetle of your wide experience cannot have passed through the world without

some love adventures. I strongly suspect you fell in love with your lady-bird hostess. Pray allay my curiosity."

THE SUFFERINGS OF A BEETLE. 125

The little green Beetle hereupon bestowed one searching look upon the Owl, and drawing in his legs and horns, lapsed into silence, simulating death so cleverly that his interrogator became alarmed. The Owl put on his spectacles to examine the insect more closely. He then saw for the first time that it was an emerald mounted on an enamelled leaf. The sun beginning to appear, he became drowsy, and pulling his hood over his eyes, fell into a profound sleep.

Awaking at last, he discovered that the story of the green Beetle was but a dream, and returning the pin to, Violet, he recounted the history of the transformed jewel as if it had been his own invention.

A Fox in a Trap.

HE following story was found among the papers of a distinguished "Orang-Outan" member of the Academies :—

"No, decidedly not!" I cried; "it shall never be said that I chose for the hero of my tale a cowardly, sneaking, voracious brute, whose name has become synonymous with cunning, hypocrisy, and knavery—a fox, in fact."

"You are wrong," replied one whose presence I had overlooked.

I must tell you that my lonely hours had been beguiled by a creature of a species hitherto undescribed by the naturalist, who performed slight services, and was at that moment engaged in arranging the books in my library. The reader will no doubt be surprised to learn that an orang-outan—literally, man of the woods or wilds—possessed a library. His astonishment will be still greater when he is informed that the chief works in my collection were penned by philosophic apes, and that most of them contain elaborate disquisitions on the descent of apes from the human species. This by the way.

Perhaps the dependant who addressed me would be called a "familiar spirit." Although spirits are not totally unknown, I am unacquainted with those of the familiar type; I will therefore, with your leave, name this one Breloque.

"You are wrong," he repeated.

"Why?" I indignantly inquired. "Will your love of paradox tempt you to defend the cursed, corrupted race?"

"I think," replied Breloque, leaning on the table with an air of arrogance most ludicrous to behold, "that bad reputations, as well as good ones, are sometimes usurped, and that the species in question, or at least one example with whom I became acquainted, is the victim of an error of this sort."

"So then," I said, "you are speaking from personal experience?"

I.I.G.

"Quite so, sir; and were it not that I fear wasting your precious moments, I would try and convince you of your error."

"I am willing to listen, but what will the result be?"

"Nothing."

"That is satisfactory. Sit down in this arm-chair, and should I go to sleep, do not stop, I pray you, as that would awake me."

After taking a pinch of snuff from my box, Breloque, nothing loath, commenced thus:—

"You are fully aware, sir, that notwithstanding the affection which attaches me to your person, I have never submitted to the slavery that would have been distasteful to both. I have my leisure hours, when I think of many things; just as you have yours, when you think of nothing. Oh, I have many ways of passing my time. Have you ever been out fishing with the line?"

"Yes," I replied; "that is to say, I often used to go in a costume expressly suited to fishing, and sit from sunrise to sunset on the borders of a stream. I had a superb rod mounted with silver, like an Oriental weapon, but without its danger. Alas! I have passed many sweet hours, and made many bad verses, but I never caught a single fish."

" Angling, sir, appeals to the imagination in your case, and has nothing to do with the happiness of the true angler. Few persons are so framed as to appreciate the charms of which you speak. Your mind, filled with dreamy, vague hope, follows the soft motion of the transparent water, marks and profits by the events of the insect world

that clouds its clear face. To the fisher of poetic mind the capture of one of the silver dwellers in the stream can only bring regret, remorse."

I made a sign of assent.

" Yet," he continued, " few persons regard the sport in this light."

" That is true," I replied.

Breloque, unaccustomed to find one entering so fully into his views, felt flattered.

" Sir," he said in a tone marked by perfect self-satisfaction, " I have thought deeply on subjects most profound, and I feel convinced, if the world would only give me a fair hearing, I could earn a wide reputation—nor would it be a borrowed one."

"Apropos of borrowed fame,' let us hear the history of your fox. You abuse the privilege granted by thus trifling with my patience."

"Ah, sir, you misjudge me. This is only a subtle, roundabout way of leading your mind up to the theme. I am now all for you, and will only permit myself to put one question—What do you think of butterfly-catching?"

"Wretch!" I exclaimed, "am I here to discuss the fortunes of all

created things before the one which occupies me? You forget the hatred that fills my breast, the mask of hypocrisy which the fox craftily assumes to attract tender chickens, lambs, doves, and his thousand victims."

"What calumnies!" replied Breloque. "I hope to avenge the fox of all his enemies by proving that in love he is stupid, unselfish, and tender-hearted. For the moment I have the honour of returning to the butterfly-hunt."

I made an impatient gesture, to which he replied with such a look of supplication that I was completely disarmed. Besides, I had the imprudence to let him see that the exciting pastime interested me.

I

Breloque satisfied, took a second pinch of snuff, and half lay down in his arm-chair.

"I am happy, sir," he said, "to see you take delight in the truly worthy pleasures of life. Can you point out a being more to be envied or recommended to the consideration of his fellow-creatures than the one we encounter early in the morning, joyous and breathless, beating the long grass with his stick? In his button-hole hung a bit of cork armed with long pins used to spike—without pain—his lovely victims. He soothes himself with the notion that these little insects, brought by the zephyrs, cannot suffer pain, as they never utter a complaint. For my part, I think the butterflies rather enjoy the prospect of being dried like mummies, and displayed in choice collections. But we are off the line of our subject."

"You are right for once," I said.

"I shall return to it. As speaking in general terms pains you, I will talk of my own experiences in the field. One day, when carried away by the ardour of the hunt. It is altogether different from fishing, of which we were just talking."

I rose to go, but he quietly made me resume my seat.

"Do not be impatient. I only spoke of fishing as a comparison, for you to note the difference. Fishing with bait requires the most perfect rest, while the hunt, on the contrary, demands activity."

"You have fairly caught me and pinned me down," I replied, laughing.

"That is a cruel remark; but I shall now be careful to stick to my narrative. You are as capricious as the gay butterfly I was engaged in pursuing. He was a marvellous *Apollon* in the mountains of Franche Compté. I stopped quite out of breath in a little glade into which he had led me, thinking he would profit by this moment to escape; but, either from sheer insolence or frolic, he alighted on a long stem of grass, which bent under his weight, seeming to set me at defiance. Collecting all my energy, I determined to surprise him. I approached with stealthy steps, my eyes riveted on him, my legs strained in an attitude as uncomfortable as it was undignified, my heart swelling with an emotion more easily imagined than described. At this moment a horrid cock crowed lustily, and away flew my coveted prize. Inconsolable, I down upon a stone and expended my remaining breath in heaping invective on the head of my musical enemy, menacing him with every kind of death, and I own, to my horror, even mentioning a poisoned pill. I was delighting in guilty preparations to carry my threats into effect, when a paw was placed on my arm, and I beheld two soft eyes looking into mine, those of a young fox, sir, of charming form. All his externals were in his favour, betokening a loyal noble character. Although you yourself are against his species, I somehow contracted a liking for the fox before me. This modest animal heard my menaces against the cock.

"'Do not give way to passion, sir,' he said in such a sad tone that I was moved even to tears. 'She would die of grief.'

"I did not quite understand. 'Who do you mean?' I inquired.

"'Cocotte!' he replied with sweet simplicity.

"I felt still in the dark; yet conjectured it was some love story. I have always been passionately fond of romance, and you?"

"That depends entirely on circumstances."

"Say at once you detest love tales. However, you must resign yourself to hearing this one."

"I should name my objections at once, were I not afraid of wounding your feelings, so I prefer bravely taking my part and listening to your story; ennui does not kill."

"So it is said, yet I have known people who have almost succumbed to ennui. But to return to the fox.

"'Sir,' I said, 'you interest me deeply. You seem unhappy. Can I serve you in any way?'

"'Thank you,' he replied, 'my grief must remain unalleviated. No one has the power to make her return my love.'

"'Cocotte?' I said quietly.

"'Cocotte,' he replied, sighing.

"The greatest service one can render a disconsolate lover, next to destroying him, is to listen to him. He is happy while recounting his troubles. Knowing the truth of this, I asked and obtained his confidence.

"'Sir,' said this interesting quadruped, 'since you wish me to relate some of the incidents of my life, I must go back several years, as my misfortunes commenced with my birth. I owe my introduction into life to one of the choicest foxes of the time. For all that, I am happy to say I inherit almost nothing of the subtle nature of my parents. My utter abhorrence of their ways inspired me with tastes opposed to the interest of my family. A large dog with whom I became acquainted taught me to befriend the weak and helpless. Many hours

have I spent, not only listening to his counsel, but observing how careful he was to put his virtuous maxims into practice. He won my gratitude by saving my life. A country steward caught me in his master's vineyard beneath a vine, where I had taken shelter from the heat of the sun, after quenching my thirst with a grape. I was ignominiously arrested and brought before the proprietor, a "justice of the peace," whose fierce aspect did not calm my fears. But this powerful, superb animal proved most kind; he forgave me, admitted me to his table, where, in addition to more substantial fare, I was fed on the precepts of virtue and morality. To him I owe the sensibility of my heart, the culture of my mind, and even the pleasure of being able to relate my experience in intelligible language. Numerous griefs and wrongs chequered my existence up to the fatal hour when, like Romeo, I gave my heart to a creature from whom our family feuds seemed to have parted me for ever. Less fortunate than Romeo, I was not loved in return.'

"'Who,' I said, 'is the fair charmer so insensible to your love? Who is the lover preferred before you?'

"'The charming one,' he replied with humility, 'is a hen, and my rival a cock.'

"I was confounded. 'Sir,' at last I said to him, 'do not for an instant attribute my remarks to our newly-formed friendship. I for one have always looked with scorn and contempt on individuals of this vain type. What more stupidly pretentious, what more ridiculous than a cock, whose stiff strut of pride causes him to stumble in his sublimest moods? The unbridled pomp and vanity of the cock renders him the meanest and most ridiculous of birds.'

"'There are many hens, sir, who are not of your opinion,' said my young friend, sighing. 'Alas! the love of Cocotte is a proof of the value of a picturesque physique coupled with bold assurance. I hoped that my boundless devotion would one day be rewarded by her love. I had spiritualised an attachment which generally displays itself in a rather material fashion when the fox woos the hen. But happy love knows no pity! Cocotte saw me suffer without remorse. My rival enjoyed my troubles, for in the game of insolence and fatuity he has no rival. My friends scorned and abandoned me, and, to crown all, my noble protector ended his days in an honourable retreat. Alone now, I would feel wretched but for the memory of this fatal passion, which has still its inexplicable charm. I am bound to Cocotte, and to the end of my days must defend her against my fellows, and wear the chains she has coiled around me. I would die happy if only I could prove to her that I am not unworthy of her pity! You are so indulgent, sir, I venture to think that the circumstances which introduced me to Cocotte may not be indifferent to you. I first beheld her during a blood conventicle held last summer, at which I unwillingly assisted. It was through my father's influence that I was admitted. I was detested by my friends, and could take no part in eating feathered creatures like the one I loved. A number of my relations had agreed among themselves to seize a farmyard during the absence of the master and dogs. You may descry the house not far from here. The most careful preparations, such as would make your hair stand on end—(pardon me, I did not notice your wig) —were made for a general slaughter of the dwellers in the yard. In spite of my tender heart I lent myself with a rather good grace to aid in carrying out their schemes. It may have been with some touch of pride more worthy of men than foxes, I felt prepared to prove, dreamer as I was, that in the hour of danger I could be trusted. The plot, the memory of which makes me shudder, did not seem at all odious at the time. At last, under cover of night, we made a triumphant entry into the ill-defended yard. Our victims were asleep—hens go to roost early. One only remained watching—that was Cocotte. The first glance of her fair form floored me—to make use of a vulgar phrase. Here I was, a fox in love. I breathed soft words to the night air; she listened to me as one accustomed to homage. I retired to devise some means of saving her. Do not fail to note that my love began in an unselfish thought. This is so rare as to be worthy of special remark. When I approached the bloodthirsty foxes, I advised them to begin decently and in order by devouring the eggs. My proposal was adopted by a large majority. Thus gaining time to reflect, I had decided on nothing when I had to mount guard; the thought then flashed across my mind that a false alarm would save my darling, I at once cried, "Flee who may!" Most of the robbers were already laden with spoil, some had nothing, yet they fled, all of them, leaving me master of the field. The cock awoke, and discovering that his harem had been invaded, crowed lustily, compelling me to retreat. I kept watch over that farmyard for many days, but could never win a kind look from Cocotte, who, although frequently beaten by her unfaithful lord, seemed daily to grow fonder of his society. Nevertheless, I would not have tried to gain her love by unveiling the character of my rival, and depriving her of her dearest illusions.

"'The image of my old instructor often rises before me, and I feel, while he raised me out of my own level by education, he rendered me more unhappy than the most ignorant and besotted of my kind. What more can I say? the incidents of an unrequited love are so few that I

am surprised at the brevity of my tale when recalling the misery of my life. Now, I shall leave you, the sun is going down; think of me, sir, when you hear it said 'that foxes are wicked. Do not forget that you have met a kindly-disposed, sensitive, and therefore miserable fox."

"Is that all?" I said.

"Of course," replied Breloque, "unless the interest you feel in my story prompts you to inquire what became of the different personages."

"Interest never prompts me to do anything," I replied; "I like everything to be in its proper place. It is therefore better to know what the characters are now doing, than to risk meeting them in places where they are least expected."

"The fox," continued Breloque, "came across our common enemy. One day venturing to carry off Cocotte, he was shot by the farmer, who hung his tail up as a trophy."

"What became of the cock?"

"Listen; he is crowing, the cowardly, stupid, selfish rascal!"

"Have you not for the fox the same hatred I have for the cock?"

"Do not deceive yourself; the fox was the craftiest rogue you ever met. Had he succeeded in deluding the farmer as he deceived you, his thirst would have been slaked with the blood of Cocotte. He would have proved as benevolent as a Bashi-Bazouk in Bulgaria."

"I don't doubt that," said Breloque, "but I am sorry for it."

TEXT-BOOK

FOR THE GUIDANCE OF ANIMALS STUDYING FOR HONOURS.

MR. EDITOR,—DONKEYS have long felt the need of asserting their rights before the tribunal of animals, and putting down the injustice which has made them the living types of stupidity.

If skill is wanting in the writer of this manuscript, courage is not. Moreover, let me conjure the silent sage to examine himself in order to find out the secret of his success in society, and ten chances to one he will admit that it all comes of his being an ass. Without donkeys in political circles, majorities would never be obtained, so that an ass may pass as a type of those governed.

But my intention is not to talk politics. I only wish to prove that we have many more opportunities, were they rightly used, of securing honours than fall to the lot of highly gifted and cultured creatures.

My master was a simple schoolmaster in the environs of Paris. He was a good teacher, and a thoroughly miserable character. We had this peculiarity in common, if we had our choice, we would have decided to live well and do nothing. This characteristic, common both to asses and men, is vulgarly called ambition, at the same time I think it is only the spontaneous growth of modern society. I myself had opened a class, and taught in a manner which excited my master's jealousy, although he acknowledged himself struck by the results of my method.

"Why is it," he one day said to me, "that the children of men take so much longer to learn to read, write, and become useful members of society, than young donkeys do to learn how to earn a living? How is it that asses have so profited by all that their fathers knew before them, that their education is, so to speak, born in them? So it is, indeed, with every species of animal excepting the human. Why is man not born with his mind and faculties fully developed?"

Although my master was quite ignorant of natural history, he imagined that these questions in themselves were so thoroughly scientific and posing as to entitle him to a place under the Minister of Public Instruction, where he might extend his valuable reflections at the expense of the State.

We entered Paris by the Fabourg St. Mareian. When we reached the elevated ground near the Barrier d'Italie, in full view of the metropolis, we each delivered an oration in our own way.

"Tell me, O Sacred Shrine wherein the budget is cooked, when will the signature of some *parvenu* professor obtain for me food, raiment, and shelter, the cross of the Legion of Honour, and a chair of no matter what, no matter where, &c. ?

"Believe me, I should say so much good of every one that no harm could be breathed against me.

"Tell me how shall I reach the Minister and convince him of my fitness to wear my country's honours."

I followed my master's eloquent appeal.

"O charming Jardin des Plantes, where animals are so well fed, will you never open to me your stables of twenty feet square? your Swiss valleys thirty yards wide? Shall I ever be one of those happy animals who roll on the clover of the budget, or stalled beneath graceful trellis-work bearing the superscription, 'An African donkey, presented by So-and-so, captain of a ship, &c.?'"

After saluting the city of acrobats and fortune-tellers, we entered the noxious defiles of a celebrated fabourg famed for leather and science. At last we found shelter in a wretched inn crowded with Savoyards with their marmots, Italians with their monkeys, Avergnats with their dogs, Parisians with their white mice, harpers with their stringless harps, and husky-voiced songsters. My master had with him six francs, the only barrier between us and suicide. The inn called The Mercy is one of these philanthropic establishments where one may sleep for a penny a night, and enjoy a meal for fourpence halfpenny. It also boasts a stable, where all sorts of animals may be lodged promiscuously. My master naturally placed me there.

Marmus, such was my master's name, could not avoid contemplating the throng of depraved beasts to which I was added. A monkey in marquis furbelows, plumed head-dress, and gold waistband; quick as gunpowder, was flirting with a military hero of popular burlesque; an old rabbit, well up in his exercises; an intelligent poodle of modern dramatic fame spoke of the capriciousness of the public to an old ape seated on his troubadour's hat; a group of grey mice were admiring a cat taught to respect canaries, and engaged in conversation with a marmot.

"Confound these creatures!" exclaimed my master; "I thought I had discovered a new science, that of comparing instincts, now I am cruelly undeceived by this stableful of beasts, who are all of them the same as men!"

"Ah, sir," said a shaggy-looking young man, "you desire to gain a reputation for learning, and yet you pause at trifles. Know, ambitious one, that in order to succeed you must allow your external appearance to indicate the height of your aspirations. The traveller who seeks to make his way into a *terra incognita* must not encumber himself with baggage. Our great explorers were men who wore an expression of resolute earnestness, and carried an umbrella and a tooth-pick. They penetrated to the heart of savagedom, and brought back to civilisation a wayworn exterior and the power of discoursing on the perils of their journeys."

"To what great genius have I the honour of speaking?"

"A poor fellow who has tried everything, and lost everything except his enormous appetite, and who, while waiting for something to turn up, lives by selling newspapers, and lodges here. Who are you, pray?"

"A resigned elementary teacher, who naturally does not know much, but who has asked himself this question, 'Why is it that animals possess à *priori* the special science of their lives called instinct, while man learns nothing without extraordinary toil?'"

"Because science is in its infancy!" exclaimed the adventurer. "Have you ever studied 'Puss in Boots'?"

"I used to tell it to my pupils when they had been good."

"Well, my dear sir, it points the line of conduct for all to follow who wish to succeed. What did the cat do? He told every one that his master possessed lands; he was believed. Do you understand that it is enough to make known that one is, one has, one intends to have? What does it matter, if you have nothing, if others believe that you have all?"

"But '*væ soli!*' says the Scripture. In fact, in politics, as in love, two are better than one. You have invented Instinctology, and you shall have a chair of *Comparative Instinct;* you shall be the great modern sage, and I shall announce it to the whole world—to Europe, to Paris, to the Minister, to his secretary, his clerks and supernumeraries. Mahomet became a prophet, not because he was gifted with prophetic inspiration, but because his followers proclaimed him prophet."

"I am quite willing to become a great *savant*," said my master resignedly, "but I shall be asked to explain my theories."

"What! would it be a science if you could explain it?"

"Yet a point to start from will be necessary."

"Yes," replied the young journalist, "we ought to have some animal that would upset all the theories of our learned men. Baron Cerceau, for example, has devoted his life to placing animals in absolute divisions. That is his plan, but now other great naturalists are knocking down all the strongholds of the Baron. Let us take part in the war of words and hypothetical ideas. According to us, instinct will be the leading feature in animals, by which alone, according to the degree of instinct, they must be classified. Now, although instinct will submit to infinite modifications, it is nevertheless still *one* in its essence, and nothing can prove the unity of all things better than this. We shall thus say there is only one animal, as there is only one instinct, the instinct which characterises all animal organisations. The, so to speak, appropriation of the element of life which circumstances change without affecting the principle. We come in with a new science opposed to the Baron, and in favour of the new school of philosophy which advocates zoological unity. We shall no doubt sell our discoveries in a good market; our opponents must buy us up."

"Well," said Marmus, "science has no conscience. But shall I have no need of my donkey?"

"What! have you a donkey?" exclaimed the adventurer; "we are saved!! We shall turn him into an extraordinary zebra, and puzzle the whole learned world by some singularity which shall derange their most cherished conclusions. *Savants* live by nomenclature, let us reverse it; they will be alarmed, they will capitulate, they will try to gain us over, and, like so many who have gone before, we may be gained over at our own price. There are in this house mountebanks who hold wonderful secrets, men having dwarfs, bearded women, and a host of monstrosities. A few politenesses will win us the means of concocting revolutionary matter such as shall astonish the world of science."

To what science was I to become a prey? During the night several transversal incisions were made in my skin, after my coat had been clipped. To these a gipsy vagrant applied some strong liquor, and a few days afterwards I became celebrated. In the papers Parisians read as follows:—

"One of our most courageous travellers, Adam Marmus, after passing through the central wilds of Africa, has at last returned, bringing with him from the Mountains of the Moon a Zebra so peculiar as to derange the fundamental principles of naturalists who advocate a system of merciless division, not even admitting that the horse, in its wild state, was ever found with a black coat. The singular yellow bands of the new Zebra are most puzzling, and can only be explained by the learned Marmus in the work he is about to give to the world. This work, the result of many years' toil and observation, will be devoted to an elucidation of *Comparative Instinct*.

a science discovered by the illustrious author and traveller. The Zebra, the only trophy of a journey unparalleled in the annals of discovery, walks like a giraffe. Thus it is proved beyond doubt that instinct modifies the forms and the attributes of animals, which are also greatly affected by geographical position. From these hitherto unknown facts the zoologists will be enabled to lay a new foundation of truth upon which to raise the fabric of natural history. Adam Marmus has consented to make known his discoveries in a course of public lectures."

All the papers repeated this audacious fable. While all Paris was occupied with the new science, Marmus and his friend took up their quarters in a respectable hotel in the Rue de Tournon, where I was carefully kept in a stable under lock and key. All the learned societies sent delegates, who could not disguise the anxiety caused by this blow to the doctrine of the great Baron. If the forms and attributes of animals changed with their abodes, science was upset! The genius who dared to maintain that life accommodated itself to all should certainly be upheld. The only distinctions now existing between animals could be understood by all.

Natural science was worse than useless; the Oyster, the Lion, the Zoophyte, and man all belonged to the same stock, and were only modified by the simplicity or complicity of their organs. Saltenbeck the Belgian, Vos-man-Betten, Sir Fairnight, Gobtonswell, the learned Sottenbach, Craneberg, the beloved disciples of the French professor, were ranged against the Baron and his nomenclature. Never had a more irritating fact been thrown between two belligerent parties. Behind the Baron were the academicians, the university men, legions of professors, and the government, lending their support to a theory, the only one in harmony with Scripture.

Marmus and his friend remained firm. To the questions of academicians they replied by bare facts, avoiding the exposition of their doctrine. One professor, when leaving, said to them—

"Gentlemen, the opinion which you hold is without doubt directed against the convictions of our most reliable men of science, and in favour of the new schism of zoological unity. The system, in the interest of science, ought not to be brought to light."

"Say, rather, in the interest of scientific men," said Marmus.

"Be it so," replied the professor; "it must be nipped in the bud, for after all, gentlemen, it is Pantheism."

"You think so?" said the journalist. "How can one admit the

existence of material molecular force which renders matter independent of the Creator."

"Why should not the Creator have ordered that everything should be subject to, and dependent upon, one universal law?" said Marmus.

"You see," said his friend in a whisper to the professor, "he is as

profound as Newton. Why do you not present him to the Minister of Public Instruction?"

"I shall do so at once," rejoined the professor, happy to make himself master of the owner of the Zebra. "Perhaps the minister would be pleased to see our curious animal before any one else, and you will of course accompany him."

" I thank you."

" He would then be able to appreciate the service which such a journey has rendered to science," continued our friend. "Mr. Marmus has not visited the Mountains of the Moon for nothing. You shall see this for yourself; the animal walks like a giraffe. As to the yellow bands, they are caused by the temperature, which was found to be several degrees Fahrenheit, and many degrees Reaumur."

" Perhaps it is your intention to engage in public instruction ? "

"Splendid career!" cried the journalist starting.

"I do not allude to the profession of noodles, which consists in taking the students out for an airing, and neglecting them at home; but to teaching at the Athenæum, which leads to nothing, save to securing a professorship and pupils, which pave the way to all sorts of good things. We will talk of that again. All this took place early in the nineteenth century, when ministers felt the need of making themselves popular."

The partizans of zoological unity learned that a minister was about to inspect the precious Zebra, and fearing intrigue, the worthy disciples of our great opponent flocked to see the illustrious Marmus. My masters obstinately refused to exhibit me, as I had not acquired my giraffe step, and the chemical application to my Zebra bands had not yet completed the illusion. A young disciple discoursed on the new discovery with eloquence and force, and my cunning masters profited by his learning."

"Our Zebra," said the journalist, "carries conviction to the most incredulous."

"Zebra," said Marmus. "It is no longer a Zebra, but a fact which engenders a new science."

" Your science," responded the unitariste, "strengthens the ground taken up by Sir J. Fairnight on the subject of Spanish, Scotch, and Swiss sheep, who eat more or less, according to the sort of herbage in pasture lands."

"But," exclaimed our friend, "the products, are they not also different in different latitudes and under different atmospheric conditions. Our Zebra explains why butter is white in the Brie in Normandy, and the butter and cheese yellow in Neufchâtel and Meaux."

"You have placed your finger on the point of greatest vitality,"

K

cried the enthusiastic disciple; "little facts solve great problems. The question of cheese bears a subtle affinity to the greater questions of zoological form and comparative instinct. Instinct is the entire animal, just as thought is man concentrated. If instinct is modified and changed according to the latitude in which it is developed, it is clear that it must be the same with the *Zoon*, with the exterior living form. There is but one principle of instinct."

"One for all beings," said Marmus.

"Then," continued the disciple, "nomenclatures are all very well for us to indicate the different degrees of instinct, but they no longer constitute a science."

"This, sir," said the journalist, "is death to the Mollusks, the Articulata, the Radiata, Mammifera, Cirropedia, Acephala, and Crustacea. In fact, it breaks down all the strongholds of natural history, and simplifies everything so thoroughly as to destroy accepted science.

"Believe me," said the disciple, "men of science will defend their position. There will be much ink spilt and pens spoiled in the contest, to say nothing of the reams of paper that will be destroyed in keeping the wounds open. Poor naturalists! No, they will hardly allow a single genius to wrest from their hands the labours of so many lives."

"We shall be as much calumniated as your great philosopher himself. Ah! Fontenelle was right. When we have secured truth, let us close our fists tightly over it."

"Shall you be afraid, gentlemen?" said the disciple; "shall you be traitors to the sacred cause of the animals?"

"No, sir," cried Marmus, "I shall never abandon the science to which I have devoted the best days of my life; and to prove my sincerity we must conjointly edit the history of the Zebra."

"We are saved," exclaimed Marmus, when the disciple had gone.

Soon after, the ablest pupil of the great philosopher drew up a notice of the Zebra. Under the name of Marmus he launched out boldly, and formed the new science. This pamphlet enabled us at once to enter into the enjoyable phase of celebrity. My master and his friend were overwhelmed with invitations to dinners, dances, receptions, morning and evening parties. They were proclaimed learned and illustrious everywhere. They indeed had too many supporters, ever for a moment to doubt their being geniuses of the highest order. A copy of the work by Marmus was sent to the Baron. The Academy of Science then found the affair so grave that not a member dared give his opinion."

"We must see, we must wait," they said. Sathenbeck, the learned Belgian, is coming by express, Vas-man-Bitten from Holland, and the illustrious Fabricus Gobtouswell are on their way to see the Zebra. The young and ardent disciple of zoological unity was engaged on a memoir which contained terrible conclusions, directed against the Baron's dogmas. Already a party was forming to promote unity applied to botany. The illustrious professors, Condolle and Mirbel, hesitated out of consideration for the authority of the Baron.

I was now ready for inspection. My mountebank artist, in addition to finishing my bands, had furnished me with a cow's tail, while my yellow stripes gave me the appearance of an animated Austrian sentry-box.

"It is astonishing," said the minister, as he gazed upon my coat for the first time.

"Astonishing!" echoed the professor; "but, thank goodness, not inexplicable."

"I am puzzled," said the minister, "how best to reconcile this new discovery with all our preconceived notions of zoology."

"A most difficult problem," suggested Marmus.

"It seems strange," said the great man, "that this African Zebra should live in the temperature of the Rue de Tournon."

This was treading on delicate ground, but my master was equal to the occasion, although on hearing the remark I began to walk like an ass.

"Yes," replied Marmus, "I hope he may live until my lectures are over."

"You are a clever fellow, but bear in mind that your new and popular science must be moulded to fit in with the doctrines of the worthy Baron. Perhaps it would lend dignity to your cause were you represented by a pupil."

Here the Baron entered, and overhearing the remark, said:—

"Ah, sir, I have a pupil of great promise, who repeats admirably what he is taught. We call this sort of man a vulgariser."

"And we," said the journalist, "call him a parrot. Those men render real service to science as they talk it down to the level of the popular mind."

"Well, that is settled," said Marmus, taking the Baron's hand; "let us pull together."

The minister said: "Marmus, you deserve, and shall receive, the substantial reward of genius in such honour and support as your country has to bestow."

The Geographical Society, jealously wishing to imitate the government, offered to defray the entire cost of the journey to the Mountains of the Moon, which offer was ultimately carried into effect. These timely aids came in opportunely as my master had been burning the financial candle at both ends.

The journalist was placed as librarian in the Jardin des Plantes, and abused the opportunity which leisure afforded him by running down my master and his science. Nevertheless Marmus coined a wide reputation out of the base metal of the parrot's jargon, and sustained his hard-earned fame by discreet and modest silence. He was elected professor of something somewhere, and would no doubt have filled the post honourably had a time and place ever been named when he would be required to fill a chair.

As for myself, I was bought for the London Zoological Gardens, where change of climate and kind treatment rendered me the wonder of the world, as I gradually changed from a strange Zebra to a domesticated Cockney ass.

The Inconsistencies of a Greyhound.

THE theatre has always had a peculiar charm for me, and yet there are few persons who have greater reason to hold it in utter abhorrence, for it was there at about nine o'clock one evening that I first beheld my husband. As you may well suppose every detail of our meeting is indelibly fixed in my mind. I have indeed many grave reasons for not forgetting it. In all frankness, I wish to accuse no one, but I was never meant for married life. Elegant, attractive, fitted only to revel in the pleasures of the world, and feast on the joys of a great life, space, luxury, brilliancy, were necessary to me. I was born to be a duchess, and married—O heavens! the first clarionet player at the Dogs' theatre. It was a serious joke! Was it not? It has moved me to laughter times without number. Yes! he really played the clarionet every evening from eight to eleven, the easy parts too, at least, he told me so. I daresay it was not true for I never found that he played false to me.

During the day he was second trombone to the parish of dogs, and above all, his greatest ambition was a hat in the National Guards.

These details may seem grotesque. Pray forgive me if they are, as I only wish to discharge my duty.

One evening when I was at the theatre, I noticed between the acts a big burly dog in the orchestra wearing spectacles, a cap, and blowing his nose in a checked cotton handkerchief. He made so much noise that all heads were turned towards him. Had any one said that that creature would be my future husband I should not have replied. I should have treated the remark with silent contempt. Yet under the most embarrassing circumstances, with all eyes turned upon him, and amid a peal of laughter my future spouse slowly and carefully folded his handkerchief, looking at the company over his spectacles, at the same time changing the mouthpiece of his instrument with a calmness perfectly charming to behold. This singular proof of *sang-froid* caused me to turn my eye-glass upon him. He no doubt remarked this movement, for he immediately took off his cap, adjusted the short hair on his big head, replaced his spectacles, settled his tie, and pulled down his waistcoat. There is no monster, however ugly, who would not do the same, in his position. His eye which caught mine seemed to me most brilliant.

There was as little doubt of his ugliness as of his strange emotion. I was young, silly and coquettish, so it amused me to be looked at like this. The chief mounted his throne and the music commenced anew. The fat clarionet player cast a last glance at me, and then pulled himself together for work. He had started a trifle behind-hand, and galloped over his part to make up for lost time—turning over two pages at once, and running up and down with his big fingers on his unfortunate pipe, producing the most hideous snortings imaginable—the conductor, red as a peony flower, called to him in the midst of the noise menacing him with his bow. His neighbours pushed him, trod on his toes, hooted him, and showered invectives on his head, but he calmly pursued his notes, no doubt blowing through his pipe a hurricane of rage. Knowing I was the sole cause of the delirium I felt flattered; I pitied and loved him! After about a quarter of an hour he stopped, and placing his clarionet between his legs, proceeded to rub his round head with his cotton handkerchief.

On leaving the play, at about half-past eleven, it rained slightly, and on passing the stage entrance we were nearly knocked down by an individual wearing a white hairy hat. I can still see him coming out of the door and bearing down upon us—I say us, because my mother was with me; I had not yet ventured to the theatre alone.

"Ladies," cried the Bull-dog, "you have, I daresay, already guessed that the white hat shelters the clarionet. Ladies, stop for heaven's sake!"

"Why? how? How dare you accost us in this manner; stand on one side, sir, stand on one side!" said my mother with a lofty air.

Before such a show of nobility the musician stammered, only taking off his hat. "It rains, ladies, and you have no umbrella, deign to accept mine."

My mother who has always been careful, feared water quite as much as she did fire, and accordingly was fain to accept this umbrella, never dreaming that it would lead me to the altar of Hymen.

I purposely refrain from dwelling on details as uninteresting to the reader as they are irritating to myself. The bold musician taking advantage of the introduction afforded by an unlucky shower of rain had paid us several visits, when at last my mother said to me,

"Eliza, tell me frankly, what do you think of him?"

"Who, mamma?" I said inquiringly; "the musician?"

"Yes, little rogue, the clarionet, the young Bull-dog who wants your hand. You know quite well I am speaking of him."

"But, mamma, I find him so horribly ugly."

"So do I, my dear; but you have not answered my question."

"Oh! ah! well! he is vulgar, grotesque, and is as disagreeable as the rain."

"Quite so," said my mother; "but again that is not the point. Does he please you when viewed as a sober, steady, desirable husband?"

"I won't say he does not," and I burst into tears.

"Come, no nonsense," said my mother; "I know you would like to be married, and this Bull-dog has many advantages. His double position as clarionet and trombone to the parish secures for him a comfortable living. What more can one require of a husband? I think, my child, that physical beauty and grace are only fleeting, besides you yourself have beauty enough and to spare to adorn a whole family. It is by the intelligent union of opposite natures that conjugal felicity is best secured. Well, that being so, it becomes a positive advantage for you to acquire a thoroughly ugly husband, a heavy, taciturn, serious, hard-working husband, who is certain to be a model of economy and affection."

I saw at a glance that my mother was right, and gave my consent. Had it all to be done over again, I think now I should do exactly as I did then. A sure, steady husband is a great prize in life. It is always good to have bread on the shelf, and one must be very stupid indeed not to be able to get little luxuries.

I therefore said: "Let us marry!"

Do not human beings say: "Let us take our degree; it will be the making of us."

To say my honeymoon was long and delightful, or that I discovered a hitherto unknown mine of devotion and romance beneath the hard crust of my husband's unsightly exterior, would be simply fiction. It is much nearer the mark to say at once that the coarse nature of my spouse soon revealed itself in all its odiousness. His every look, every movement, wounded my refined susceptibility. He rose at daybreak, and awoke me with the snorting of his clarionet, which he played with that degree of obstinacy and labour which belongs to mediocrity.

"Softly, my dear, softly; I tell you it would be better so," I would say.

He strove with all his might to modulate the notes, but for all that his tenderest passages made everything tremble. I even shook with rage! What irritated me most was that his instrument monopolised his whole attention.

"Won't you take a walk? have a little fresh air?" I would say to him. "You must feel tired, dear."

I could have beaten him. When we walked out together he used to stop and gossip at all the street corners, turning up all sorts of filthy heaps. Oh, how he made me suffer; he was born to be a butcher's dog. How many times has he not left me to pick up a bone, or quarrel with some inoffensive dog? His loud laugh and vulgar conversation with ill-conditioned curs, and . . .

I began to hate him; he bothered me, irritated me beyond measure. I own he would have cut himself in quarters to make our home happy, and he worked like a slave. But, alas! money can never compensate for a badly-assorted match. Little by little I withdrew myself from his company, and took to loitering about alone. I frequented a public garden, the resort of the aristocratic world, where every one was seen to advantage. My delight knew no bounds when I discovered that I was much noticed. I had found my own set at last.

One day I remember walking along a shady alley when I heard a voice whisper, "Oh, madam, how happy would he be who, in the midst of the crowd, could attract your attention." These words, so respectfully uttered, and so full of a something, a sort of passionate earnestness, pleased me immensely. I turned and beheld a well-dressed, beautiful insect flying near me. His manner was so graceful and his flight so fashionable, that I at once perceived he had moved in the higher circles of the air-istocracy; besides, he seemed to me to know his value, and to account himself a very fine fellow indeed.

"Ah, Greyhound!" he said, "how beautiful you are. What a fine head you have—a true type of the classic. Your feet would hardly soil a lily-leaf. Your silky dress, too, is so simple; yet it is enough to set off such charms as yours."

I quickened my pace, trembling at the audacity of this polished flatterer. Still he followed, and his voice vibrated in my ear like delicious music. He had evidently no ordinary appreciation of the beautiful.

"You are married, sweet one?" he added.

I could not resist the temptation of fancying that my fetters were broken, so I replied gaily, "No, I am a widow, sir!"

I saw no harm in this flirtation. What danger was there, after all, in the fact that an insect thought me pretty, and expressed his admiration? It cannot be too well impressed, upon all whom it may concern, that beauty must be appreciated; the public gaze is the sun, which warms it into bloom, and sustains its vitality; cold indifference first mars, and then destroys it. Our coquetry simply expresses a natural craving for being seen, a thoroughly honest and respectable ambition. I had no shade of guilty intention, or exaggerated pride; it was only the consciousness of a tribute, paid daily by the sun to the flower which opens to display its charms to the heavenly gaze. I looked upon this tribute of the world as my right. To prove that I was the most virtuous greyhound in Paris, I felt intoxicated by the words of my new admirer.

"Your eyes are terribly bright," said my husband on my return home. He was polishing a bone in a corner of our kennel—where he had picked it up, I do not know—"your voice is sweeter than usual."

"To please you, my eyes must grow dim and my voice husky," I replied.

Nothing is more galling than these simple remarks some people are always making, and asking why you detest them. My spouse was growing more and more distasteful to me. The trouble he takes to please me is most annoying. I hate to profit by his ridiculous labour, to eat his bread; all the time thinking that I owe it to the infernal clarionet he plays so badly. His irritating temper is killing me, his unutterable calm and absolute self-control compel me to shut up within myself all my bad temper, my indignation, my scorn! This sort of thing is perfectly frightful when one is nervous.

Life became a burden, and the polished insect soon found it out, for he followed me about with his dreamy, delicious buzzing.

"Greyhound, you are unhappy! you are suffering! I feel it, I see it. Grief ought not to touch a heart so tender," he said in tones so pathetic, that I looked upon him as a deliverer.

"Care will line your forehead and tarnish your beauty!"

I shuddered. What he said was, alas! too true, anxiety would certainly rob me of my charms, clog my steps, and veil my eyes. His words kindled my wrath against my husband, who would surely bring this grief upon me.

"Well," pursued the insect, "why not amuse yourself, come with me into the woods. Go on in front, and I shall follow, so that I may admire you, and drive away your gloom with my songs. Come, let us fly from the city-throng, and fill our breasts with the pure air of the fields."

I was choking; air I must have, air at any price. "To-morrow at such an hour, be at such a place, and we shall go out together."

It must not be thought, that by granting a rendezvous to this insect, I yielded to foolish sentiment. I simply did it to oblige him, because he rendered justice to my charms, and spoke ceaselessly about me.

When I reached home that evening, I suppose my face must have expressed more than usual disgust, for my musician stood looking at me for several minutes without uttering a single word, and then two large tears rolled down his cheeks; he was grotesque. Nothing is more dreadful than an ugly animal, who adds to his ugliness the horrors of grief. I expected a scene and reproaches, my heart swelled within me, as I said to myself, "Let him but speak, get angry, curse me; I will do the same, and oppose anger to anger. Passion is like a storm, when it has burst and is over, it refreshes the earth. I began to sing snatches of songs, like little bits of forked lightning, to bring about the crisis. But he did nothing, and said nothing, two or three times he sniffed badly, and carefully placing his clarionet in its dirty case, put on his cap, and said—

"Good night, my dear, I am going to the theatre."

What did these tears mean; did he think that he was odious to me? He did not seem jealous; how could he be so? was I not the most irreproachable, and, at the same time, most miserable of wives? Oh, if I had only something to break, scratch, or bite! How he does make me suffer!

Next day at the appointed hour, we met at our rendezvous. My fine companion, who had been impatiently waiting for me, exclaimed, "How beautiful you are! let us start for the woods."

"Yes," I replied, quite flattered, "I am ready."

So off we started. Although my mind was made up, a certain foreboding of evil troubled me. I could not throw it off. It occurred to me that I had gone too far, and was approaching the edge of a volcano.

"What is the matter, dear?" said the insect.

"Do you not see those ambulating musicians over there at that window?"

"Yes; they are showing performing Beetles to the inmates of the house. It seems to me they have to work hard for a living."

"Doubtless, but I am afraid, they look so strange. Please let us go some round-about way; I am trembling."

We followed a street to the left, and continued our course, yet I felt uneasy. It was a presentiment, for that day I had one of the most disagreeable meetings imaginable. We were just emerging from the suburbs when I descried in a corner an obscure mass, which turned out to be one of those performing Bears who figure at fairs and markets. He was making a Tortoise go through all sorts of wonderful exercises. Nothing was more natural than to meet this Bear, and yet I shivered all over. As my fears seemed unfounded, we continued to advance, and came close to the performer. The keen eye of this monster shot forth fire, and he sprang forward to bar my way.

"What are you doing here, madam?" he exclaimed, crossing his arms.

"Pray what does it matter to you what madam is doing here?" said my protector. "On my honour you are a bold fellow. Who are you, I pray? Speak! Who are you?"

"Who am I?" he breathed heavily. "I am the husband of this lady."

Saying which, he threw off the bearskin disguise, and revealed the clarionet, the musician, the Bull-dog, my husband, in fact, pale as death and a prey to horrible passion. He was frightful; although, to tell the truth, I liked him better excited, furious, grinding his teeth with rage, than calm and resigned, with tears in his eyes. He was really not so ugly as usual. Unfortunately the picture was spoilt by the cap which he kept on his head. That was a fault not to be pardoned. Readers of the opposite sex will hardly understand how it is that no detail escapes us.

"Madam," said my husband gravely.

This was another defect of his, to be grave! It was evident that he had prepared a speech, and weighed its effects. The insect hidden behind my ear said in a low voice: "What! is it possible, my queen of beauty, that you are married to this brute?"

I blushed to the tip of my nose.

"Madam," continued my master. 'Mada"—
Here he sneezed in the most comical manner. Perhaps a hair of the bearskin had got lodged in his nose. I laughed loudly, and quite as involuntarily as he had sneezed.

"Madam, follow me," continued my husband, quite losing his head. "This is too much; follow me!"

"I advise him not to touch you," said my protector, still hiding behind my ear; "as I really think I should not be responsible for my actions. I feel savage!"

He had not time to finish his sentence. My husband, as quick as lightning, seized him as he was flying, and mutilated him horribly. I do not know what followed. I became mad, and by a violent effort disengaged myself from my husband's paws, and jumping over his head, started off. I soon turned to look back, and saw the Bull-dog struggling with the police, making desperate efforts to get free, but the bearskin got entangled about his feet, and paralysed his movements, and at last he was carried off prisoner, followed by a jeering crowd.

So, I reflected, I am free; and pursued my way. The pure bracing air and deep blue of the sky had lost their charm. My breast was filled with indignation. I felt humiliated by this absurd jealousy, this scandalous outburst at once comic and tragic. The comic element annoyed me most. This prosaic clariouet appearing all at once upon the scene to dispel the dream of my life—can he ever be forgiven? After wandering about till I was giddy, I bent my steps homeward, and on entering found the place empty. It seemed to me I had lost something or some one. In truth, the deserted kennel filled me with strange longings for my poor husband. One gets used even to ugly, awkward things. If camels were at one fell swoop deprived of their humps, they would feel strange without them.

At this moment a letter was handed to me, ornamented with an imposing seal. It was an invitation from the authorities to be present at my husband's examination. The disguise in which he had been found, as well as a weapon discovered in his shoe, told badly against him.

Next day after breakfast—I had risen very late—and after finishing my toilet set out for prison to cheer my husband. It proved a great trial to my nerves. I passed through damp, dark corridors, enormous keys grating in horrible locks; heavy doors barred with iron were opened, and I entered a place crowded by miserable, ill-conditioned, dirty, repulsive animals.

Picking my steps into the midst of this filthy den, afraid to breathe

the vitiated air, I beheld my husband seated in a corner. Expecting reproaches and a tragic scene, I held myself in readiness to stand my ground. But contrary to my expectations he lay down at my feet and sobbed, begging my forgiveness.

I was quite touched—although the scene afforded amusement to the other prisoners—and resolved to do my best to obtain his release. I am naturally tender-hearted, too much so indeed. It was most proper on his part, that he owned his faults and ugliness, and rendered homage to my beauty.

I went at once to the presiding judge, who, viewing me over his spectacles, was astonished at my attractive appearance. He was clever, amiable, and leisurely, so that the trial of my husband lasted a long time.

Now is the moment when I must own a strange fact, and let in the light on a hitherto dark recess in my heart. Hardly was my Bull-dog incarcerated than my hatred of him changed to affection. He was no longer there for me to grumble at, and every time my eyes caught his clarionet in the corner they filled with tears. I was almost frightened at the power this morally and physically imperfect creature had over me, and the place he had filled in my life. His comical face, his cap, even his silence were wanting. I never knew where to vent my bad temper, which at times made me feel fit to burst. I tried to distract my attention, fearing lest my health should give way, but it was of no avail. I hardly dare to say it, I loved my Bull-dog, the jealous clarionet, I loved him! For all that, consideration for my feelings prevented me repeating my visit to the noxious prison which caused me a dreadful attack of neuralgia.

Thanks to my keeping him out of sight, his image became idealised in my imagination. In my dreams he appeared clothed in charms not his own. The news of his release was such a shock to my nerves that I nearly fainted. I rejoiced in his freedom. Soon after he arrived, but oh dear, how ugly he was! His coat was dirty, and his whole being steeped in an odour most offensive. A block of ice had fallen on my heart.

"My Greyhound! my wife! my darling!" he cried, running to meet me.

"Good morning, my friend," I replied, averting my nose. I had no courage to say more, my dreams had vanished.

All this passed long ago. Now my indignation brings the smile to my lips. Nothing more. I have learned to make the most of my bargain. If I made a mistake, and married a clarionet in place of a first-class tenor, I determined not to die of grief, but rather to be as brave as beautiful, and devote myself to cultivating all that was good in my Bull-dog. He has left off wearing his cap, and positively plays better; his walk is improved, and, by the dim light of the lamp, his profile is marked by a certain character.

"How pretty you are, little heartless one," he sometimes says. I reply in the same tone, "How ugly you are, my fat jealous one."

TOPAZ THE PORTRAIT-PAINTER.

AM his heir, I was his confidant, so that no one can better relate his history than myself.

Born in a virgin forest in Brazil—where his mother rocked him on interlacing boughs—when quite young he was caught by Indian hunters and sold at Rio, with a collection of parrots, paroquets, humming-birds, and buffalo-skins. He was brought to Havre in a ship, where he became the pet of the sailors, who, in addition to teaching him to handle the ropes, made him acquainted with all manner of tricks. His sea-life was so full of fun and frolic, that he would never have regretted quitting his forest home had he not left the warm sunshine behind.

The captain of the ship, who had read "Voltaire," called him Topaz, after Rustan's good valet, because he had a bare, yellow face. Before arriving in port, Topaz had received an education similar to that of his fellow countryman on the barge, Vert-Vert, who shocked the nuns by his manner. That of Topaz was also decidedly briny, as was quite natural from his nautical experience. Once in France, he might easily have passed for a second Lazarelle de Tormes, or another Gil Blas, if one cared to name all the masters under which he studied up to the time of full-grown Monkeyhood.

Suffice it to say, that as a youth he lodged in an elegant boudoir in the rue Neuve-Saint-Georges, where he was the delight of a charming personage, who finished his education by treating him as a spoilt child. He led an easy life, and was happier than a prince. In an unlucky hour he bit the nose of a respectable old dotard called the Count, the protector of his fair mistress. This liberty so incensed the old gentleman, he at once declared that the lady must choose between him and the beast, one of the two must leave the house.

The tyranny of a rich, old husband prevailed, and Topaz was secretly sent to the studio of a young artist, to whom the lady had been sitting for her portrait.

This event, simple in itself, opened up for him a new career. Seated on a wooden form in place of a silken couch, eating crusts of stale bread and drinking plain water instead of orange syrup, Topaz was brought to well-doing by misery, the great teacher of morality and virtue, when it does not sink the sufferer deeper into the slough of debauchery and vice. Having nothing better to do, Topaz reflected on his precarious, dependent position, and his mind was filled with a longing for liberty, labour, and glory. He felt he had come to the critical point of his life, when it was necessary for him to choose a profession. No career seemed to offer the same freedom and boundless prospects as that followed by the successful artist. This became a settled conviction in his mind, and, like Pareja the slave of Velasquez, he set himself to picking up the secrets of the limner's art, and might be seen daily perched on the top of the easel, watching each mixture of colour, and each stroke of the brush. As soon as his master's back was turned, he descended, and going over the work with a light hand, and a second coat of colours, retired one or two paces to admire the effect. During such moments he might be heard muttering between his teeth, the words used by Corregio, and later by the crowd of youthful geniuses with which Paris is inundated : *Ed io anche son pittore*. One day, when his vanity caused him to forget his usual prudence, the master caught him at work. He had entered his studio elated with joy, having received a commission to paint a cartoon of the Deluge, for a church at Boulogne-sur-Mer, where it rains all the year round. Nothing renders one so generous as self-satisfaction; instead, therefore, of taking the mahl-stick and beating his disciple, "In good faith," he said, like a second Velasquez, "since you wish to be an artist, I give you your liberty, and, instead of my servant, I make you my pupil."

Here Topaz became an historical pilferer; he arranged his hair like the powdered wig of a country priest, caught together the straggling hairs of his beard into a point, put on a high-peaked hat, dressed himself in a tight-fitting coat over which the ruffle of his shirt fell in folds, and, in short, tried to look as much as possible like a portrait of Van Dyck. Thus attired, with his portfolio under his arm, and colour-box in hand, he began to frequent the schools. But, alas! like so many apprentice artists, who are men with all their faculties fully developed, Topaz followed the empty dreams of his ambition, rather than the teaching of common sense. It was not long before he found this out. When the works of his master were not available, he had to begin with the bare canvas, and unaided lay in outline, form, light, shadow, and colour; when, in fact, instead of imitation, originality and talent were required, then, alas! good-bye to the visions of Topaz. It was no good his working, perspiring, worrying, knocking his head, tearing his beard. Pegasus, always restive, refused to carry him to the Helicon of fortune and renown. In plain English, he did nothing worth the materials wasted in its production: masters and pupils urged him to choose some other means of making a living.

"Be a mason, or a shoemaker; your talent lies more in the direction of trade!" It was in truth a pity that Topaz—full-grown ape as he was—should have been the slave of his narrow pride and vanity. That he should have aspired to fill a grand, generous, imposing, humanlike roll. I have often heard him say he would follow the example of the men of the Middle Ages, study medicine among the Arabs; and then return to teach it to the Christians. His foolish ambition was to transmit, from cultured men to apes, the knowledge of art, and, by idealising his fellows in portraiture, to place them on the level of the Lords of Creation. His chagrin was as profound as his project had been visionary. Wounded by the dreadful fall his vanity had sustained, sulky, ashamed, discontented with the world and with himself, Topaz, losing his sleep, appetite, and vivacity, fell into a languishing illness which threatened his life. Happily he had no physician, Nature fought out the battle for herself, and won.

About this time Daguerre, a scenic artist, completed the discovery which has rendered his name famous. He made an important step in science by fixing the photographic image, so that objects, animate and inanimate, might be caught on a silver plate. Thus photography became the handmaid of science and art. I had just made the acquaintance of a musical genius—human—to whom nature had refused both voice and ear; he sang out of tune, danced out of time, and for all that, was passionately fond of music. He had masters for the piano, flute, hunting-horn, and accordion. He tried the different methods of Wilhem, Paston, Cheve, and Jocotot. None of them answered, he could neither produce time nor harmony; what did he do in order to satisfy his taste? He bought a barrel-organ and took his money's worth out of it, by turning the handle night and day. He certainly had the wrist of a musician.

It was a similar expedient which brought back Topaz to life, with its hopes of fame, fortune, and apostolic insignia. The Jesuits and Turks say the end justifies the means, so, acting on this philosophic saying, Topaz adroitly stole a purse from a rich financier who was sleeping in his master's studio, while the latter was trying to paint his portrait. With this treasure he bought his barrel-organ, a photographic camera, and learning how to use it, he all at once became artist, painter, and man of science.

This talent acquired, added to a brace of fine names, he felt already half way towards reaching the coveted goal. To realise his hopes, he took his passage at Havre in a ship about to cross the Atlantic, and after a prosperous voyage, again set foot on the shore where, only a few years before, he had embarked for France. What a change had come over his position. From Monkey-boy he had become Monkey-man. In place of a prisoner of war he had become free, and above all, from an ignorant brute—the condition in which Nature sent him into the world—he had developed into a sort of civilised ape. His heart beat fast as he landed on his native soil. It was sweet to visit familiar scenes, after so long an absence. Without losing so much time as I take to write, he started off, camera on back, to seek the grand solitudes of his infancy, where he hoped to become the pioneer of progress. In his secret heart—he owned it to me—there was still the burning desire for fame. He hoped to create a sensation, to be regarded as more than a common beast; to enjoy the victory he would so easily win, over the natives of the country, by his title of Illustrious Traveller, backed by his knowledge and his wonderful machine. These were his true sentiments, but he cherished the delusion that he was impelled onwards by the irresistible force which urges forward the predestined ones—the leaders of mankind—to play their part in the world. Arrived at the scene of his birth, without even looking up his friends and relatives, Topaz pitched his camp in a vast glade, a sort of public common which Nature had reserved in the forest. There, aided by a black-faced Sapajo called Ebony, after the other servant of Rustan, who became his slave after the manner of men, who find in colour a sufficient reason for drawing the line which separates master from slave, Topaz set up an elegant hut of branches beneath an ample shade of banana leaves, and above his door he placed a signboard, bearing the fable, "Topaz, painter after the Parisian fashion;" and on the door itself, in smaller letters, "Entrance to the Studio." After sending a number of magpies to announce his arrival, to all the country round, he opened his shop.

In order to place his services within the reach of all—as no currency had ever yet been instituted—Topaz adopted the ancient custom of receiving payment in kind. A hundred nuts, a bunch of bananas, six cocoa-nuts, and twenty sugar-canes, was the price of a portrait. As the inhabitants of the Brazilian forest were still in the golden age, they knew nothing whatever about property, heritage, or the rights of mine and thine. They knew that the earth and its fruits were free to all, and that a good living might be picked off the trees, and an indifferent living off the ground. Topaz had many difficulties to contend against; by no means the least was the fact that no one is great in his own country, and especially among his own friends. The first visits he received were from monkeys, a quick and curious, but also a very spiteful, race.

Hardly had they seen the camera in action before they set to work to make spurious imitations of the dark box. Instead of admiring, honouring, and recompensing their brother for his toil in bringing this art-treasure to their country, they strove to discover his secret, and reap the profits of his labour. Here, then, was our artist at war with counterfeiters. Happily it was not a simple case of reprinting an English book in Germany or America. The apes might puzzle their brains, and toil with their four feet, and even combine one with the other—

amongst them, as elsewhere, one can easily find accomplices to carry out a bad scheme,—all they could do, was to make a box and cover like the camera and focusing cloth of Topaz; but they had neither lens nor chemicals. After many trials and as many failures, they became furious, and planned the ruin of Topaz; thus proving the truth of the saying, "One must look for enemies among one's fellow-countrymen, friends, and relations; even in one's own house"—

"Araña; quien te araño Otra araña como yo."

But no matter, merit makes its own way in defiance of envy and hatred, and finds its true level like oil that rises to the surface of water. It so happened that a personage of importance, an animal of weight, a Boar in fact, passing through the glade and seeing the signboard, paused to reflect. It seemed to this Boar that one need not of necessity be a quack or charlatan, because one comes from a distance, or because one offers something new and startling; also that a wise, moderate, impartial spirit always takes the trouble to examine things before condemning them. Another and much more private reason tempted the thoughtful Boar to test the stranger's talent; for side by side with the great actions of life there is frequently some petty, contemptible secret, and personal motive which, as it were, supplies the mainspring of action. This little motive is always studiously concealed, even from its owner's view, like the mainspring of a watch in its shining case. But the little spring, true to its work, marks the time on the dial, the hour, minute, and second, which heralds the birth of all that is noble, and all that is mean in life. This applies with kindred force to the instinct of brutes, and aspirations of men.

Our Boar was a lineal descendant of the companion of Ulysses who, touched by the wand of Circé, is supposed to have addressed his captain thus—

"How am I changed? My beauty as a boar I'll prove,
How knowest thou, one form is worst, another best?
Grace and good breeding are in my form express'd,
At least it has been said so by those who know."

He was a trifle foppish and very much in love. It was to make a gift to his betrothed he wished for a portrait.

Entering the studio he paid down double the usual price, as this Boar was the most liberal member of his government. He then seated himself solidly down in his appointed place where his steadiness and unconcern rendered him a capital subject for the camera. Topaz on his part exercised all his skill in posing, lighting, and photographing.

The portrait was a perfect gem, his lordship was delighted. The little image seemed to reduce his bulk in every way, while the silvery grey of the metallic plate replaced with advantage the sombre monotony of his dark coat. It was a most agreeable surprise, and fast as his bulk and dignity would permit him, he hastened to present the picture to his idol. The loved one was in rapture, and by a peculiar feminine instinct she first suspended the miniature round her neck, then, as instinctively, called together her relatives and friends to form an admiring circle around her lover's portrait. Thanks to her enthusiasm, before the day was over, all the animal inhabitants for miles round were appraised of the marvellous talent of Topaz, who soon became quite the rage. His cabin was visited at all hours of the day, the camera was never for a moment idle. As for Sapajo he had more than enough to do in preparing the plates for every new comer. With the exception of the apes there was not a single creature in earth, air, or water, who had not sat for a likeness to the famous Topaz.

One of his chief patrons was a Royal bird, the sovereign of a winged principality, who arrived surrounded by a brilliant staff of general officers and aide-de-camps. The artist was greatly annoyed by the remarks of a group of obsequious courtiers who bent over the desk alternately praising the prince, and criticising the portraits. The finished work, nevertheless, afforded satisfaction to the potentate who, proud of his tufted crown and brilliant feathers, gazed fondly down upon his image.

His conduct was quite different from that of the Boar. Although the king was accompanied by a splendid pea-hen, his wife by morganatic marriage, he himself retained the portrait, and, like Narcissus, before the fountain, fell in love with his own image. Happy are they who love themselves. They need not fear coldness, or disdain. They can feel no grief of absence, or pangs of jealousy. If the sayings of human philosophers are true, love is only a form of self-esteem which leaves its habitual abode, seeking to extend its dominion over the passions of another.

To return to Topaz, he touched up his portraits to suit the taste and vanity of his customers. In this, it must be owned, he did not always succeed. Some of his clients were all beak, and had no focus in them; others could not sit steady for a second, the result was, they figured on the plate with two heads, and a group of hands like Vishnu, the heathen god. They jerked their tails at some fatal moment, rendering them invisible in the photograph. Pelicans thought their beaks too long. Cockatoos complained of the shortness of theirs. Goats said their beards had been tampered with. Boars held that their eyes were too piercing. Squirrels wanted action. Chameleons changing colour; while the donkey thought his portrait incomplete without the sound of his mellifluous voice. Most comical of all—the owl, who had shut his eyes to the sun, maintained that he was represented stone-blind, thus destroying his chief attraction. In the laboratory of Topaz, as in the painter's studio, might be seen constantly in attendance a troop of young lions, the sons of the aristocracy, who came to loiter away their leisure. They prided themselves in being judges of art, called all the muscles of the face by their anatomical names; and spoke of graceful sweeps, handling of the brush, tooling, modelling, breadth of expression, &c., &c. Under pretext of enjoying the society of the artist, they twitted and laughed at his clients. To the crow, if he showed face at the entrance with his glossy black coat, and gouty, magisterial step, they cried in chorus—

"Oh! good morning, Mr. Crow, come in, nothing shows up so well as a good, black coat." Then they gently reminded him of his adventure with the fox and the stolen cheese.

One day a good fellow, a duck, left his reeds and swamps, and came with much ado to the studio, desirous of seeing his image to greater perfection than in his native stream. As soon as he appeared, one of the clique approached and taking off his cap, said—

"Ah, sir, you must be a great observer, you constantly move from side to side. What is the news?"

No one escaped their sarcasm; many were offended, many more lost their temper, and as for Topaz, he lost some of his best customers. But he really could not afford to offend the lions, as they belonged to good families, and were careful to flatter his vanity; besides, they were by no means bad fellows, when in their generous moods.

In spite of these petty troubles and annoyances—who is exempt from them in this world?—Topaz filled his barns; and his fame increased, keeping pace with his fortune. He perceived that the time had arrived for him to fill a larger field. His own industry had secured for him riches and honour, but the dream of his life was yet unfulfilled. Why should he not embrace the golden opportunity, and become a great teacher, a benefactor of his kind? His fame had reached the ears of a distant potentate, an Elephant-sovereign whose territory was somewhere—no matter where—it had never found its way into any

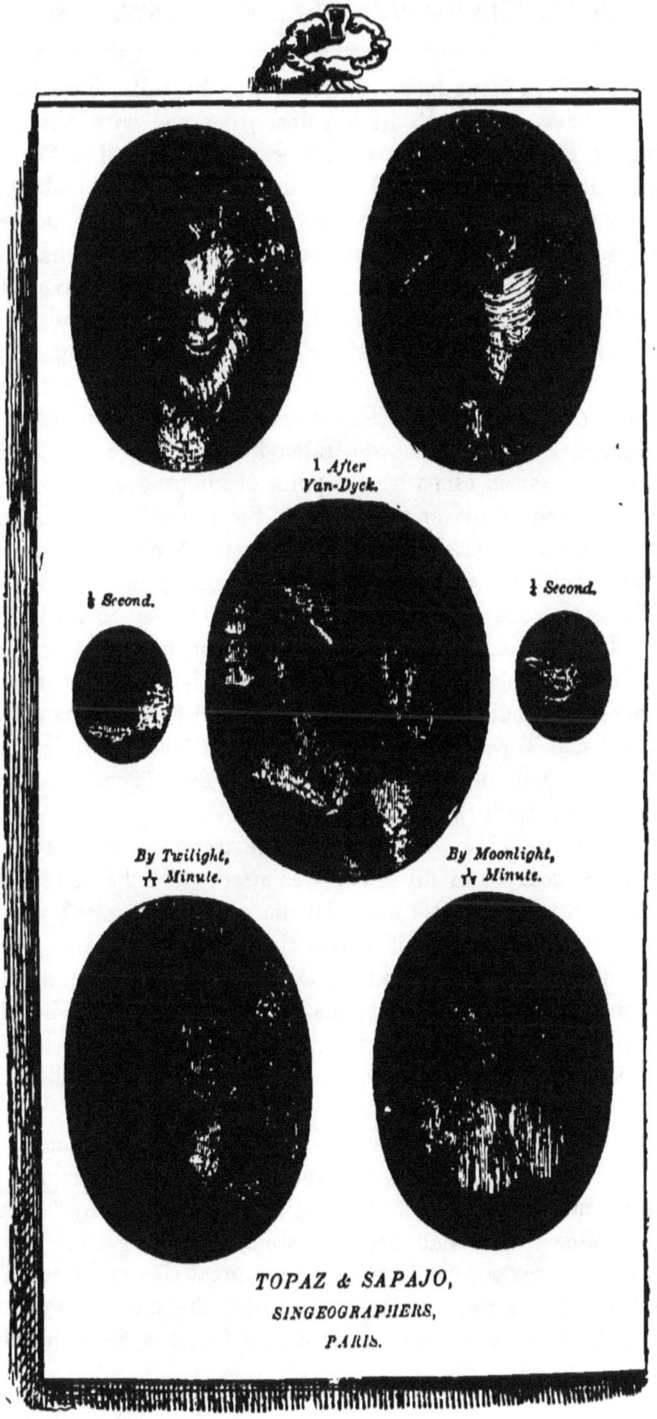

1 After Van-Dyck.

½ Second. ½ Second.

By Twilight, 1/10 Minute. By Moonlight, 1/10 Minute.

TOPAZ & SAPAJO,
SINGEOGRAPHERS,
PARIS.

map; no civilised being had ever set foot on his soil. This Elephant sent an embassy to the Parisian painter, charged with the mission of bringing Topaz to his court. He was an elephantine Francis I., calling to his presence another Léonardo da Vinci. His brilliant offers were at once accepted. This is how absolute monarchs proceed in their caprices, Topaz was promised, besides a considerable share of the native produce, the title of Cacique, and the ribbon of the ivory tooth. The artist set off mounted on a horse, and followed by a mule, bearing his faithful Sapajo and his precious machine. He at length arrived without accident at the court of the Sultan Poussal. Topaz was at once introduced to his Royal Highness, by the usual Minister of Rites and Ceremonies. The artist prostrated himself before the potentate, who gracefully raised him with the point of his proboscis, and allowed him to kiss one of his enormous feet, the same foot which later— but I must not anticipate events. His Massive Majesty was in such a ferment of impatient curiosity, that before taking any rest or refreshment, Topaz was requested to unpack his box and set to work without delay. He accordingly prepared his instrument, heated his drugs, and selected his finest plate for the royal image. The plate was small, but it was necessary that the entire elephant should figure on its surface.

"Good," said Topaz, "since it is a miniature His Majesty requires, I am certain he will be delighted with the result (Topaz recalled his early experience with the Boar).

He placed the king as far as possible from the camera so as to diminish his image and fill the plate, after which he conducted his operations with the nicest care. All the courtiers awaited the result with anxiety as profound as if it were the casting of a statue. The sun was scorching. After a few minutes the artist took up the plate lightly, and triumphantly presented it to the gaze of His Majesty; hardly had the king cast his eyes upon it, when he burst into a loud laugh, and without knowing why, all the courtiers joined in the royal hilarity. It was like an Olympian scene.

"What is this?" roared the Elephant as soon as he could speak. "That is the portrait of a rat, and you presume to say it is me? You are joking, my friend" (the laughter still continued), "why," continued the king after silence had been restored, his tone getting gradually more and more severe, "it is owing to my great size and strength that I have been chosen king. Were I to exhibit this miserable portrait to my subjects they would imagine I was an' insect, a weak, hardly perceptible, creature, only fit to be dethroned and crushed. The interest of the State, sir, forbids my taking this course," saying which, he

hurled the plate at the artist, who bowed down to the ground, not so much from humility as to escape a shock that would have been fatal to him. "I should have tested the truth of the stories so freely circulated about you."

The king and his ministers were becoming furious.

"Ugh! you are one of the hawkers of inventions and secrets, one of those innovators we have heard so much of, who prowl about seeking what good old institution they can devour; fellows who would bring down our constitution, and heaven itself about our ears, with their infernal machines. Bah!"

Here the mighty king stepped over the still prostrate body of the artist, and approaching the innocent machine—in his eyes big with the darkest plots ever brewed in the heart of a State—full of a no less legitimate wrath than Don Quixote, when breaking the marionettes of Master Peter, he raised his formidable foot, and crushed the camera to atoms.

Adieu fortune, honour, fame, civilisation! Adieu art! adieu artist! At the sound of the smashing which announced his doom, Topaz sprang to his feet, and starting off like a man, ended his sorrows in the waters of the Amazon.

He who became his heir and confidant was Ebony, the poor black Sapajo, who came over to Europe and studied at one of the universities, in order to qualify himself to write this history.

Journey of an African Lion to Paris,
and what came of it.

In which the political reasons for the visit of Prince Leo shall be fully discussed.

At the foot of the Atlas, on its desert side, there reigns an old Lion. Much of his youth was spent in travelling. He had visited the Mountains of the Moon, lived in Barbary, Timbuctoo, in the land of the Hottentots, among the republicans of Tangier, and among Troglodytes. From his universal benevolence he acquired the name of Cosmopolite, or friend of all the world. Once on the throne, it became his policy to justify the jurisprudence of the lions; carrying this beautiful axiom into practice—"To take is to learn." He passed for one of the most erudite monarchs of his time, and, strange as it may seem, he utterly detested letters and learning. "They muddle still more what was muddled before." This was a saying in which he took peculiar delight.

It was all very well; his subjects, nevertheless, were possessed by an insane craving for progress and knowledge. Claws appeared menacing him on all points. The popular displeasure poisoned even the members of the Cosmopolite's family who began to murmur. They complained bitterly of his habit of shutting himself up with a griffin, and counting his treasure without permitting a single eye to rest upon the heap.

This Lion spoke much, but acted little. Apes, perched on trees, took to expounding most dangerous political and social doctrines; tigers and leopards demanded a fair division of the revenue, as indeed, in most commonwealths, the question of meat and bones divided the masses.

On various occasions the old Lion had to resort to severe measures to quell the public discontent. He employed troops of savage dogs and hyenas to act as spies, but they demanded a high price for their service. Too old to fight, the Cosmopolite was desirous of ending his days peacefully—as he said, in Leonine language—"to die in his den." Thus his difficulties and the instability of his throne set him to scheming.

When the young princes became troublesome he stopped their allowance of food, wisely reflecting that there is nothing like an empty stomach for sharpening instinct, and sending the young lions to seek food abroad. At last, finding Liona in a state of hopeless agitation, he hit upon a very advanced policy for an animal of his age, viewed by diplomatists as the natural development of the tricks which rendered his youth famous.

One evening while surrounded by his family, it is recorded that the king yawned several times. In the annals of a less enlightened State this important fact might have been overlooked. He then uttered these memorable words: "I feel age and infirmity creeping on apace. I am weary of rolling the stone called royal power. My mane has grown grey in the service of my country; I have spent my strength, my genius, and my fortune; and what, my children, is the result? Simply nothing! nothing, save discontent! I ought to lavish bones and honours on my supporters. Should I succeed in this, it would hardly stifle the national discontent. Every one is complaining, I alone am satisfied; but, alas! infirmity gains upon me so surely, that I have resolved to abdicate in favour of my children. You are young, you have energy and cunning; get rid of the leaders of popular discontent by sending them to victory, to death!" Here the venerable potentate, recalling his youth, growled a national hymn, and ended by urging his tender-hearted sons to "sharpen their claws, and bristle their manes."

"Father," said the heir-apparent, "if you are really disposed to yield to the national will, I will own to you that the lions from all

parts of Africa, furious at the *far niente* of your Majesty, were about to take up arms against the State."

"Ah, my fine fellow," thought the king, "you are attacked by the malady of royal princes, and would wish for nothing better than my abdication. I shall teach you a lesson."

"Prince," replied the Cosmopolite in a roar, "one no longer reigns by glory, but by cunning. I will convince you of this by placing you in harness."

As soon as the news flashed through Africa, it created a great sensation. Never before, in the annals of history, had a Lion of the desert been known to abdicate; some had been dethroned by usurpers, never had a king of beasts voluntarily left the throne. The event was therefore viewed with some apprehension, as it had no precedent.

Next morning at daybreak, the Grand Dog Commander of the Life Guards appeared in his gay costume, fully armed, and around him the guard ranged in battle-array. The king occupied the throne, surmounted by the royal arms representing a chimera pursued by a poignard. Then, before all the birds composing his court, the great Griffin brought the sceptre and crown to the king who addressed the young lions in these words, first giving them his benediction—the only thing he cared to bestow, as he judiciously guarded his treasures —"Children, I yield you my crown for a few days; please the people, if you can, but do not fail to report progress." Then turning to the court, he said in a voice of thunder, "Obey my son, he has my instructions!"

As soon as the heir was seated on the throne, he was supported by a band of young, ardent, ambitious followers, whose pretentious doctrines led to the dismissal of the ancient counsellors of the crown. Each one desired to sell his advice, so that the number of places fell far short of the number of place-hunters. Many were turned back, fired with hatred and jealousy which they poured forth to the masses in eloquent harangues, stirring up the mud of popular corruption. Tumults arose; schemes for the destruction of the young tyrant were everywhere secretly discussed; and the youthful sovereign was privately informed that his power was built over a mine of political petroleum and social nitro-glycerine. Alarmed, he at last sought the counsel of his father who, cunning old rogue, was busy stirring up the slough of popular disorder and discontent. The people clamoured for the reinstatement of the venerable Cosmopolite, who, yielding to the pressure, again received the sceptre from the hands of his son who was thus completely outwitted by his crafty parent. The worthy king, moved no doubt by parental love, determined to rid himself of his dutiful heir by sending him on a foreign mission. If men have their Eastern question to settle, the lions also find matters no less pressing to draw their attention to Europe, where their names, their position, and habits of conquest, have so long been usurped. Besides, by instituting international complications, the Cosmopolite succeeded in engaging the attention of his people, and securing the tranquillity of the State. Accordingly, the heir-apparent, accompanied by a Tiger in ordinary, was sent to Paris on a diplomatic mission.

We subjoin the official despatches of the prince and his secretary.

FIRST DESPATCH.

"SIRE,—As soon as your august son had crossed the Atlas Mountains, he was warmly received by a discharge of loaded muskets presented by the French outposts. We at once understood this to be a graceful mark of the homage due to rank. The government officials hastened to secure him, and even placed at his disposal a carriage decked with bars of solid iron. The prince was constrained to admire the conveyance as one of the triumphs of modern civilisation. We were fed with viands the most delicate, and so far, can only speak in praise of the manners of France. My master and your slave were conveyed on board ship and taken to Paris, where we were lodged, at the expense of the state, in a delicious abode called the King's Garden. The people flocked to see us in such crowds that our staff of men attendants had to put up strong iron rails to protect our royal master from the vulgar throng. Our arrival was most fortunate, as we found an unusually large gathering of ambassadors from the animals of all nations collected in the garden. In a neighbouring palace I perceived Prince Beanokoff, a white Bear from the other side of the ocean, who had visited Paris on behalf of his government, and who informed me that we were the dupes of France, that the lions of Paris dreading the result of our embassy had shut us up; made us prisoners!

"'How can we find these so-called lions of Paris,' I inquired—Your Majesty will appreciate the action I have taken, in order to uphold your high reputation for boldness and fair dealing—This Bear, seeming to divine my thoughts, replied, that 'Parisian lions dwell in regions where asphalt forms the pavement; where the choicest veneers and varnishes of civilisation are produced, and guarded by spirits called the municipal authorities. Go straight on, and when you reach the quarter St. Georges, you will find them abounding.'

"'You ought to congratulate yourself, Prince Beanokoff, to find that your name and northern characteristics are not burlesqued in this capital.'

"'Pardon me, the Beanokoffs are no more exempt from the evil than are the lions of Leona.'

"'Dear Prince Beanokoff, what possible advantage can man derive from imitating our attributes?'

"'Ah! you have a great deal to learn. Why, look around at the pictorial representations of all sorts of animals that figure on the scutcheons of the nobility. There you will find that the proudest families claim us as their ancestors.'

"Wishing to make myself fully acquainted with the policy of the north, I said to him, 'I suppose, my dear Prince, you have already represented the matter in a proper light to your government?'

"'The Bears' cabinet is above dealing with such drivelling questions. They are more suited to the capacity of the lower animals, to Lions!'

"'Do you pretend, old iceberg, to ignore the fact that my master is the king of beasts?'

"The barbarian remained silent and looked so insulting that with one bound I broke the bars of my prison, his Highness, your son, followed my example, and I was about to avenge the insult when the Prince judiciously interfered, saying, 'We must for the present avoid conflict with the northern powers, our mission is yet unfulfilled.'

"As this occurred during the night, under cover of darkness, we made our way into the Boulevards, where at day-break we heard the passing workmen exclaim, 'Oh, what heads! would any one believe they were not real animals?'"

SECOND DESPATCH.

Prince Leo in Paris during the carnival, His Highness's opinion of what he saw.

"YOUR son, with his usual discernment, perceived that we had gained our liberty just as the carnival was at its height, and thus might come and go without danger. We felt excessively embarrassed, not knowing the manners, the usages, or the language of the people. Our anxiety was relieved in the following manner:—

"Interrupted by severe cold."

Prince Leo's first letter to his father, the King.

"MY DEAR AUGUST FATHER,—When I left the palace, you, with true paternal affection, bestowed almost nothing on me save your blessing. Without undervaluing that inestimable gift, I am bound to say I can raise hardly anything on it among the miserable money-lenders of this city. My dignity must be maintained on something more closely resembling coin than a father's benediction. Paris is unlike the desert; everything here is bought and sold. I could even find a ready market for my skin, if I could only get on without it. To eat is expensive, and to starve, inconvenient.

"Conducted by an elegant Dog, we made our way along the Boulevards where, owing to our likeness to men, we almost escaped notice. At the same time we kept a sharp look-out for the Parisiens they call lions. This Dog, who knew Paris perfectly, consented to become our guide and interpreter. We were thus enabled like our adversaries to pass for men in the disguise of brutes. Had you known, sire, what Paris really is, you would never have troubled me with a mission. I often fear being compelled to sacrifice my dignity in order to satisfy you. On reaching the Boulevard des Italiens it became necessary for me to follow the fashion and smoke a cigar, which caused me to sneeze so violently as to create a sensation. A popular writer passing, remarked, 'These young fellows are well up in their parts!'

"'The question is about to be settled, I said to my Tiger.'

"'Rather,' suggested the Dog, 'let it remain for a time like the Eastern question—diplomatic, vague, doubtful, open! It will pay better in the end.'

"This Dog, Sire, is constantly affording the most astounding proofs of his intelligence. It will therefore hardly surprise you, to learn that he belongs to a celebrated administration, situated in the Rue de Jerusalem, devoted to the guidance of strangers in France.

"He led us, as I have just said, to the Boulevard des Italiens, where, as indeed all over this large town, Nature's share is very small. There are trees, but such trees. Instead of pure air, smoke; instead of rain, dust; so that the leaves are bronzed, and the trees are mere sticks, supporting a tuft like the crown of leaves on the brows of the bronze heroes of France. There is nothing grand in Paris; everything is small, and the cooking is execrable! I entered a café for breakfast, and asked for a horse, but the waiter seemed so astonished that we profited by his surprise, took him round the corner and devoured him. The

Dog cautioned us not to make this a rule, as it might be misunderstood. He nevertheless accepted a bone which he polished with manifest joy.

"Our guide rather likes talking politics, and his conversation is not without its fruit. I have picked up wonderful scraps of knowledge from him. On my return to Leona no tumult shall disturb me, as I have discovered the best mode of governing the world. The chief in Paris does not rule; the business of governing and collecting the revenue is entrusted to a body of senators. Some of whom are descended from sheep, foxes, and donkeys, but the title of statesmen has made them lions. When any important question has to be settled, they all speak in turn, without paying the slightest attention to the views of their predecessors. One discusses the Eastern question, after some member who has exhausted himself on the subject of cod-fishing. When they have all done talking, it is not unfrequently discovered that the wise ones have carried through some important measure, while the donkeys have been braying to their heart's content.

"I noticed a sculpture in the palace, wherein you were represented struggling with the revolutionary serpent, a work infinitely superior to any of the statues of men by which it was surrounded. Many of these poor devils are represented with long dinner-napkins over their left arms, just like waiters; others, with pots on their heads. Such a contrast proves our superiority over men, whose imagination delights in building stones one upon the other, and cutting on their surface the finest flowers and forms of Nature.

"My Dog informed me that he would take us to a place where we would behold lions, lynxes, panthers, and Paris birds of night.

"'Why,' I inquired, 'does a lynx live in such a country?'

"'The lynx,' replied the Dog, 'is accustomed to appropriating. He plunges into American funds; he hazards the most daring actions in broad day and darts into concealment. His cunning consists in always having his mouth open, and strangely enough, doves, his chief food, are drawn into it.'

"'How is that?'

"'He has cleverly written some word on his tongue which attracts the doves.'

"'What is the word?'

"'I ought rather to say words. First, there is the word *profit*; when that has gone it is replaced by *dividend*; after dividend comes *reserve*, or *interest*. The doves are always caught.'

"'Why so?'

"'Ah! we are in a land where men have such a low opinion of each other, that the most foolish is certain to find another more foolish still—some one simple enough to believe that a slip of printed paper is a mine of gold. Human governments cannot be held altogether blameless, as they have too frequently misled the people by their paper. The operation is called "founding public credit." When it happens that the credit exceeds the public credulity, all is lost.'

"Sire, credit does not yet exist in Africa. We might occupy the malcontents there by getting them to found a bank. My *détaché*—I can hardy call my Dog an *attaché*—took me to a public café, and, by the way, explained many of the faults and frailties of beasts. At this famed resort there were a number of the animals we had been looking for. Thus the question is being cleared up little by little. Just imagine, my dear father, a Parisian lion is a young man who wears patent-leather boots worth about two pounds, a hat of equal value, as he has nothing better to protect in his head than in his feet; a coat of six pounds, a waistcoat of two pounds, trousers, three pounds, gloves, five shillings, tie, one pound; add to these rags about one hundred pounds for jewellery and fine linen, and you obtain a total of about one hundred and sixteen pounds, five shillings. This sum distributed as above, renders a man so proud that he at once usurps our name. With one hundred and sixteen pounds, five shillings, and, say, ninepence for pocket money, one rises far above the common herd of animals of intellect and culture, and obtains universal admiration. If one can only lay one's claws on that sum, one is handsome, brilliant. One may look with scorn upon the unfortunate poet, orator, man of science, whose attire is humble and cheap. You may indeed be what you like; if you do not wear the harness of the authorised maker, of the regulation cut and cost, you are certain to be neglected. A little varnish on your boots, and the other etceteras make up the roaring lion of society. Alas, Sire, I fear the same varnish and veneer conceals the hollowness of human vanity. Tear it off, and nothing remains.

"'My lord!' said my *détaché*, seeing my astonishment on beholding this frippery, 'it is not every one who knows how to wear these fine things. There is a manner, and here, in this country, everything resolves itself into a question of manners.'

"I sincerely wish I had stayed at home!"

THIRD DESPATCH.

"SIRE,—At the ball, Musard, His Highness, came face to face with a Parisian lion. Contrary to all dramatic rules, instead of throwing himself into the prince's arms, as a real lion would have done, the Parisian counterfeit almost fainted, but plucking up courage he had recourse to cunning, and by this talent, common to all low animals, wriggled out of the situation.

"'Sir,' said your son, 'how is it you take our name?'

"'Son of the desert,' replied the child of Paris in a humble tone, 'I have the honour of observing that you call yourselves lions. We have adopted your name.'

"'But,' said His Highness, 'what right have you, any more than a rat, to assume our name?'

"'The truth is we are like yourself, flesh eaters, only we eat our flesh cooked, you eat yours raw. Do you wear rings?'

"'That is not the question.'

"'Well then,' continued the Parisian fraud, 'let us reason, and clear the matter up. Do you use four different brushes; one for the hair, another for the hands, a third for the nails, and a fourth for the skin? Have you nail scissors, moustache scissors? Seven different sorts of perfume? Do you pay a man so much a month for trimming your corns? Perhaps you do not know what a chiropodist is. You have no corns, and yet you ask me why we are called lions. I will tell you why. We mount horses, write romances, exaggerate the fashions, strut about, and are the best fellows in the world. You are happy having no tailor's bill to pay.'

"'No,' said the prince of the desert.

"'Well then, what is there in common between us? Do you know how to drive a tilbury?'

"'No.'

"'Thus you see the strong points in our character are quite different from yours. Do you play whist, or frequent the Jockey Club?'

"'No,' said the prince.

"'Well, your Highness, with us whist and the club are everything.'

"This polite nonsense became so aggravating that His Highness replied—

"'Do you, sir, deny that you had me shut up?'

"'I had not the power to shut you up. It was the government. I am not the government.'

"'Why did the government impose on His Highness?' I inquired.

"'Exactly,' replied the Parisian. 'Why? hem! the government

takes no notice of popular whys and wherefores, it has its own political reasons for action, which are never divulged.'

"On hearing this, the prince was so utterly astounded that he fell on all fours. The Parisian lion, profiting by the prince's blind rage, saluted His Highness, turned a pirouette, and escaped.

"Your august son, deeming it wise to leave men alone to enjoy their illusions—the gilded toys, the pomp and tinsel, the borrowed names and nameless follies which make up the happiness and misery of their existence—prepared to quit Paris. A few days later one read in the 'Semiphone' of Marseilles—

"'Prince Leo passed here yesterday *en route* for Toulon, where he embarked for Africa. The news of his father's death is assigned as the reason of his sudden departure.'

"Tardy justice too often yields its tribute to greatness after death. This trustworthy organ even gave a picture of the consternation which your Majesty's untimely end spread through Leona. 'The agitation is so great, that a general rising is feared, and a massacre of the ancient enemies of the crown. It is asserted that the Dog, the prince's guide and interpreter, was present when His Highness received the fatal news, and bestowed the following advice, so characteristic of the utter demoralisation of the dogs of Paris: Prince Leo, if you cannot save all, *save the treasury!*"

Adventures of a Butterfly.

RELATED BY HER GOVERNESS.

Her infancy.—Youth.—Sentimental Journal.—From Paris to Baden.—Her wanderings, marriage, and death.

EDITORIAL PREFACE.

IN studying the manners and customs of the insect world, naturalists have brought to light many most curious and interesting facts. In the case of the three genders of Hymenoptera, each gender performs its allotted functions with a degree of care, tenderness, and precision that mimics the complex organisation of human society.

The neuter Hymenoptera are the working members of the insect world, and enjoy a greater share of life than either the males or females of their kind, outliving, indeed, two or three successive generations. In His infinite wisdom, God has denied them the power of reproduction, and at the same time entrusted to them the care and rearing of the young. Nothing in nature is without design. The neuter Hymenoptera bring up the orphan larvæ of their relatives who invariably die after giving birth to their young. It falls to the lot of the neuters to provide food for the larvæ who, thus deprived of the care of their parents, find in the neuter Hymenoptera the nurses who, with the most tender solicitude, take the place of sisters of mercy among men. Our correspondents' account of the life of a Butterfly will embody some interesting facts relative to the habits of this beautiful family.

EDITORS.

"DEAR SIRS,—Had I been requested to write down my personal experiences I should have declined the task, as it seems to me impossible to write an honest history of one's own career. The following biographical sketch is the fruit of moments stolen from the active hours of a busy life. I stand alone in the world, and shall never know the happiness of being either a father or a mother; I belong to the great family of neuter Hymenoptera. Feeling the misery of a solitary life, you will not be surprised to learn that I consented to become a tutor. An aristocratic Butterfly who lived near Paris in the woods of Belle Vue, had once saved my life, and as a token of gratitude I consented to become the foster-parent of the child he would never live to see. The egg was carefully deposited in the calyx of a flower, and hatched by a ray of sunlight the day after the parent's death. It pained me to see the youth begin life by an act of ingratitude. He left the flower that had found a place for him in her heart without saying a word. His early education was most trying to one's temper; he was as capricious as the wind, and of unheard-of thoughtlessness. But thoughtless characters are ignorant of the harm they do, and as a rule, are not unpopular. I loved the little orphan, although he had all the faults of a poor caterpillar. My instruction, advice, and guidance seemed to be thrown away upon him. Full of vivacity and light-heartedness, he embraced every opportunity of following the bent of his own reckless will. If I left him for an instant, on my return I never found him in the same place. He would venture to climb almost inaccessible plants, and risk his neck along the edges of leaves that hung over a yawning precipice. I remember being called away on important business, at a time when his sixteen legs would hardly carry him. On my return, I in vain searched for my charge, until at last I found him up a tree whose topmost branch he had reached, at the peril of his life.

"He was scarcely out of his babyhood when his vivacity suddenly left him. It seemed to me that my counsels were beginning to bear fruit, but I was soon undeceived. What I had mistaken for signs of repentance was the chrysalis malady, common to the young. He remained from fifteen to twenty days without moving a muscle; apparently asleep.

"'What do you feel like?' I asked him from time to time. 'What is the matter, my poor child?'

"'Nothing,' he replied in a husky voice. 'Nothing, my good tutor.

I cannot move about, and yet feel sensations of life and motion all over me. I am weary, weary, do not talk to me! Keep quiet, do not stir!'

"He became quite unrecognisable; his body swollen and of a yellow hue, like a faded leaf. This latent life so much resembled death, that I despaired of saving him; when one day, warmed by a splendid sun, he gradually awoke. Never was transformation more startling, more complete; he had lost his worm-like mould, and rose from his shell like a disembodied spirit, glorious in prismatic hues Four azure wings, as if by enchantment, had been placed upon his shoulders, feelers curved gracefully above his head, while six dainty legs peeped out beneath his velvet coat. His eyes, bright as gems, sparkling with the boundless prospect his new attributes had brought with them, he shook his wings and rose lightly in the air.

"I followed him as fast as my worn wings would carry me. Never was a course more erratic. Never flight more impetuous. It seemed as though the earth belonged to him, and all its flowers were designed for his pleasure; as though all created things, edged with the roseate light of his new being, were made to minister to his joy. He seemed to have risen from the grave to flit through a paradise all his own.

"Soon weary of caprice, fields and flowers lost their enchanting lustre, and ennui crept on apace. Against this evil, riches, health, the joys of liberty, all the pleasures of nature, were powerless. He alighted, choosing the plant of Homer and Plato, the daffodil, only to leave it for the lichen of bare rocks, where, folding his wings he remained the prey of discontent and satiety.

"More than once, dreading his desperate mood, I hid away the dark poisonous leaves of the belladona and hemlock.

"One evening he came in a state of great agitation, and confided to me that he had met in his wanderings a most amiable Butterfly who had just arrived from distant lands, bringing tidings of the wonders of the world.

"A craving for exploration had seized upon him. 'I must either die or travel,' said he.

"'Do not die,' I replied; 'self-inflicted death is only fit for the sneak and coward. Let us travel!'

"My words filled him with new life; he spread his wings, and we started for Baden.

"It is impossible to describe his joy at our departure, his delighted ecstasy. He was full of young life, its hopes and aspirations. As for myself, grief had enfeebled my wings, so that I found it hard to follow him. We only stopped at Chateau Thierry, the birthplace of La Fontaine, not far from the vaunted borders of the Marne.

"Shall I tell you the true cause of our stoppage? He caught sight of a humble Violet in the corner of a wood.

"'Who could help loving you, little Violet,' he exclaimed, "with your face so sweet and dewy? If you only knew how charmingly honest you look, decked with your border of little green leaves, you would then understand my love. Be kind, consent to become my dear sister. See how calm I remain when near you! How I love these sheltering trees, the peaceful freshness, and the sacred perfume you breathe around. How modestly you hide your beauty in this delicious shade. Love me! love me in return, and make life happy!"

"'Be a poor flower like me,' replied the Violet, 'and I will love you; and when winter comes, when the snow covers the ground, and the wind whistles through the leafless trees, I will hide you under my leaves, and together we will forget the cold that spreads death around. Fold your wings, and promise to be always faithful.'

"'Always?' he repeated, 'that is too long. Besides, there is no winter!' and he flew away.

"'Don't grieve,' I said to the Violet, 'you have escaped misery.'

"Our way lay over wheat-fields, forests, towns, villages, and the sad plain of Champagne. Not far from Metz, attracted by a sweet smell, he exclaimed, 'The gardens watered by these clear springs must indeed be beautiful!' Here he winged his way to a single Rose, growing on the banks of the Moselle.

"'Beautiful Rose,' he murmured, 'never has the sun shone on a flower more lovely. I have travelled far, suffer me to rest on one of your leaves.'

"'Stay!' replied the Rose, 'presumptuous flatterer, do not approach me!'

"Nothing daunted he touched a branch and retreated, exclaiming, 'You have pricked me!' and he showed his wounded wing. I no longer love wild roses, they are cruel, devoid of heart. Let us fly, to be happy is to be unfaithful!'

"Not far from the Rose he saw a Lily whose form charmed him. While its stateliness, purity, and cold, aristocratic bearing, filled him with mingled fear and admiration.

"'I do not dare to love you,' he said in his most respectful voice, 'for I am nothing more than a Butterfly, and I fear even to disturb the air you have glorified by your presence.'

"'Be spotless, pure, and unchangeable,' replied the Lily, 'and I will befriend you.'

"'Never change! In this world few Butterflies are sincere.' He

really could not promise. A puff of wind carried him away to the silvery banks of the Rhine. I soon joined him.

"'Follow me,' he was addressing a Daisy, 'follow me, and I will love you for your simplicity. Let us cross the Rhine and go to Baden. You will enjoy brilliant concerts, routs, dances, gay palaces, and the great mountains you can descry on the distant horizon. Leave these tame banks and shine as the queen of flowers in the smiling country yonder.'

"'No,' replied the virtuous Daisy. 'No! I love my native land, my sisters around me, and the mother earth that nourishes me. Here I must stay, must live and die. Do not tempt me to do wrong. The reason why Daisies are loved, is because they are the emblems of constancy. I cannot follow you, but you can remain with me, far from the noise of the world of which you speak. I will love you. Believe me, happiness is within the reach of all who are true and contented.

What flower will love you better than I ? Here, come, count my petals. Do not forget a single one, and you will find that I love you, and that I am not loved in return.'

"He hesitated an instant, and the eye of the tender flower dilated with hope. 'What are my wings made for ?' he said, and left the ground.

"'I shall die,' said the Daisy, bending low.

"'Nay,' I replied, 'thy grief will pass away.'

"A tiny Forget-me-not whispered, 'Daisy queen ! you have our love, our admiration ! Why break our harmony ? Why cast your pure heart away on a worthless Butterfly, whose flight and fancy follow every breath of wind, who is as swift to change his loves as evil tidings to fly abroad.'

"Following my young scapegrace, I observed him dart down towards a stream as if fired by a sudden resolution to end his days. 'Good heavens !' I cried, 'what has he done ?' as, descending to the water, I beheld nothing but the floating leaves on its surface. Shall I own it ? my blood froze with terror and apprehension. Fool that I was, he was enjoying the joke all the while through a tuft of reeds. 'Come, my tutor, come. I have found her at last.' He was dancing like a lunatic round a bulrush. My temper was sorely tried ; I nearly swore on observing this fresh token of folly.

"The young rogue continued: 'She is no flower this time; a real

treasure, a daughter of the air, winged like an angel, and jewelled like a queen.'

"I then perceived at the top of the reed, softly swaying in the wind, a graceful Dragon-fly of many colours.

"'Allow me to present my betrothed,' continued my pupil.

"'What? Already!' I exclaimed.

"'Yes,' said the Fly. 'Our shadows have grown, and these flowers have closed, since we became acquainted. I seem to have known and loved my charmer all my days.'

"Soon setting out for Baden, they gratified every caprice, arranged their wedding, and issued formal invitations to the gayest of the gay among the insect aristocracy. It was a civil marriage, advertised with all the pomp of a royal union, and attended by the cream of the native and foreign nobility. Certain clauses in the marriage code, touching the obedience and constancy of the wedded pair, gave offence to the lady, as she deemed them superfluous; she, however, modestly kept her views on these subjects to herself. The ceremony was so imposing that I employed a spider to make a sketch of the scene.

"The wedding was followed by rejoicing, feasting, and gaiety.

Pleasure parties thronged the ruts in the fields, making their way onward to congratulate the happy pair. The Snail drove over in her carriage, while the Hare mounted his thorough-bred Tortoise, and the Ant his Centiped, to pay their formal visits. Even the rustics held high holiday, and thronged to witness the marvellous performances of a troop of acrobats on the verge of a corn-field. Here, a Grasshopper displayed wonderful dexterity in dancing with and without a pole on a horizontal stem of grass; and a showman cricket was blowing a blast of music through the corolla of a tricoloured convolvulus.

"A ball had been arranged, for which great preparations were made.

A large Glow-worm, aided by a staff of Fire-flies, was charged with the illumination. The Glow-worm produced the central light, while his assistants, the Fire-flies, stood around the open cups of flowers with such marvellous effect, that every one thought a fairy had passed that way. The golden stems of astragalus were of such dazzling brightness that even the Butterflies could hardly bear its light; while many nocturnal insects retired, without being able to congratulate the married couple. Some remained from sheer politeness, veiling their eyes with their velvet wings.

"When the bride appeared, the whole assembly burst into transports of admiration. She was certainly a georgeously-dressed, charming-looking creature. She never rested for a second, but kept up with the

music and dance. 'Waltzing much too frequently,' said an old neuter, 'with a magnificent cousin in the Guards.' Her husband, my pupil, was the heart and soul of the party; he was everywhere, dancing and conversing.

"The orchestra, led by a humble Bee, a clever pupil of Da Costa, performed admirably a number of new waltzes and field-flower dances. Towards midnight the Signora Cavelleta, dressed in rather a transparent costume, danced a satarelle, which was only moderately successful. The ball was then interrupted by a grand vocal and instrumental concert, in which figured a number of celebrated artists who had followed the fine weather to Baden. A young Cricket played a solo on the violin, which Paganini had also executed just before his death.

"A Grasshopper, who had created a *furore* at Milan, the classic land of grasshoppers, sang a song of her own composition with great effect. Others followed, rendering some of the finest music of modern times in a manner unsurpassed. At the close of the concert a supper, ingeniously prepared from the juice of jessamine, myrtle, and orange blossom, was served in pretty little blue and rose-coloured bells. This delicious repast was prepared by a Bee, whose secret even the most renowned makers of bon-bons would have been glad to know.

"At one o'clock dancing recommenced with renewed vigour. The fête was at its height. Half an hour later strange rumours arose. It was whispered that the husband, in a transport of rage and jealousy, was searching everywhere for his missing wife. Some friends, with the intention, no doubt, of reassuring him, said she had danced constantly with her handsome, dashing cousin, and was seen to elope with him.

"'Ah! the false one!' cried the poor, despairing husband; 'I will be revenged!'

"I pitied his despair, and coaxed him away from the scene, at once so gay and so tragic. 'You have sown,' I said, 'and you have reaped. It is now not a question of cursing life, but of bearing it.'

"We left Baden that night, and, contrary to my expectation, my pupil never recovered the humiliating shock his own folly had brought upon him, by 'marrying in haste, and repenting at leisure.' True to his weak nature, easily attracted by glitter and flare, he at last flung himself into a lamp at Strasbourg, and perished with a comforting belief in the doctrine of transmigration of Buddha and Pythagoras.

The fate of the runaway Dragon-fly is a warning to weak wives. She and her admirer were caught in the net of a princely bird, and pinned down on a board, in a museum, two days after their elopement.

The Misfortunes of a Crocodile.

You see in me, gentlemen, a very unfortunate animal. Under the circumstances, I think I am justified in maintaining that no reptile has the same reason to complain. Judge for yourselves! What do I ask? Simply to be left alone to eat, digest, sleep, and warm my thick coat in the sun. If other animals are foolish enough to display their restless activity, and wear themselves out, in order to earn a miserable living, that is their business, not mine. I await my prey quietly, in a manner becoming the descendant of the illustrious Crocodiles worshipped by the Egyptians. Faithful to my aristocratic origin, I detest anything more intellectual than a good dinner, and the full enjoyment of the senses. Why will men pester me with their schemes for the extension of my mud bank by warfare, or harass me with their brand new measures for pacific financial reform? My privacy is perpetually invaded; I have hardly an hour I can call my own.

One bright summer morning my history began, like the first part of a novel, all perfume and roses, steeped in the social tranquillity which precedes the storms and heart-breakings of closing volumes.

The primary event of this important history was the breaking of my egg, which led to my taking bearings. Daylight for the first time fell upon my young life, casting its shadow across the desert covered with sphinxes and pyramids. The great Nile lay unexplored at my feet—a glorious expanse of turbid water, edged with corn-fields, and swollen by the tears of slaves. On its bosom reposed the lovely Isle of Raondah, with its alleys of sycamore and orange groves. Without pausing—as a historian ought to do—to admire this sublime spectacle, I advanced towards the stream, and commenced my gastronomic career by swallowing a passing fish. There still remained on the sand about a score of eggs similar to the one I had left. Have they been dissected by Otters and Ichneumons? or have they burst into life? No matter; free Crocodiles have no family ties.

For ten years I lived by fishing and capturing stray birds and unhappy dogs that mistook me for a mud bank. Arrived at this mature age, it occurred to me that philosophic reflection would aid digestion. I therefore reflected after a fashion common in the world. Nature has loaded me with her rarest gifts, charm of face, elegance of figure, and great capacity of stomach. Let me think how I may wisely use her gifts.

I belong to horizontal life, and must abandon myself to indolence. I have four rows of sharp teeth, I shall therefore eat others and endeavour to escape being eaten myself. I shall cultivate the art of enjoyment, and adopt the morals of good living—whatever they may be—and shun marriage. Why should I saddle myself with a wife to share my prey, when I myself can eat the whole, or with a pack of ungrateful children?

Such were my thoughts about the future, and all the Saurians in the great river could not shake my resolution to remain single. Only once I thought I was seriously in love with a young Crocodile of about sixty summers. Her laughing mouth seemed as wide as the entrance to the pyramid of Cheops, her little, green eyes were shaded by eyelids, yellow as the waters of the Nile in flood. Her skin, hard and rough, was adorned with green spots. Yet I resisted her blandishments and severed the ties that menaced our lives.

For many years I contented myself with the flesh of quadrupeds and fish of the stream, never daring to follow the example of my ancestors and declare war on man. One day, however, the Sheriff of Rahmanich passing near my haunt, I drew him under the water before his attendants had time to turn their heads. He proved as tender a morsel as any dignitary ought to be who is paid for doing nothing.

How many high and mighty men there are who could thus be spared for my supper! From this time forth I became a man-eater; men are tender, and besides they are our natural foes. It was not long before I acquired amongst my fellows a high reputation for audacity and sybaritism. I became the king of their feasts, and presided at many banquets.

The banks of the Nile often witnessed our convivial meetings, and echoed with the sound of our songs.

About the beginning of the moon of Baby-el-Alonel, the year of Higera 1213, otherwise 3d Thermidor, year VII., otherwise 21st July 1798, I happened to be reposing on a bed of reeds, and was awakened by a strange noise. Clouds of dust rose round the village of Embabeh. Two great armies were advancing to close in battle. On the one side the Arabs, the Mamelouks with breastplates of gold, the Keayas and the Beys mounted on superb horses. The other was a foreign army, made up of soldiers wearing black felt hats with red feathers, blue or rather dirty white uniforms and trousers. The commander was a slight, short, thin man. I pitied the human beings who were led by such a weak creature, hardly a mouthful for a Crocodile.

The little man uttered a few words, at the same time pointing to the pyramids, after which the cannonade began, the guns belched forth their fire and shot, while shells whistled and exploded among the Crocodiles, laying some of them low. That was a fatal day, the turning point in my history. The invaders carried off a gigantic column, placed it on board ship and transported it to one of the finest cities in Europe. The inscriptions on this stone have never been deciphered; I am told the meaning runs thus :—

> " Worship good living,
> Let your belly be your god.
> Selfishness is a virtue
> When practised voluntarily.
> You must never take the obelisk
> By force or by consent,
> Two millions must you pay
> If you take it unjustly."

Some of the new comers took it into their heads to hunt and shoot our noble selves. I was captured, but not killed, and became a prisoner at the disposal of man, and was conveyed to El-Kahiret—which the infidels call Cairo—and there provisionally lodged at the consulate. The tumult of war was as nothing compared to the clamour of disputants discussing the Eastern question in this house. Fighting was carried on with the sharpest weapon known—the human tongue. They squabbled from dusky dewy morn till eve. It was truly unfortunate that no free Crocodile was there to end the disputes by devouring Consul, swords, tongues and all. Had I been free, this useful office should have been performed and that speedily. My sailor captor, judging me unfit for a museum, handed me over to an adventurer. On our arrival at Havre—oh misery! my jaws were paralysed with cold. I was placed in a huge tub and exposed to the vulgar gaze of the crowd. The showman stood at the door of his hut bawling out this terrible fiction, "Walk in, ladies and gentlemen, now is the time when this interesting reptile is about to feed!"

He pronounced these words in a tone so delusive that I instinctively opened my jaws, to receive, what? nothing!

The traitor fearing to put my strength on an equality with my ferocity subjected me to systematic starvation.

An old money-lender, who had advanced a sum to my master, delivered me from this slavery by seizing the menagerie of which I was the chief ornament—all the other animals were stuffed. Two days later he handed me over, instead of money, to a man he was piously engaged in ruining. I was placed in a large pond near the sea, where my new owner possessed a villa. I gathered from the servants—internal enemies, as yet happily unknown amongst the Saurians—that my master was a young man of forty-five years, a distinguished gastronomist, the possessor of twenty-five thousand pounds a year—indulgent tradesmen allowing him to spend two hundred thousand pounds.

He had remained a bachelor, wisely viewing marriage as the closing scene in the comedy of life. The only thing remarkable about him was his stomach, of which he was very proud, "I have made it what it is," he would say, "it cost me a good bit, but I have not lost my money. Nature intended me to be thin and dry, but, thanks to an intelligent regimen, in spite of Nature I have acquired this honourable *embonpoint*. The cheapest dinner of this truly great man, cost him at least fifty francs. He used to say with great feeling, " only fools die of hunger."

One summer evening, after dinner, my master visited me with a numerous company of guests, some of whom found my countenance most prepossessing; others thought me hideous, and all agreed that I bore a strong resemblance to their host.

"Why do you delight in rearing such a monster?" said an old toothless man, who in truth, himself merited this insulting appellation. "Were I in your place, I should have him killed and sent to the kitchen. I have been told that crocodile's flesh is very much sought after by certain African and Cochin Chinese tribes."

"Upon my honour," said my patron, "your idea is original; notwithstanding his resemblance to me, I will sacrifice him to your palates. Cook, to-morrow you will make a crocodile pie with Egyptian onions." All the parasites clapped their hands, the cook bowed, and I disappeared to the bottom of my pond. After a terrible night, the first rays of the morning sun revealed the cook sharpening an enormous knife. He approached me, followed by two assistants who unlocked my chain and beat me with a stick about the head. I was lost, had not a sudden noise attracted the attention of my executioners. I beheld my master struggling with four unknown bull-dog-looking men, who had just arrived from Paris. One of them held a watch in his hand. Five o'clock had just struck, when I heard the words "*En route* for Clichy." A carriage appeared, and without pausing to make further notes, profiting by the excitement, I left my pond and gained the sea.

After many perils, I at last reached my native shore, where I found civilisation and M. de Lesseps were turning everything upside down. Should this rage continue for steam traffic, cutting canals, negotiating loans, and generally playing the mischief with all our ancient institutions, what will become of Crocodiles? Who knows, before long the Nile may be found to flow back to its source—wherever that may be—and the world itself, propelled by steam, may make its way to the sun, or take its enchanted inhabitants on a tour through space.

Progress is most annoying to a conservative Crocodile!

The Funeral Oration of a Silkworm.

The sun, having done his day's work of shining right well, suddenly and wearily retired to rest. The last notes of the birds' song of praise were still lingering in the echoes of the woods, and the earth, wrapping herself in her dark mantle, was preparing for repose. The death's-head Moth giving the signal of departure, the little cortége set out on the march for the purple heath. Field-spiders, whose work consisted in clearing the road, preceded the corpse which was surrounded by beetles, in black, carrying the bier of mulberry leaf. These were followed by tail-bearing mutes, next came the Ants, and lastly the Grubs. When at some little distance from the sacred mulberry tree, around which were assembled the relatives of the deceased, the Cardinal Pyrochre gave orders that the hymn of the dead should be intoned by the choir of Scarabs, and afterwards sung by Bees and Crickets.

At intervals, when the harmony ceased, one could hear deep sighs and sobs, bearing evidence of the universal grief caused by the loss of the humble insect, whose remains were being borne to their last resting-place. The procession at length reached the cemetery on the

heath, where the sextons were still bending over the new dug grave. Sighs and sobs were hushed in that profound silence which betokens the deepest sorrow. But when the bearers had laid the body in the tomb, and the yawning earth closed over it, the air was rent with a piteous wail, for the mourners had seen the last of a true friend.

An insect, robed in black, advanced to the grave-mound, saying:

"Why this outburst of bitter grief? Why weep for one who has been delivered from the trial and burden of life. Yet," he added, "weep on, for he who lies there can feel no pang of sorrow; no tears, no loving tones, can wake a responsive throb in his cold breast, nor bring him back to his earthly home!" They would not be comforted.

"Brothers," said another, advancing in turn, "it is at the birth of a silkworm one ought rather to mourn. His life was one of ceaseless toil. By leaving this earth he has left his misery behind; neither joy nor sorrow can follow him beyond the grave. I tell you simple truth; this is no time for hypocrisy. Why should worms mourn this event? Death has no terrors for us!" They still wept.

One of the mourners said with faltering voice: "Brother, we know that there is a beginning, and alas! an end, to everything, and that all must die; we know, too, the sorrows of our life, the labour of gathering our food leaf by leaf; we know the toil that transforms a mulberry leaf into a shining silken robe; we know the dangers that beset our lives; and the doom of the silken shroud that at last imprisons and blights the dreams of our young lives; we know that to die is to cease to toil, death being the end of the silken thread which began with our birth—we know all this; but, oh, we know, too, that we loved our brother, and who can console us for so great a loss?"

"We loved him! we loved him!" cried the mourners.

"I wept like you," said the Cardinal, "for our brother who is gone; yet, when I meet death face to face in the silkworm, my heart expands. 'Go to the other world,' I say, the better world; there the gates will open for the good, both high and low; there you will rejoin your lost loved ones in a land where flowers breathe an eternal fragrance; where the mulberries bordering the glassy streams are ever green. Ah, brothers, tell them to wait for us there, for to die is to be born to a better life!"

With these words the weeping ceased. The moon broke out, silvering the heath with a chaste glory.

The good insect added: "Go back to your homes; our brother has no longer need of you."

Each of the mourners, after placing a flower on the grave, left the scene, feeling comforted.

TO THE READER.

DEAR READER,

We are now halfway on our journey, and feel confident that you will place confidence in us as your guides during the second part of our expedition. Be assured of this, while we lead you into the unknown regions of the animal kingdom, we are prepared to shield you from the dangers of contact with its uncivilised or purely savage races. At the same time, your well-known craving for all that is marvellous has been fully considered, and shall be duly gratified.

Our correspondents have sharpened their wits and pens, and are impatient to lay open a perfect mine of treasure.

Good evening, dear friends. Go home, bar your doors well! One never knows what may happen. The calmest nights are frequently the harbingers of storms. Sleep with one eye open. At any rate, sleep well. Pleasant dreams!

THE MONKEY, PAROQUET, AND COCK,
Editors in Chief.

Part II.

Public
and
Private
Life of Animals.

Part Second.

JARDIN DES PLANTES, PARIS.

IN preparing the second part of our work for press, we were about to discharge the sacred duty of congratulating ourselves upon having laid the solid foundation of the animal constitution, when our pen was arrested by rumours of sedition and conspiracy. Dark clouds have been observed on the horizon; but our astronomers—creatures of true instinct—by their forewarnings, have hitherto enabled us to weather the worst storms, while at the same time, they have greatly increased our store of knowledge by clearing up some obscure points of siderology. They have further invented the seasons, and assured us that days and nights shall succeed each other as long as the observatory is properly endowed. They have decreed that the sun shall be free to all who pay the constitutional rates for the maintenance of paupers, of police, and of the state.

The wide experience and sagacity of these creatures have led them to investigate various natural phenomena, which they do not understand, nevertheless, with the innate modesty of votaries of science, they have compelled nature to bend to their conclusions and have accordingly arrived at certain incontestable facts.

The following communication has just been received from the observatory:

"We have discovered the true cause of alarm. Unless we are mistaken, the clouds that obscure the political horizon consist of swarms of flies and other winged insects—whose political opinions change with the wind—all of them armed to the teeth and tips of their tails.

"This rising is the result of social decomposition among the masses, and a breeze of false doctrine which threatens the glorious fabric of the animal constitution, founded by our first assembly.

"Conspiracy broods over the land. For all that, as the swarms have never been known to pursue any definite policy, we hope to be enabled to contradict the news, which to-day we announce as certain. —In any case : *Caveant consules !* do not slumber."

No, we will not sleep ; and as we have great faith in the wisdom of

our brothers. Since anarchy watches, we shall watch with and against her.

As a first measure, to maintain order, we propose to issue a daily bulletin of events, which will, at any rate, supply material for gossip to the various members of our league.

EXTRACT FROM THE "DAILY MONITEUR" OF THE ANIMALS.

Our worst fears are confirmed. Grave disorders of a seditious character have broken out. A band of rioters, numbering about three thousand, have detached themselves from the army, with the avowed intention of exciting the animal kingdom to revolt. Sword in hand, or sting in tail, they clamour for what they are pleased to term "general reform." This band is led by a notorious Wasp, famed for his poison and the purity of his principles. In vain have a number of venerable flies striven to calm the popular tumult. Their words have been misunderstood. Happen what may, we are prepared to tide over the storm, and to defeat these odious attempts to uproot the constitution. "Troubles," said Montesquieu, "build up empires."

The captain of our winged guards, Lord Humble Bee, has not succeeded in dispersing the rioters; he thought—and rightly—that it would be advisable to withdraw before shedding blood, contenting himself by cutting off the food supplies and hemming in the insurgents, who, after a few hours, would thus be compelled to capitulate or starve. The humanity of this noble leader is worthy of all praise.

The insurgents are throwing up barricades of grass and dried twigs, and are prepared, it is said, to sustain a regular siege. The field they occupy is at least eighteen inches wide by ten inches long.

The most contradictory rumours are spread abroad. Some of the rebels accuse us of indirectly stirring up revolt. "Tyrants of the deepest dye," said one, "maintain their power by setting their subjects one against the other, so that in their petty strife they may overlook the defects of government." What can we say of such absurdities. If the rulers of states had nothing to fear save the unity of the people, they would sleep on downy pillows!

It is reported that the disaffected flies are everywhere rousing the

nation. One of them the Clarion, a clever musician, has composed a war march entitled, "The Roll Call of the Flies." We can now hear the tones of this impious music floating over Paris. It is wafted from a thousand instruments at the Pantheon, the Val de Grace, the tour Saint Jacques la Boucherie, the Salpîtrière, the Père Lachaise, where the emissaries have been stationed by the leaders of the movement.

A number of prisoners have been arrested, but they refuse to disclose their principles.

"We are of snow-white purity!" say they. "Why should such innocents be arrested? Take our heads!"

"Your heads! what can we do with a fly's head? Nevertheless we will consider this proposition."

The pretensions of the rebels are now known, "*the common good*" serves them as a pretext for personal ambition and private hatred. Revolution means nothing more than the relinquishing of our posts to others who are not so well qualified to fill them. If we refuse to yield to their demands—as we intend to do—we are doomed, so they say. Our posts and emolu-

EXAMINING THE FLY'S HEAD.

ments will be sold with our lives! We owe this as a tribute to the animal kingdom.

For what are we reproached? Have we been unjust, or partial? Have we not followed our programme and printed all contributions without preference, or selection, blindly as every just editor ought to do? We are over head and ears in paper, knee deep in ink; we have burned the midnight oil, endeavoured to please everybody, entertained foes in the guise of friends, and in short, succeeded so well in our various duties as to secure the envy and hatred of an ungrateful rebel.

The chief of the insurrection is a Scarab! the Scarab Hercules! This is no doubt a very fine name for a leader. Have you made the

acquaintance of this Scarab? We for our part might scorn the attacks of such a grovelling fellow, did we not know that the bite or sting of the meanest of God's creatures is always most venomous and destructive.

We have therefore pleasure unalloyed in issuing the following orders:—

1st. A price is placed upon the head of the Scarab Hercules; a suitable reward will be paid to any one who will bring him dead or alive (we would prefer him dead).

2d. Measures will be immediately taken to raise a large body of troops; a force of nine hundred thousand flies fully equipped to fight the rebels in the field or in the air.

218 PUBLIC AND PRIVATE LIFE OF ANIMALS.

3*rd*. The commissioners of police are required to carry one or more lengths of rope as their means will permit.

4*th*. All honest subjects are required to remain at home, go to bed early, get up late, and to see or hear nothing. Such a line of conduct

will prove to the rioters that their projects find no favour among slumbering citizens.

5*th*. Animals found in pairs, or in groups, shall be cooked, or dispersed

by force. This notice concerns Ostriches, Ducks, gregarious and socially-disposed animals.

A Kite was sent to us bearing a flag of truce. We deigned to receive and listen to him. He said, "You, sirs, have spoken and managed affairs after your own fashion; now listen, we must each one have our turn. Over there, we number thirty three million free subjects, God's creatures, and every one as ambitious as yourselves to make a stir in the world; to write and speak fearlessly, Equality is our divine right!"

"What is a right?" inquired an old Crow whose acquaintance the reader has already made, "*summum jus, summa injuria!* If you must all write, the folios of the whole world would not be sufficient to contain the manuscript, not even if each one restricted himself, not to his history, nor to a page, line, word, letter, or even a comma."

This judicious refutation was deemed simply absurd, and the foolish Kite replied by asking another question. "That is enough! who endowed you with your power of reckoning? Has the God of Scarabs not made earth, sky, light, trees, and even leaves, that every one who has an equal stake, may have an equal share in all created things?"

O folly! the victory of such reasonable kites and scarabs is certain. Go back to your camp.

Alas! civil war is making its way into the most peaceful valleys. The spirit of revolt has spread from the insects to the birds, and even to the quadrupeds. Alarm is everywhere abroad. The doors of the cages have to be kept shut, a proceeding most galling to those animals who sit outside watching their neighbours. Let the peacefully disposed take courage, the geese are still guarding the capital.

The insurgents have replied to the articles of our journal, in a paper they have established, called " The Guardian of Freedom ;" or, " Review of Animal Reform."

Yesterday, the friends of liberty assembled in the Hall of Natural History, where stuffed animals are preserved.

This preliminary meeting was held at a late hour. One by one the members assembled, and silently exchanging tokens of recognition, seated themselves in the galleries opposite their preserved ancestors. The stillness was such, that one could hardly distinguish the dead from the living. The Elephant, Bear, Buffalo, Bison, and the Eagle all arrived at the same moment, as if drawn thither by some power supernatural. But who can deny that love of liberty moves mountains, and at once explains the presence of these noble beasts.

"Brothers," said an orator at last, "we have remained silent, and yet we know full well the cause of our meeting. Fellow elephants, apes, birds, and beasts! I crave your forbearance—(cheers)—while I point out to you the only true elements of reform. (Loud applause.) Our proceedings last year have let us in for a rather bad thing; the animals elected to edit our proceedings, and to conduct the affairs of our kingdom, have tampered with our liberty. Visit their chambers—there you shall behold histories without number, rejected and shelved; shelved to suit the editor's caprices! (Cheers.) Many of the pages thus consigned to

oblivion, are very mirrors of light and liberty that would have shed a glorious lustre over the ages. Ah! I see, in the cultured faces around, the lineaments of all that is noble and patriotic in the land! I hear in those deep drawn sighs, harrowing tales of genius neglected and suppressed by the jealousy of those who are set over us! (Thunders of applause.) I read the sentiments of true hearts, roused by oppression, in the fervour of your wagging tails and glorious gnashing of incisors! Brothers, let calm and tranquil sagacity resume its throne in your breasts, which are torn with righteous indignation! Listen—words must express pent-up thoughts! I must speak! you must act!! The course we are pursuing is leading us to ruin! What has the publication of our history done for us? For us? nay, not for us; for the few—the select favoured ones whose stories have appeared in its pages. What has it done for us? simply nothing. In these pages the wrongs of all, high and low, should find a place. Has it been so? I ask you. (Shouts of 'No! no! no! down with the editors!') Down with them! the tyrants!! they have abused the power we placed in their hands! served their friends, and calmly said, 'All is well.' What has come of it all? Has our world ceased to be a vale of tears? Have our homes been happier? Our prospects brighter? Has our fame been spread abroad? ('The stag, elk, and calf, No! no!!') Brothers, since that memorable night, when the first outcry for liberty and reform was hailed by the acclamations of the whole world, our rights and liberties have been systematically betrayed. We have been sold! sold!! sold to men!! ('True, true! they sold us,!') sold to men!!! But let us leave these inferior animals alone, they are not our worst enemies. Our leaders have betrayed us for a caress from their keepers, or a miserable subsidy of nuts and crusts. Whither shall we direct our steps? shall it be back to our narrow prisons, or lonely desert wastes? (All the animals, 'Alas! alas!') Will the clouds be our canopy and the earth our pillow? I tell you, friends, we shall all of us die in irons. (In chorus, 'O misery, misery!')"

The orator, turning towards the remains of countless generations of animals, continued—

"Remains of our illustrious ancestors, you who once lived and breathed. Miserable mummies! ghosts of all that is beautiful in our vitality and action. Did you voluntarily relinquish the care of the creator to play your part in this ghastly mimicry of life? Were we created to be stuffed and preserved in cases, side by side with the poor works of man, in place of returning to your parent earth after fulfilling your destinies ? Brothers, let us escape from men and the doom that awaits us. The way to liberty may be narrow and well-guarded; it is our only way! we must follow it, force the passes, water them with our blood, and gain the glorious grassy plains and wooded vales of freedom!"

If one may credit the report of this pompous oration, the effect it produced was perfectly marvellous. We need only notice one point in this wicked dithyrambic. You say, Mr. Bison, the speaker, that we have sold you—you are right we have sold you! and what is more we are proud of it! No less than 20,000 copies. Could you have done so much ? You owe us your thanks for raising your market value.

The dean of the Jardin des Plantes—a venerable Buffalo—whose personal character we esteem, replied thus to his cousin the Bison :—

"My children, I am the oldest slave in this garden, and have the sad honour of being your dean. Of my early days I have but a dim recollection, indeed I can only recall the days of my freedom. Sweet days they were, and in spite of my twenty odd years of bondage the young blood comes back to my heart as I reflect on the prospect of renewed liberty. (Cheers.) I speak of your liberty, my children, not of my own, for my eyes will close in death long before the dawn of that glorious day. Slave I have lived, and slave I shall die. (Shouts of 'Long live the Buffalo.') My good friends," replied the speaker, "it is not in your power to add an hour to my life. It is not the selfish freedom of one, or of many, but of all that we must seek. I therefore beseech you to remain united. (Murmurs of dissent.) My children, do not plunge into the misery of civil strife. Do not cavil over the mean rags of power. When you have changed your one-eyed house for a blind mock, what benefit will the change confer ? Think of the misery you may bring upon the poor and helpless ones, and how that a little power, more or less, vested in the hands of my hearers can never effect the good of all."

The closing words of this speech were listened to coldly, the respect due to the speaker alone preventing a demonstration.

"Civil war leads to despotism and not to liberty," said the dean, as he sadly resumed his seat.

"Are we here to listen to a sermon ?" roared the Lynx.

A number of agitators followed. It is necessary here to remark that the more indifferent the cause to be advocated the greater the crowd of speakers.

The Boar proceeded to address the assembly in a flow of eloquence, until domestic duties called him to the bosom of his numerous family.

Here we end our quotations from the "Journal of Reform," and in justice to the rioters, will conclude with a literal account of the proceedings, furnished by a Ferret who was present at the meeting.

"For three hours the rioters, irrespective of the place, or the sacred presence of the dead around, kept up an incessant thunder of inarticulate sounds, stamping, groaning, and applauding. Sixty-three speakers addressed the audience simultaneously. The result of this tumult of voices may be more easily imagined than described."

Our correspondent adds: "The art of whistling and howling has made such astonishing progress among the audience as to suggest a mass meeting in England!"

One of those doubtful dogs who have no political opinions, and who are to be found in every popular assembly attempted to gain a hearing.

"If we are vanquished!" he said.

"Vanquished! bah! Out with the cur!" cried the Bear, with that air of brutality so peculiarly his own.

"Out with him!" growled the Hyena; "barking is not enough, we must bite!"

"Beware of the spy," shrieked the Weasel.

The prudent brute waiting to hear no more, tucked his tail snugly between his legs and bolted through a window.

Here the Ram ventured to point out that the editors had gained the confidence of the people.

"Popularity is no proof of genius," said the Wolf. "The people will forget their idols."

"And hate them," growled the Hyena.

"If they neglect their love, they will nurse their hatred!" hissed the Snake.

The Fox perceiving that unanimity of sentiment was hopeless, adjourned the meeting by proposing that the rioters should refresh themselves by a night's repose. So they departed each one to his den, and there dreaming of reform and rapine, rose with the sun to renew the conflict. They awoke to arms and assaulted the amphitheatre. The onslaught was severe, and in our extremity we inquired for Prince Leo.

"They have taken the amphitheatre," said that great general, "and what is more they shall keep it."

The prince's firm attitude proved reassuring, for this renowned tactician had taken timely measures to teach the traitors a terrible lesson. He shut them in and secured the approaches, so that the stronghold was like to become the tomb of the insurgents. All attempts to relieve their position were vigorously repulsed by Prince Humble-Bee.

An audacious Ape mounted the amphitheatre roof and raised the standard of revolt; while a Mole proposed to entrench the army within its hill. The proposal was negatived, as the position was deemed already too strong.

A celebrated engineering Spider offered to spin a suspension bridge over which the insurgents might escape during the night. To this the Fly objected, while the Elephant urged that the work should be at once proceeded with.

The extraordinary simplicity of this giant of the forest inspired one of our friends with the idea for the following couplet, which we gladly

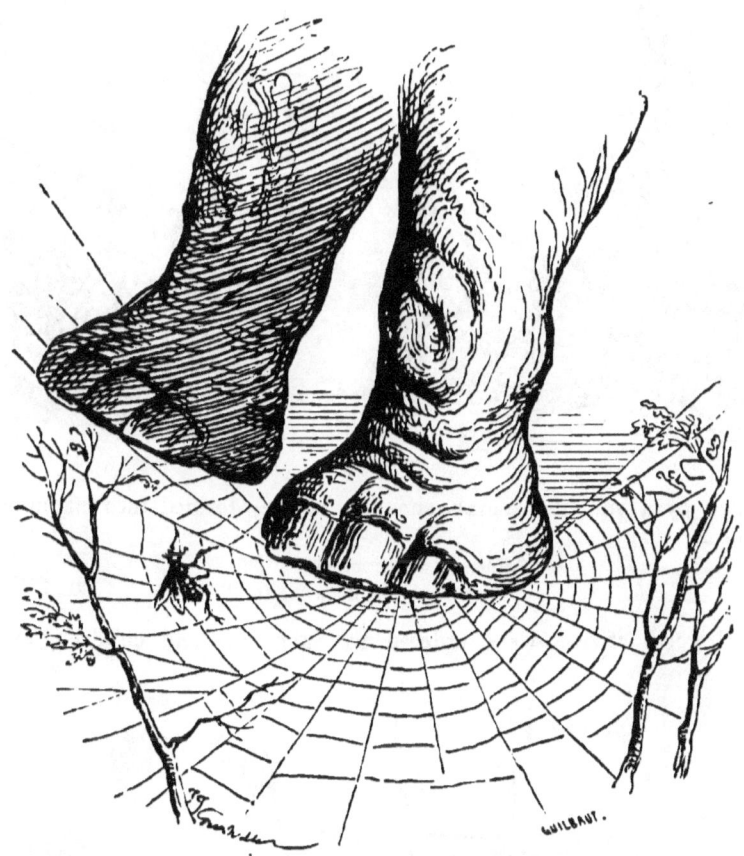

insert (as it ought not to be lost to posterity), regretting, at the same time, that the gifted poet insists on remaining anonymous :—

   Air—" *Femmes, voulez-vous éprouver.*"

    " Un Éléphant se balançait
     Sur une toile d'Araignée;
    Voyant qu'il divertissait,
     Une Mouche en fut indignée :
    ' Comment peux-tu te rejouer,'
     Dit-elle, 'en voyant ma souffrance
    Ah ! viens plutôt me soucourir,
     Ma main sera ta recompense.' "

We secured a number of brave auxiliaries in the shrimps, who,

headed by a valiant sea-crab, shouted, as they formed into marching order—
"Forward let us march
With our backs upon the foe."

All good citizens were ordered to leave wife and children, and

prepare to be everywhere at a moment's notice, ready to fight for their country. Notwithstanding the happy stratagem which shut in the rebels, we were doomed to defeat. A company of the enemy's flies, mechanics, were drafted to place the guns so as to command our position. The coolness of these creatures, foes though they were, won our admiration. They planted the weapons with an unconcern as complete as if preparing to storm the calix of a flower, while the result of their manœuvres soon told terribly on our left wing. Our swarms, impatient for the fray—displaying more valour than discretion—fell upon the foe in disorganised detachments. The right attacked the enemy's left under the leadership of the Goliaths, but the light infantry under Prince Humble-Bee were as waves against a rock scattered in boiling foam. Our left was opposed by the mining, cutting, and carpentering Andrines, and the corporation of Rhinoceros-Beetles, who having only one horn, obeyed the mighty two-horned Stags. Flies, Moths, Grubs, and other insects attacked and routed our centre. Prince Humble-Bee calculated on the Rhinoceros-Beetles attacking his heavy troops, compelling them to traverse the field, separating the two armies; but the Beetle, who had been apprised of the plan of campaign by a deserter, commanded his troops to close their ranks and their wings, thus to await the enemy's shock.

The colours floated in the wind, the sun shone brightly on the

insects ranged in battle array, while martial music fired our foes with

desperate resolve. From time to time grains of balsam, projected into the air by Stag-Beetles with much precision, fell among our troops, exploding and scattering death and dismay around. The enemy's forces stood firm as a rock. Our army, thoroughly demoralised, made a final attack, and were beaten off with great loss. Bruised wings, scattered mandibles and limbs impeded their movements, till at last they fell back in disorder. As a climax to our misfortunes, the general of the May Bugs, rolling over on his back, was pierced by the sting of a rebel Wasp. It was a lost battle—the Waterloo of our cause! Prince Humble-Bee, not caring to survive his defeat, plunged into the thick of the fray, when, after performing prodigies of valour, he died the death of the brave, pierced by twenty-nine wounds.

Notes by the Office-Boy.

Knowing the anxiety of my chiefs to keep our readers posted up in news, I take the liberty of writing in my turn, and shall go on until I am arrested.

My masters had just finished speaking, when the door flew to atoms. The Elephant had rung out the hour of doom at the door bell, and shivered the door with his foot. The pen fell from Mr. Parroquet's claw, and his eyes closed as if in deep thought.

" What do you see ? " he inquired of Mr. Cock, who stood at the window.

" I see trouble upon trouble; we are menaced on all sides! Confound them!! " cried he bravely; " why should we yield ? "

" Yield only to reason ! " said the Monkey; " never to force ! "

" What ! " crowed the Cock, jumping on the back of the Ape; "you cowardly, man-like animal, reason would tempt you to yield up your post ? "

" No doubt about it," replied the Ape, who became as livid as this paper; " if I am "——

He had no time to finish his sentence; the cabinet door flew open and the Fox entered.

" Arrest these gentlemen," said he to the Dogs who followed him, pointing to the trio of editors.

The Parroquet flew up the chimney, the Monkey hid beneath his arm-chair, while the Cock stood defiant, his comb never having assumed a hue so red. They were arrested.

" What are you doing here ? " said the Fox to me.

THE BELL OF DOOM.

"Whatever you choose, my lord," I replied.

"Well, remain here," he continued.

Many others had entered with the speaker, and shouted, "Long live my lord the Fox!" They were right, for never had I beheld so affable a prince.

"My friends," he said, "nothing in this office is changed; only one additional animal appears." (Cheers.)

The Fox, taking up the abandoned pen of the Ape, sat down to write his first proclamation.

FIRST PROCLAMATION.

"Inhabitants of the Jardin des Plantes, the editors having been removed, all cause for disorder has ceased."

"THE FOX,
"Provisional President and Editor."

"Read and sign this document," said he to the ex-editors.

Whereupon the Cock replied, "Sir, I shall not dishonour myself by such a treacherous act."

"We shall see," replied the Fox.

He then proceeded to draw up another proclamation.

SECOND PROCLAMATION.

"Citizens, while you were asleep you were being betrayed, but friends were watching for you. Too long had we bowed our heads without murmuring; the time had come for us to assert our dignity. The traitors who governed and sold you breathe no more! The records of our nation will teach the world how the animal kingdom redresses its wrongs. During this hour justice has been executed, the work is finished, the culprits have paid with their lives the penalty of their guilt—they have been hanged!

"*N.B.*—Out of sacred regard for our ancestors who suffered the extreme penalty of the law, they have been hanged on new gibbets.

"THE FOX."

The Cock listened unmoved to the reading of this second document.

"But," said the Monkey, "my lord, we are not hanged."

"Are you really thinking of hanging us?" cried the Parroquet, weeping at the prospect.

"No," replied the Fox, "it is a proceeding I do not care to carry out, only you must appear to have been hanged."

The shouts of the populace outside could be plainly heard, demanding the heads of the editors.

"Patience," replied the Fox, addressing the people from time to time—"patience, if you are wise. You shall have some medals to

commemorate this event. [*Aside.*] To refuse nothing, and to give nothing, is the way to govern wisely and well."

The shouts, "Death to the tyrants!" "Death to the editors!" redoubled.

"You hear, gentlemen," said the Fox. "It is necessary to do something for the people; yet," he added, "if you can find means to deceive them by preserving your lives, you may do so."

"Means!" screamed the Monkey; "I have found them," and in his joy he turned three somersaults.

Mr. Monkey had got possession of the stuffed body of an ancestor, no doubt with the intention of honouring his race. He at once produced the relic, and it was decided that this defunct relative should figure on the gibbet in place of his erring descendant. To better deceive the multitude, before sending the mummy to martyrdom the Monkey attired it in his coat and well-known cap; this he did, not without tokens of genuine grief.

"Now, my dear sir," continued the Fox, "you must seek retirement for fifteen days, after which I think you may venture to show yourself again. There is no dead man or monkey who in Belle France has not the right to come to life audaciously at the end of a fortnight. The people are the most magnanimous of enemies—they forget everything."

"They are also the most fickle friends," replied the Ape; then, casting a last fond look on his boxes, his table, and his office, he vanished.

The Parroquet found means of communicating with an old friend, an ardent admirer of his talent, who volunteered to be hanged in his stead. A quarter of an hour after the execution, the ungrateful Parroquet was joking with his wife about the folly of martyrdom.

The Cock, who remained true to his principles, suffered death, much to the regret of a numerous circle of female admirers.

The crowd, drawn together with the view of seeing such mighty personages dangling in the air, had its wish gratified. Some silent worshippers of the illustrious dead could scarcely believe their eyes.

"Is it possible," they said, "that animals of such influence can be hanged like common felons? What is the world coming to? They, only the other day, seemed to be the mainsprings of life!"

A bird whose name remains unknown published a pamphlet on this subject, in which he developed this proposition: "Is it good that he who governs is not the State? for should misfortune befall him, there would be an end to the State."

After the executions had taken place the Fox thought proper to make the two proclamations public, and being in a mood for proclamations, issued a third.

THIRD PROCLAMATION.

"Inhabitants of the Jardin des Plantes, invested by your confidence with a post so important as that of directing the second and last part of our National History, it is needless here to expose the principles which obtained for me your suffrage. It is by my work you shall judge me. I shall make no pledges, although pledges cost nothing. I shall not tell you that the golden age is about to begin for you, whatever the golden age may be; but I can assure you that when you find neither pen, ink, nor paper in my office, it will be because they are not to be had at any price. My advice for all is to observe justice and sincerity. Remember, were these words blotted out of the dictionary, you would still find them indelibly engraved on the heart of a Fox.

"Your brother and director,

"THE FOX."

The effect of these proclamations, which were circulated everywhere, was almost magical. Perfect tranquillity reigned; the politest civilities were exchanged by all; a little dust sprinkled over the dead, and one would imagine that neither war nor bloodshed had ever disgraced this smiling land. Some disagreeable animals who sneak about and ferret out everything, having no fault to find with the chief editorship of the Fox, inquired by whom he had been elected chief? What can it matter to them, so long as he has been elected? One names one's self, but one is no less editor-in-chief for all that.

My lord, casting his eyes over my work, was pleased to inform me that I gave him satisfaction, and that he intended to recompense me. Yesterday I was office-boy, to-day I am His Highness's private secretary! Yesterday my feet were trod on, to-day they are licked! I am evidently somebody, and can do something. I embraced the occasion to inform him I had been yard-dog in a college.

"I congratulate you on your university training. Even if one knows nothing on leaving the walls of such an institution, one is credited with profound knowledge. The important part of life consists not in being, but in appearing to be."

It is said that I sold myself; it is a mistake, I was bought, that was all. Besides, the advantageous post just given to me belonged to no one; it was made expressly for me. There is a ring at the bell, it is a deputation of animals.

"We come," said the chief of the deputation humbly, "to represent to your Highness that something is wanting in our glorious constitution."

"What?" said the Fox.

"Sir," replied the deputy, "what will posterity say to our pulling through a revolution without eating or drinking?"

THE DEPUTATION.

"Gentlemen," said His Highness President Fox, "I note with pleasure your attention to important details, and that the country may rely upon your practical common sense. Go and dine."

GOING TO THE BANQUET.

A great public dinner was prepared, in token of rejoicing, in a field in front of the amphitheatre. As on all similar occasions, there was much speech-making and little food, at least for many of the most deserving supporters of the republic. The Insects were relegated to an obscure position, politely called the place of honour, where they feasted on fine phrases. In consideration of his position, the Fox, as President, was supported by a Duck and Indian Hen, who kept a respectful distance from His Excellency. It was a most amicable gathering. The views expressed were as diverse as the individuals present. One said white, another black; one red, another green; and all agreed that the speakers were the living representatives of worth, genius, and national progress. The Fox was everything to every one. He had a smile and kind word for each guest. "You do not eat," he said to the Cormorant. "Are you ill?" to the White Bear; "you seem pale." To his vis à vis, "Have the Wolves no teeth now?" To the Penguin, who was yawning, "You require rest after your exploits." To the Blackbird, "You seem silent." And to all, "My good friends, use your pens freely." At last came the toasts, the time for oratorical display. You should have watched how each one retired within himself, scratched his head or pensively caressed his tail as a means of inspiration, how each silently rehearsed his little speech. Unfortunately the order of the toasts had been arranged beforehand—not only the order, but the number as well. Splendid fasting might be forgiven, but the cancelling of a cherished toast—never! In spite of this wise precaution, there were so many speakers that my pen and patience alike failed to enumerate them. As may be imagined, the first toast was Liberty; this is traditional, and it is no fault of those who dine if liberty makes a poor show on such occasions. By courtesy the second was the Ladies, couched in these terms, "To the sex that adorns and ennobles life!" This toast, proposed by an amiable Hippopotamus well known for his gallantry, was greeted with applause.

Towards the close of the evening wine flowed freely, and as the contents of the cask fell, the spirits of the party rose to that pitch when all things earthly seemed steeped in the roseate light of a glorious dawn. The repast ended like all others of the kind, when the face of the universe is proposed to be changed, and the world forced backwards by eating and drinking. But the morning revealed the marvellous fact that the world still revolved in its old way, and that recourse must again be had to the common, traditional, time-honoured modes of life, at least so thought the Fox, who replaced his cap by a little crown, declaring at the same time that in future he would shun popular feasts as he would the devil.

"I am about to draw up a charter. A nation that has a charter wants for nothing. Here is my charter:—

"All animals who can read, write, and especially count, who have hay in their racks, and powerful friends, being all equal before the law, shall receive protection. The great ones of the Jardin des Plantes may therefore enjoy their ease. The lesser ones are requested to give up what little they have, and to become so small as to be imperceptible and impalpable.

"It is impossible to please every one; those who are displeased ought not to be astonished, as they have a right to complain. The right of drawing up petitions is solemnly recognised. But as it is well known that the moments of a ruler are precious, and as it would be impossible for him to receive all the petitioners, it is forbidden for any one to bring his petition to the august arm-chair. They will only be received when sent by post, postage prepaid, and will only be read when convenient to do so."

The animals required no second telling. Every one having some source of complaint, petitions arrived in cartloads. The earth and air were thronged with messengers and couriers of every description. The charter had not been published two hours before the house, cellars, and lofts were packed full of petitions. They were even piled up against the outside door.

"Fools!" said the Fox, laughing in his sleeve to see they had taken him at his word. "How long will they imagine that governments are made to protect them? Yet I must look at these petitions, and in order to observe the strictest impartiality, will close my eyes."

He opened one written by a Bittern, signed and crossed by many supporters. It ran as follows:—

"The undersigned declare that they have had enough of civil discords and of preliminary proceedings, and suggest that the white Blackbird should now be called upon to relate his history."

"I like this petition," said the Fox, "as it enables us to dispense with opening the others. The others may make a bonfire."

No sooner said than done. They were burned.

History of a White Blackbird.

How glorious and yet how painful it is to be an exceptional Blackbird! I am not a fabulous bird. M. de Buffon has described me. But, alas! I am of an exceedingly rare type, very difficult to find, and one that ought, I think, never to have existed.

My parents were worthy birds, who lived in an old out-of-the-way kitchen-garden. Ours was a most exemplary home. While my mother laid regularly three times a year, my father, though old and petulant, still grubbed round the tree in which she sat, bringing her the daintiest insect fare. When night closed round the scene, he never missed singing his well-known song, to the delight of the neighbourhood. No domestic grief, quarrel, or cloud of any sort had marred this happy union.

Hardly had I left my shell, when my father, for the first time in his life, thoroughly lost his temper. Although I was of a doubtful grey, he neither recognised in me the colour nor the shape of his numerous posterity.

"This is a most doubtful child," he used to say, as he cast a side glance at me, "neither white nor black, as dirty-looking as he seems ill-begotten."

"Ah me!" sighed my mother, who was always coiled up in a ball on her nest. "You yourself, dear, were you not a charming good-for-nothing in your youth? Our little pet will grow up to be the best of our brood."

While taking my part, my mother felt inward qualms as she saw my callow down grow to feathers; but, like all mothers, her heart warmed to the child least favoured by nature, and she instinctively sought to shield me from the cruel world.

When I was moulting, for the first time my father became quite pensive, and considered me attentively. While my down fell off he even treated me with some degree of favour, but as soon as my poor cold wings received their covering, as each white feather appeared, he became so furious that I dreaded his plucking me alive. Having no mirror, I remained ignorant of the cause of his wrath, and was at a loss to account for the studied unkindness of the best of parents. One day, filled with joy by a beam of sunlight and the warmth of my new coat, I left the nest, and alighting in the garden, burst into song. Instantly my father darted down from his perch with the velocity of a rocket.

"What do I hear?" he cried. "Is that meant for a Blackbird's whistle? Is it thus I sing? Do you call that song?"

Returning to my mother with a most dangerous expression lurking round his beak, "Unfortunate! who has invaded our nest? who laid that egg?"

At these words my good mother jumped from her nest fired by proud resentment. In doing so she fell and hurt her leg; she wished to speak, but her heart was too full for words. She fell to the ground fainting.

Frightened and trembling, I cast myself at my father's feet. "O my father!" I said, "if I whistle out of tune, and am clothed in white, do not punish my poor mother. Is it her fault that nature has not tuned my ear like yours? Is it her fault that I have not your yellow beak and glossy black coat, which recall a sleek parson swallowing an omelette? If Heaven has made me a monster, and if some one must bear the punishment, let me be the only sufferer."

"That is not the question," said my father. "Who taught you to whistle against rule?"

"Alas! sir," I said humbly, "I whistled as best I could, because my breast was full of sunshine and stomach full of grubs."

"Such whistling was never known in my family," he replied. "For untold centuries we have whistled, from father to son, the notes alone

by which we are known. Our morning and evening warblings have been the pride of the world since the dawn that awoke us to the joys of paradise. My voice alone is the delight of a gentleman on the first floor and of a poor girl in the attic of yonder house. They open their windows to listen to me. Is it not enough to have your whitened clown-at-a-fair coat constantly before my eyes? Were I not the most pacific of parents, I should have you plucked and toasted on the poor girl's spit."

"Well," I cried, disgusted with my father's injustice, "be it so, I will leave you—deliver you from the sight of this white tail you are constantly pulling. As my mother lays three times a year, you may yet have numerous black children to console your old age. I will seek a hiding-place for my misery; perchance some shady spout which shall afford flies or spiders to sustain my sad life. Adieu!"

"Please yourself," replied my father, who seemed to enjoy the prospect of losing me; "you are no son of mine—in fact, you are no Blackbird."

"And who may I be, pray?"

"Impossible to say; but you are no Blackbird."

After these memorable words, my unnatural parent with slow steps left me, and my poor mother limped into a bush to weep. As for myself, I flew to the spout of a neighbouring house.

II.

My father was heartless enough to leave me in this mortifying situation for some days. In spite of his violence he was naturally kind-hearted, and had he not been prevented by his pride, he would have come to comfort me. I saw that he would fain forgive and forget, while my mother's eyes hardly left me for an instant. For all that, they could not get over my abnormally white plumage, and bring themselves to own me as a member of the family.

"It is quite evident I am not a Blackbird," I repeated to myself, and my image, reflected in a pool of water in the spout, confirmed this belief.

One wet night, when I was going off to sleep, a thin, tall, wiry-looking bird alighted close by my side. He seemed, like myself, a needy adventurer, but in spite of the storm that lifted his battered plumage, he carried his head with a proud and charming grace. I made him a modest bow, to which he replied with a blow of his wing, nearly sweeping me from the spout.

"Who are you?" he said with a voice as husky as his head was bald.

"Alas! good sir," I replied, fearing a second blow, "I have no notion who I am; I imagine myself to be a Blackbird."

The singularity of my reply, together with my simple artlessness, interested him so much that he requested me to tell him my history, which I did.

"Were you like me, a Carrier-Pigeon," said he, "all the doubtings and nonsense would be driven out of your head. Our destiny is to travel. We have our loves—we also have our history; yet I own I don't know who my father is. To cleave the air, to traverse space, to view beneath our feet man-inhabited mountains and plains; to breathe the blue ether of the sky, in place of the foul exhalations of the earth; to fly like an arrow from place to place, bearing tidings of peace or war,—these are our pleasures and our duties. I go farther in one day than a man does in six days."

"Well, sir," I replied, a little emboldened, "you are a Bohemian bird."

"True," he said; "I have no country, and my knowledge is limited to these things—my wife, my little ones; and where my wife is, there is my country."

"What have you round your neck?"

"These are papers of importance," he replied proudly. "I am bound for Brussels with news to a celebrated banker which will lower the interest of money one franc seventy-eight centimes."

"Ah me!" I exclaimed, "you have a noble destiny. Brussels must, I suppose, be a fine city? Could you not take me with you? as I am not a Blackbird, perhaps I am a Carrier-Pigeon."

"Were you a Carrier you would have returned my blow."

"Well, sir," I continued, "I will return it, only don't let us quarrel about trifles. Morning dawns and the storm has abated, pray let me follow you. I am lost, have no home, nothing in the world; should you leave me, I shall destroy myself in the gutter."

"Come along, follow me if you can."

Casting a last look at the garden where my mother was sleeping, I spread my wings and away I flew.

III.

My wings were still feeble, and while my guide flew like the wind, I struggled along at his side, keeping up pretty well for some time. Soon I became confused, and nearly fainting with fatigue, gasped out, "Are we near Brussels?"

"No, we are at Cambray, and have sixty miles to fly."

Bracing myself for a final effort, I flew for another quarter of an hour, and besought him to rest a little as I felt thirsty.

"Bother! you are only a Blackbird," replied my companion, continuing his journey as I fell into a wheat-field.

I know not how long I lay there. When at last I made an effort to raise myself, the pain of the fall and fatigue of the journey so paralysed me that I could not move. The dread of death filled my breast when I saw approaching me two charming birds, one a nicely-marked coquettish Magpie, the other a rose-coloured Ringdove. The Dove stopped a few paces off and gazed on me with compassion, but the Magpie hastened to my side, saying, "Ah, my poor child, what has befallen you in this lonely spot?"

"Alas! madam, I am a poor traveller left by a courier on the road; I am starving."

"What do I hear?" she exclaimed, and flew to the surrounding bushes, gathering some fruits, which she presented on a holly leaf. "Who are you?" she continued; "where do you come from? Your account of yourself is scarcely to be credited; you are so young, you have only cast your down. What are your parents? how is it they leave you in such a plight? I declare it is enough to make one's feathers stand on end."

While she was speaking I raised myself a little and ate the fruit ravenously, the Dove watching my every movement most tenderly. Seeing I was athirst, she brought the cup of a flower half full of rain-drops, and I quenched my thirst, but not the fire kindled in my heart. I knew nothing of love, but my breast was filled with a new sensation. I should have gone on dining thus for ever, had it been possible, but my appetite refused to keep pace with my sentiment, nor would my narrow stomach expand.

The repast ended and my energies restored, I satisfied the curiosity of my friends by relating my misfortunes. The Magpie listened with marked attention, while the tender looks of the Dove were full of

RESCUED.

sympathy. When I came to the point where it was necessary to confess ignorance of my name and nature, I felt certain I had sealed my fate.

"Come," cried the Magpie, "you are joking. You a Blackbird? Nonsense; you are a Magpie, my dear fledgling—a Magpie, if ever there was one, and a very nice one too," she added, touching me lightly with her fan-like wing.

"Madam," I replied, "it seems to me that I am entirely white, and that to be a Magpie—— Do not be angry, pray."

"A Russian Magpie, my dear; you are a Russian Magpie."

"How is that possible, when I was hatched in France, of French parents?"

"My good child, there is no accounting for these freaks of nature. Believe me, we have Magpies of all colours and climes born in France. Only confide in me, and I will take you to one of the finest places on earth."

"Where, madam, if you please?"

"To my verdant palace, my little one. There you will behold life as it ought to be. There you shall not have been a Magpie for five minutes before you shall resolve to die a Magpie. We are about one hundred all told, mark you, not common village Magpies who pick up their bread along the highway. Our set is distinguished by seven black marks and five white ones on our coats. You are altogether white. That is certainly a pity, but your Russian origin will render you a welcome addition to our number. I will put that straight. Our existence is spent in dressing and chattering, and we are each careful to choose our perch on the oldest and highest tree in the land. There is a huge oak in the heart of our forest, alas! it is uninhabited; it was the home of the late Pius X., and is now the resort of Penguins. We pass our time most pleasantly, our women folk are not more gossiping than their husbands are jealous. Our pleasures are pure and joyous, since our hearts are as true as our language is free. Our pride is unbounded. Should an unfortunate low-born Jay or Sparrow intrude himself, we set upon him and pick him to pieces. Nevertheless, our fellows are the best in the world, and readily help, feed, and persecute the poor Sparrows, Bullfinches, and Tomtits who live in our underwood. Nowhere can one find more gossip, and nowhere less malice. We are not without devout Magpies who tell their beads all day long, and the gayest of our youngsters are left to themselves, even by dowagers. In a word, we pass our time in an atmosphere of glory, honour, pleasure, and misery."

"This opens up a splendid prospect, madam, and I would be foolish not to accept your hospitality; yet, before starting on our journey, permit me to say a word to this good Ringdove. Madam," I continued, addressing the Dove, "tell me frankly, do you think I am a Russian Magpie?"

At this question the Dove bent her head and blushed. "Really, sir," she replied, "I do not know that I can."

"In Heaven's name, madam, speak; my words cannot offend you. You who have inspired me with a feeling of devotion so new and so intense that I will wed either of you if you tell me truly what I am." Then softly I continued, "There seems to be something of the Dove about me, which causes me the deepest perplexity."

"In truth," said the Dove, "it may be the warm reflection from the poppies that imparts to your plumage a dove-like hue."

She dared say no more. "Oh, misery!" I exclaimed, "how shall I decide? How give my heart to either of you while it is torn with doubts? O Socrates, what an admirable precept was yours, yet how difficult to follow, 'Know your own mind'! It now occurred to me to sing, in order to discover the truth. I had a notion that my father was too impulsive, as he condemned me after hearing the first part of my song. The second part, I was fain to believe, might work miracles with these dear creatures. Politely bowing by way of claiming their indulgence, I began to whistle, then twitter and make little warblings, after which, inflating my breast to its fullest, I sang as loud as a Spanish muleteer in his mountains. The melody caused the Magpie to move away little by little with an air of surprise, then in a stupefaction of fright she described circles round me like a cat round a piece of bacon which had burned her, and which proved too tempting to relinquish. The more impatient she became, the more I sang. She resisted five-and-twenty bars, and then flew back to her green palace. The Ringdove had fallen asleep—admirable illustration of the power of song. I was just about to fly away when she awoke and bade me adieu, saying—

"Handsome, dull, unfortunate stranger, my name is Gourouli. Think of me, adieu!"

"Fair Gourouli!" I replied, already on my way, "I would fain live and die with thee. Such happiness is not for me."

IV.

The sad effect of my song weighed heavily upon me. Alas ! music and poesy, how few hearts there are who understand thee ! Wrapped in these reflections, I knocked my head against a bird flying in an opposite direction. The shock was so great that we both fell into a tree. After shaking ourselves, I looked at the stranger, expecting a scene, and with surprise noted he was white, wearing on his head a most comical tuft and cocking his tail in the air. He seemed in no way disposed to quarrel, so I took the liberty of asking his name and nationality.

"I am more than astonished you do not recognise me," he said. "Are you not one of us ? "

"In truth, sir," I replied, "I do not know who I am myself, far less who you are. Every one asks me the same question, 'Who are you ? ' Who should I be if I am not one of nature's practical jokes ? "

"Come now, that will do; I am no green hand to be caught by chaff. Your coat suits you too well; you cannot disguise yourself, my brother. You certainly belong to the illustrious and ancient family called in Latin *Cacuata*, and in the vulgar tongue Cockatoo."

"Indeed, sir ? Since you have been good enough to find me a family and a name, may I inquire how a well-bred Cockatoo conducts his affairs ? "

"We do nothing, and what is more, we are paid for doing nothing ! I am the great poet Cacatogan—quite an exceptional member of my family. I have made long journeys, crossed arid plains, and made no end of cruel peregrinations. It seems but yesterday since I courted the Muses, and my attachment has been most unfortunate. I sang under Louis XVI., I clamoured for the Republic, I chanted under the Empire, discreetly praised the Reformation, and even made an effort in these degenerate days to meet the exigencies of this heartless century. I have tossed over the world clever distiches, sublime hymns, graceful dithyrambics, pious elegies, furious dramas, doubtful romances, and bloody tragedies. In a word, I flatter myself I have added some glòrious festoons, gilded pinnacles, and choice arabesques to the temple of the Muses. Age has not bereft me of poetic fire. I was just composing a song when we came into collision, and you knocked the train of my ideas off the line. For all that, if I can be of any service to you I am heartily at your disposal."

"You, sir, can serve me," I replied, "for at this moment I too feel something of the poetic fire of which you speak, although, unlike yourself, laying no claims to poetic fame. I am naturally endowed with a voice and song which together violate all the old rules of art."

"I myself have forgotten the rules. Genius may not be fettered, her flights are far beyond all that is stiff and formal in schools of art."

"But, sir, my voice has a most unaccountable effect on those who listen to its melody, an effect similar to that of a certain Jean de Nivelle whom—— You know the rest."

"Yes, yes," said Cacatogan. "I myself suffer from a similar cause, thoroughly inexplicable, although the effect is incontestable."

"Sir, you are the Nestor of poetry. Can you suggest a remedy for this peculiarity of song?"

"No; during my youth I was much annoyed by it. Believe me, its effect indicates only the public inability to appreciate true inspiration."

"That may be so. Permit me to give you an example of my style, after which you will be better able to advise me."

"Willingly," replied Cacatogan; "I am all ears."

I tuned my pipe at once and had the satisfaction of seeing that he neither flew off nor fell asleep, but riveted his gaze on me, and from time to time displayed tokens of approbation. Soon, however, I perceived he was not listening; his flattering murmurs were lavished on himself.

Taking advantage of a pause in my song he instantly struck in, "It is the six-thousandth production of my brain, and who dare say I am old? My lines are as harmonious and my imagination as vivid as ever. I shall exhibit this last child of my genius to my good friends;" thus saying he flew off without another word.

V.

Left thus alone and disappointed, I hastened my flight to Paris, unfortunately losing my way. The journey with the Pigeon had been too rapid and unpleasant to leave any lasting impression of landmarks on my mind. I had made my way to Bourget, and was driven to seek shelter in the woods of Morfontaine just as night closed in.

Every bird had sought its nest save the Magpies and Jays—the worst bedfellows in the world—who were quarrelling on all sides. On the borders of a brook two Herons stood gravely meditating, while close at hand a pair of forlorn husbands were patiently waiting the arrival of their giddy wives, who were flirting in an adjoining hedge. Loving Tomtits played in the underwood, beneath a tree where a busy Woodpecker was hustling her brood into a hollow in the trunk. On all sides resounded voices saying, "Come, my wife!" "Come, my daughter!"

"Come, my beauty!" "Here I am, my dear!" "Good-night, love!" "Adieu, my friends!" "Sleep well, my children!"

The situation for a celibate was most embarrassing. I was almost tempted to seek the hospitality of some birds of my own size, as we all looked alike grey in the dark. At last perching on a branch where there was a row of different birds, and modestly taking the lower end, I hoped to remain unobserved; but I was disappointed. My nearest neighbour was an old Dove, as thin as a rusty weather-cock. The moment I approached her, the few feathers which covered her bones became the objects of her solicitude. She pretended to pick them, but as they had only a slender hold of her skin, merely passed them in review, to make sure she had her right number. Scarcely had I touched her with the tip of my wing, when, drawing herself up majestically, she said, "How dare you, sir?" administering at the same time a vigorous British push that sent me spinning into the heath, on the top of a Hazel Hen, who would have willingly made room for me, only her spare bed was taken up by a son returned from the harvesting.

I heard myself called by the sweet voice of a Thrush, who made signs for me to join her companions. Here at last, I thought, are some birds of my feather, and nothing loath, took my place among them as lightly as a *billet-doux* disappearing in a lady's muff. Alas! I discovered that the dames had feasted freely on the juice of the grape, so I left them, to flee I knew not where, as the night was pitchy dark. Onward I sped till arrested by a burst of heavenly music. It was the song of the Nightingale, and dame Nature, attired in her sombre hues, stood listening in silence to the glorious lullaby that had soothed her children to sleep. The song recalled the first notes that doomed me to become an outcast. There was a touch of melancholy about the music, a mournful refrain that seemed to breathe forth a longing for something brighter, purer, holier than all life's experiences. My resolution to live my life out seemed to melt away in the liquid strain, and at the risk of becoming the prey of some nocturnal Owl, I plunged into the darkness determined to return to my home or die in the effort. At daybreak I descried the towers of Notre Dame, and soon perched upon the sacred building, to rest for a moment before alighting in the old garden. Alas! absence had wrought a sad change. Nothing remained to mark the site save a bundle of fagots. Where was my mother? In vain I piped and sang, and called on her to return. She had left the old familiar scene. There stood the woodman's axe that had laid low the trees and severed the ties of kindred. The shrubs of the green lane were rooted up to make way for the cold grey stones of the abodes of men.

VI.

I searched for my parents in all the gardens around, but in vain; they had doubtless sought refuge in some distant spot, and were lost to me for ever. Overwhelmed with sorrow, I lingered about the spout from which my father's wrath had exiled me. Sleep deserted me, and I lay down to die of hunger and grief. One day my sad reflections were interrupted by the jarring discord of two voices. Two slattern dames, standing slipshod, dirty, and bedraggled in the road beneath, were disputing over some point of household discipline, when one clinched the argument by exclaiming, "Egad! when you manage, you slut, to do these things, just let me know on't, and my faith, I'll bring you a white Blackbird."

Here was a discovery; probably the little unforeseen circumstance destined to turn the tide of my fortune and land me at last in Elysium. I must be a real, though rare bird of a misguided type. Thus impartial speech is sufficient to justify the conclusion. That being so, humility ill befits me. It is a mistake to cheapen what in reality are attributes as rare as they are highly prized. I am the one living illustration that in nature, as in law, nothing is impossible—that black even may become white. In law, I am told, this transformation is effected thoroughly, but at the same time at great cost to clients, and only by highly-gifted members of the bar. In my own case, natural law has been manipulated to bring about a like end, intended clearly for my gain.

These sage conclusions led at once to my assuming the airs and importance of a creature who for the first time discovers that his genius has raised him from the gutter far above all his fellows. I seemed at once to acquire a more dignified and imposing strut while parading the spout, and at the same time a capacity for looking calmly into space, towards the place of my ultimate destiny, far removed from this narrow terrestrial sphere. All this was a wonderful transformation to be wrought by the careless boast of a tawdry gossip, and clearly proves how nicely poised are the affairs of life. Such incidents are not unknown among men, as the word of a fool has been known to arrest the overthrow of a kingdom.

Among other things, it occurred to me, since Nature has gone out of her way to make me what I am, I must be a poet. I can hardly explain the process of reasoning which led to this belief; for all that, the belief became so rooted in my brain that I must needs jot down my inspiration. It is universally acknowledged that the first step to be taken towards becoming a great poet is to look like one. I accordingly studied to look genius all over, and the result was, I was accepted as my own estimate. Next I determined to go in for classical verse, and bring out a poem in forty-eight cantos, so framed as to apprise the universe of my existence. I shall deplore my isolation in such a manner as to stir up the envy of the happiest beings on earth. Since Heaven has refused me a mate, I shall utterly condemn the law which divides the bird creation into families, each having its own distinctive attributes. I will cry down everything—prove that grapes are sour, that Nightingales sing one into despair, and that Blackbirds have fallen away from their primeval whiteness. But first I must lay hold of a good rhyming companion, a handy-book to lift me out of the horrors of fishing for words of the same sound. It will also be necessary to establish about my person a retinue of needy journalists and authors as an exhaustless source of inspiration, in order to deluge the world with rhymes copied from the strophes of Chaucer, and with plays decked out from the sentiments of Shakespeare. Thus shall I ease my overburdened soul, make all the Tomtits cry, the Ringdoves coo, and the old Owls screech. Above all, one must prove one's self inexorable to the sweet sentiment of love. In vain shall I be waylaid and entreated to have compassion on maidenly hearts melted by my song. My manuscripts shall be sold for their weight in gold, my books shall cross the seas, fame and fortune shall everywhere follow me. In short, I shall be a perfectly exceptional bird, an eccentric, and at the same time brilliant writer, received with open arms, courted, admired, and thoroughly detested by a thousand rivals.

VII.

An interval of six weeks introduced my first work to the world, which turned out, as I promised myself it should, a poem in forty-eight cantos. It was slightly marred by a few negligences, the result of prodigious fertility of brain and the inability of my pen to keep pace with my inspiration. Nevertheless, I wisely concluded that the public, accustomed as they are in modern times to all that is swift in thought and action, would shield me from reproach. The success of this, my pristine effort, was simply as unparalleled as it was thoroughly deserved. The subject of the poem was my noble self; in this respect adhering to the prevailing custom, I related my sufferings and adventures, and put the reader in possession of a thousand domestic details of the most piquant interest. The description of my mother's nest filled no less than fourteen cantos. With the most graphic minuteness were noted the number of straws, grasses, and leaves of which it was composed, the whole being idealised by the tints and reflections of poetic genius. I displayed the inside and the outside, the bottom and the brim, the graceful curves and inclined planes and angles, gradually leading the reader up to the grand theme of the contents—the remains of flies, maybugs, and grubs which supplied the dainty fare of our home. Thus ascending, I reserved, with true poetic art, the dramatic incidents of my life for the grand *dénouement*.

Europe was moved by the apparition of my book, and eagerly devoured its thrilling revelations. How could it be otherwise? I had not only laid bare the facts of my existence, but pictured the dreams which disturbed my repose for many years, even introducing an ode composed in the yet unbroken egg. Of course I did not neglect the subject which interests every one—that is, the future of humanity. This problem, which for a moment had arrested my attention, was dealt with, and dashed off in outline, giving universal satisfaction.

Every day brought its tribute of congratulatory letters and anonymous love declarations, while my door was besieged by newspaper correspondents and Western tourists seeking an interview. All personal intercourse I positively declined, until forced to make an exception to a Blackbird from Senegal and another from China, who announced themselves as relatives of my own.

"Ah, sir," they said, nearly choking me with their embraces, "you are indeed a noble bird. How admirably you have painted in your immortal lines the profound sufferings of an unknown genius! If we are not already thoroughly misunderstood, we should become so after reading you. How deeply we sympathise with your griefs and your sublime scorn of vulgar opinion. Our own experience, sire, has made us familiar with all the troubles of which you sing. Here are two sonnets we humbly pray you to accept as a token of our worship."

"Here is besides," added the Chinese, "a song composed by my wife on a passage in your preface. She seems to have caught wonderfully the inspiration which it breathes."

"Gentlemen," I replied, "you seem to be gifted persons endowed with sentiments that are a credit to your nations, but permit me to inquire the reason of your manifest melancholy?"

"Ah, sir, see how I am formed. My plumage, it is true, is pleasant to behold; it is not without the tinge of emerald green, the glory of Ducks and dupes. For all that, my beak is too short and my claws too long, and whoever saw such a frightful tail as mine? I am nearly all tail. Is it not enough to give one the blues?"

"As for me, sir," said John Chinaman, "my misfortune is a still more painful one. My comrade's tail sweeps the streets, while the vulgar point the finger of scorn at me because I have only a stump."

"Gentlemen," I replied, "I pity you with all my heart. It is always painful to have too much or too little of anything, no matter what it is. But allow me to tell you that in our museums there are many examples of your class who have been stuffed and preserved in peace for years. My own case is infinitely worse than yours put together. I have the misfortune to be a lettered bird, a genius, and the only bird of my kind. In spite of my resolution to remain single, the return of spring-time caused me much uneasiness, and an event as unexpected as it was welcome decided my future. I received a letter from a young white Merle in London. It ran thus:—

"'I have read your poem, and the devotion it inspired has constrained me to offer you my hand and fortune. God created us for each other. I am like you, for I am a white Merle.'

"My surprise and joy may be imagined. A white Merle! Is it possible? I hastened to reply to the charming note—equal in terseness and fathomless sentiment to a love message in the second column of the *Times*. I besought the fair unknown to come at once to Paris, the refuge of romance-stricken young ladies. My reply had the desired effect; she came at once, or rather soon after her second letter, which informed me that she would not bother her parents with details. It was better to tell them nothing, as they might deem it necessary to send an old carrion Crow to look into my character.

"She came at last. Oh, joy! she was the loveliest Merle in the world. Was it possible that a creature so charming had lived and been reared for me? All my father's curses, and, above all, my

sufferings were welcome, since Heaven had reserved such an unexpected consolation for me. Till to-day I thought myself doomed to an eternal solitariness, but now I feel, while gazing on my lovely bride, all the nobler qualities of a father fully developed within me. Accept my claw, fair one, let us wed in the Anglo-Saxon fashion, and start for Switzerland.

"Nay," replied my love, "our wedding must be on a truly magnificent scale, all the Blackbirds of good birth must be invited. Birds in our position ought to observe the nicest ceremony, and not wed like water-spout cats. I have brought a provision of bank-notes with me. Arrange your invitations, and spare no cost in ordering the feast. I am of French origin and love display."

Blindly yielding to the wishes of my charmer, our wedding was of extraordinary brilliancy. Ten thousand flies were slaughtered for the feast, and we received the nuptial benediction from an old father Cormorant, archbishop *in partibus*, and the happy day's festivities concluded with a splendid ball.

The more I studied the character of my wife, the greater became my love. She combined in her dainty person every imaginable grace of body and mind. Only she was given to gossip, which I attributed to the influence of the English fog, and never had a moment's doubt that our genial climate would dissipate this little cloud.

There was some mystery hedging her round, which troubled me with grave forebodings. She used to shut herself up with her maids, under lock and key, for hours together, engaged, so she said, at her toilet. Husbands as a rule have no patience with such proceedings. More than a score of times have I knocked at my wife's door without receiving the slightest response. One day I insisted with such violence that she was compelled to open the door, but not without favouring me with a sample of her temper. On entering, the first thing that met my gaze was a huge bottle of a sort of paste made up of flour and whitewash. I inquired of my wife what she used that stuff for, to which she replied, it was a mixture for chilblains. This seemed rather strange, yet how could so charming a creature inspire me with anything but confidence.

Up to the present time I had remained ignorant of the fact that my wife had cultivated letters. Imagine my joy on discovering that she was the author of a romance modelled after the style of the illustrious Sir Walter Scott. I was then not only the husband of an incomparable beauty, but of a truly gifted companion. From that instant we worked

together; while I composed my poems, she covered reams of paper and displayed the rare gift of listening to my recitations without pausing in her task of composition. She composed her romances with a facility almost equal to my own, always choosing subjects of rare dramatic value; homicides, murders, and highway robberies, taking care in passing, to shoot poisoned shafts at the Government by advocating the cause of the Merula vulgaris. In a word, no efforts were too great for her mind, or tricks for her modesty. Never had she need to cross through a line, or lay her plans before beginning to work.

One day while my wife was toiling with unusual ardour, she perspired freely, and to my horror I beheld a black patch on her back. "Bless my soul, dear!" I said, "what is that? Are you plague-stricken? Are you ill?" She at first seemed frightened and speechless, but her knowledge of the world soon restored her habitual self-composure, and she replied that it was a spot of ink, a stain to which she was subject in moments of inspiration. Inwardly I was greatly troubled. Does my wife lose her whiteness? was a question which cost me many wakeful nights. The paste bottle rose like a phantom before me. Oh heavens! what doubts. Can this celestial creature, after all, only be a painting, a work of art? Is she varnished to deceive me? Had I been wooed and won by a mixture of flour and whitewash? Haunted by doubt, I took measures to lay the apparition by investing in a barometer, and watching for signs of coming rain. I planned to decoy my wife some doubtful Sunday into the country, and try the effect of an impromptu wash, but we were in the middle of July, and the weather provokingly fine. Real happiness, and long habit of writing, had much increased my sensitiveness. While at work it sometimes happened that my affections were stronger than my inspiration, and I gave way to tears, while waiting for my rhyme. My wife loved these rare occasions, and strove to soothe my masculine weakness.

One evening while dashing through my writing according to Boileu's precept, my heart opened. "Oh thou, my queen!" I said, "thou my only truly loved one, thou without whom my life is a dream, thou whose look, whose smile, fills my world with light. Life of my heart! dost thou know the height, the breadth, the depth of my love? Before thou camest to me my lot was that of an exiled orphan, now it is that of a king. In my poor breast thine image shall be enshrined till death. All! All my hopes and aspirations are centred in thee."

While thus raving, I wept over my wife, and as each tear-drop fell upon her back, she visibly changed colour. Feathers, one by one, not even black, but red appeared—she must have coloured red to fill some other rôle. Soon I found myself vis-à-vis with a creature unpasted, unfloured, and nothing more than a vulgar Blackbird. How dare I publish my shame! I plucked up courage and resolved to quit the gay world, to give up my career, to flee to a desert, if that were possible, to shun the sight of every living creature.

IX.

I flew away broken-hearted, and the wind, the good angel of birds, wafted me on its wings to a branch at Mortfontaine. It was night, the birds were asleep, but the Nightingale still sang. Alone in the darkness his heart overflowed with his song to God for His goodness, his breast expanded with the sacred theme, and with a rapture unfelt by the most gifted poets who sing for the ears of men. I could not resist the temptation of addressing him.

"Happy Nightingale, you sing because your heart is bursting with joy. You are indeed highly favoured, you have a wife and little ones which you sing to sleep on their pillow of moss. You have a full moon to cheer you, plenty to eat, and no journals to praise or condemn you. Rubini and Rosini are as nothing to you. You are equal to the one, and divine when compared with the other. I, sir, have wasted my life in pursuing the empty vanities of fame, while you have secured real happiness in the wood. May your secret be learned?"

"Yes," replied the Nightingale, "but it is not what you imagine. My wife bothers me, I do not love her! I am passionately fond of the Rose; Sadi, the Persian, has spoken of it. I sing all night to her while she sleeps and is deaf to my praise. Her petals are closed at this hour. She cradles an old Scarab, and when the gray dawn breaks sadly over the wood, and my eyes are closing in sleep, then she will open her breast, and the Bee will be welcomed with the dainty pollen from the lips of her lover.

THE QUEEN'S HUSBAND.

THE first political act in which I took part made so deep an impression on me, that I attribute the strange vicissitudes of my life to its influence. Permit me to begin my narrative without further introduction.

I had reached maturity and become a citizen of the hive, when one morning I was roused by a knocking at the partition, and some one calling on me by name.

"What is wanted?" I inquired.

"Come out at once!" was the instant rejoinder. "You are wanted. Monsieur is about to be executed, and you are required as one of the guards of honour."

These awful words, which I scarcely comprehended, filled me with horror. I was, for all that, aware beforehand of the impending doom of Monsieur, but had no notion that my services would be required at the ghastly ceremony.

"Here I am!" I exclaimed, and finishing my toilet in all haste, precipitated myself outside the hive, a prey to the strongest emotion. I was not pale, but green! Monsieur was one of the finest drones in the hive, rather stout, but, withal, well made; his physiognomy was full of a pleasing, wistful, and yet proudly aristocratic expression—as novelists would say—I had often seen him accompany the queen in her daily rounds of inspection, tormenting her with his jokes, helping her with his foot, sharing with her the prestige of sovereignty, and altogether appearing to be the happiest of princes, and most beloved of husbands. The people loved him little, but feared him much, he had the queen's ear, the queen had publicly kissed his forehead, and it was reported by one of the chamber maids that Monsieur was soon to be a father. This important news spread around, and filled each cell with joy. We saw ourselves transformed into nurses surrounded by groups of children, giving food to this one, rocking that one. Already in each chamber a soft couch was prepared to receive the new comer, and in the evening before going to sleep, certain flowers had been pointed out as those

containing the sugar which would yield the most delicate honey, as food for the youngsters when they made their appearance.

Our expectations were confirmed. Our beloved queen laid ten thousand twin eggs, all so beautiful that it was impossible to choose between them. The prince was radiant with joy, and spent his whole time in kissing the eggs one after the other. I had witnessed all this, had beheld him in his glory, and now, I was rudely awakened to see him dragged to his doom. More than that, oh horror! I was chosen to be his executioner. The prince, under the dreadful circumstances, showed decided reluctance to yield up his life. This seemed all the more pitiable as nature had deprived him of either offensive or defensive weapons. He was completely in our power.

"What have I done to deserve this doom? Oh, my queen, grant me but one hour!" he cried, kneeling before her, "but half an hour, nay, five minutes. I have revelations, confessions . . . "

"Make haste!" said the queen, striving to conceal her emotion; "we must abide by the law. Away with him; put an end to him; he is now worse than useless."

The queen retired to her chamber, still full of souvenirs of the prince, and in an instant he was pierced by a thousand darts. Should I live a century, I shall never forget the scene. I pretended to share in the outrage, yet never moved my sting from its sheath. Even among the most advanced communities there are barbarous laws. Poor Messieurs, poor Messieurs!

Of these Messieurs, vulgarly called Drones, there are from five to six hundred in one hive, each one to be called upon to mount the steps of the throne, and to pay with his life for the excess of honour thus accorded to him. The prospect of a tragic end gave many of them sad looks, which contrasted with the natural gaiety of their fellows. One could mark them crawling listlessly along among the thousands of orderly workers that thronged the streets, alleys, and cells of the city, dejected and oppressed by their coming glory. At the slightest noise they turned round tremblingly. "Is the queen calling us?" they would inquire, and speedily they hid themselves away among the crowd, and, escaping from the hive, sought the freedom of fields and flowers.

There are many troubles which fall to the lot of those in high positions. The fat, overfed idlers who strut about, are most of them merely servants and dependants, unworthy of the vulgar admiration lavished on them by the working class. This sentiment of aristocracy worship is a common folly to which I myself have been subject, and which it ill befits me to condemn. Shall I confess it? I madly loved a Drone. Yes, I loved him. He was handsome beyond description. When he entered the corolla of a flower, I trembled lest the contact with its petals should spoil his beauty. I was mad. Platonic love;

for Nature permitted us only the ideal, impossible love of the poet, the dream of the artist. I loved this creature simply for his beauty.

I admired the blue Dragon-fly with his silken wings, as I watched him skimming over the grass at the close of the day. I had, indeed, an eye for everything beautiful, and above all, for my superb Drone.

One day I found him half drunk with honey, lying fast asleep in the heart of a lily; his face, though smeared with yellow pollen, still retained its noble expression. He was snoring in a most majestic and regular manner. I stood for a moment, quite rooted to the spot by the glorious spectacle. This then, I thought, is a future husband of our queen! I at last approached him, foolishly curious to examine the details of his figure, and gently touched him, when, yawning, he said—

"What does your Majesty want now?"

Then looking at me, he perceived his mistake, and added smiling—

"I am not in your way, my child, so proceed with your work, and permit me to rest in peace."

There must have been a subtle odour in this flower which stole into my head, for I instantly forgot my work, and remained looking at him dreamily. What are we? I thought. Only miserable workers, makers of honey, moulders of wax, and neuter nurses to the children of those magnificent idlers who spend their days in sleeping in the heart of flowers, and dreaming that they hear the silvery tones of the queen's voice calling them. I own myself ashamed of my humble, laborious calling. How could he love such a simple drudge? Were I even a Wasp, scouring lanes and hedgerows, and annoying wayfarers— careless, coquettish, unkind—always armed, offensive and useless; perhaps then he might love me. Is not fear the beginning of love? Hence is it not a means of seduction? Such thoughts, and a thousand others, were buzzing in my brain; still my admiration only became all the more intense, and I exclaimed, in spite of myself—

"O Prince, most handsome Prince, you are exceedingly beautiful!"

"All right," replied the Prince, "I know it; my position requires it. Pray do not disturb my repose; go away, like a good fellow."

This strange language to a neuter disturbed me not a little. He evidently did not even know my sex, far less my love for him. That which charmed me most was—I scarce dare write it—his glorious idleness, the helplessness of his fine body, and insolent coolness of his fine language. I scorned and yet loved him. I knew he was accustomed to snore daily when in this perfumed spot; I therefore got through with my work quickly, and made the flower my resort, after dressing the little ones confided to my care, and nearly choking them with hasty meals, so that I might go and prepare his place, and sweep away with my wings any yellow powder that would soil his coat. If a few drops of water had gathered in the corolla, I pierced it with my stings and left, so that my master might repose there without fear of rheumatism.

He was none the more thankful; his requirements only increased and kept pace with my love and care for him. He would smile, blissfully stretching himself, and request me to mount guard outside the flower, so that no common insect might trouble his dreams. It tried my temper, yet I watched. One day I saw him coming; he was very pale, but his walk was steadier than usual.

"What is the matter, Prince?" I inquired anxiously.

"Go away, little one. I have need of air, and the sun will not mind seeing me face to face to-day."

I trembled for the misfortune that seemed to have overtaken him.

"To-morrow! to-morrow!!" he cried, making gestures which denoted the trouble of his mind. "To-morrow I shall be the queen's husband!"

A mist obscured my eyes; deep resentment filled my heart. I was mad with jealousy.

"From to-day till to-morrow many things may happen!" I exclaimed.

"Silence! how dare you in my presence proclaim your seditions?"

"No," I said, "you shall never wear the crown!" I flew at him, and profiting by a momentary turn of his head, pierced him to the heart with my sting. Hardly had he breathed his last, when I burst into remorseful tears.

I returned to the hive to find everything in the greatest disorder. The entire community, a prey to the deepest agitation, were jostling and knocking each other about.

"What has happened?" I inquired of the first Bee I met.

"What happened?" he replied. "Why, one of the Drones is missing."

"How is that known?" I continued with much fear.

"At the evening call there were only five hundred and ninety-nine Drones present. The queen has had a nervous attack, and one is lost in conjecture as to what will be the result."

"A dreadful affair!" I replied, and hastened to mingle with the crowd.

The queen was inconsolable, and so was I myself, for the space of two whole days.

THE LOVES OF TWO INSECTS.
PRESENTED AS AN EXAMPLE TO WISE MEN.*

SENTIMENTAL HISTORY OF ANIMALS.

I.

PROFESSOR GRANARIUS.

"CERTAINLY," said Professor Granarius, one evening while seated beneath his limes, "nothing is more curious than the conduct of Jarpeado. In truth, if the French followed his example, we should have no need of codes, mandates, sermons, or social gatherings, for the advancement of mankind. Nothing proves more conclusively that *reason* alone—the attribute of which men are so proud—is the prime cause of all the evils of Society."

Miss Anna Granarius, who was devotedly attached to a poor student, could not help blushing deeply, for her skin was fair and delicate. Anna was the typical

---

* The distinguished animal to whom we owe this history—designed to show that the creatures so boldly named stupid by men, and in reality superior to human beings—desires to remain anonymous. It may nevertheless be said, that he is a creature who held a very high place in the affections of Miss Anna Granarius, and that he belongs to the sect of reasoning animals, for whose members she had the greatest esteem.—ED.

heroine of a Scotch novel, the profound depths of her blue eyes almost betokening "Second-sight." By the candid and caught look of the professor, she perceived he had said one of those foolish things which frequently fall from the lips of scientific dreamers. Leaving her father to follow out his dream on the depravity of human reason, she bent her steps to a favourite spot in the Jardin des Plantes which was closed for the night, as the month was July and the hour half-past eight.

"What does my father mean to say about this Jarpeado who turns his head?" she inwardly inquired, seating herself outside a hothouse. Pretty Anna remained pensively rooted to the seat, while her father, absorbed in his own thoughts, never missed her presence. The maiden was endowed with a highly strung nervous temperament which, had she lived four hundred years ago, would have brought her to the stake in the Place de Grève. But happily for her, she was born in more enlightened times.

II.

That which Prince Jarpeado found most extraordinary in Paris, was himself, like the dodge of Gênes at Versailles. He was undoubtedly a fine fellow, though small, remarkable for the classic beauty of his features. His legs might have been doubtful, a trifle or so bandy, but they were encased in boots garnished with precious stones and fixed up on three sides *a la poulaine*. On his back, as was the usage of Castraine, in his country, he carried a cape which cast into the shade those worn by the ecclesiastics of Charles X. It was covered with aberesques of diamonds on a ground of lapis-lazuli, divided into two equal parts like the two flaps of a trunk. These flaps were fastened by a gold clasp, and displayed like the priestly surplice, in token of dignity, for he was prince of Coccirubri. He wore a pretty necklace of sapphire and two aigrettes infinitely finer than any of the feathers in the caps of European potentates worn on State occasions.

Anna thought him charming, only his two arms were rather short and slender for embracing. This slight defect, however, was carried off by the rich carnation of his royal blood. Anna soon found out what her father meant, by witnessing one of those mysterious things which pass unnoticed in this terrible Paris, at once so full and so empty, so foolish and so wise, so preoccupied and so much on the alert, yet always so fantastic.

III.

The three thousand windows of this glass palace exchanged glances of moonlight so bright that the edifice seemed glowing at a white heat, ablaze with the fire, kindled by the rising orb which so frequently deceives the traveller. The cactus was breathing forth a store of strange odour, the vanilla its sweet perfume. The volcaneria distilled the vinous heat from its tufts, the jessamine exhaled a poetic fragrance, the magnolia intoxicated the air, while the aroma of the datura advanced with the pomp of a Persian king, and the powerful Chinese lily sent her breath onward with an overpowering force that assimilated all the other odours of the flowery scene.

The perfume-laden air stood motionless to feast upon the spectacle presented by a troop of midnight spirits, as they rose from an enchanted spot shaded by a grove of bananas, whose wide-spreading leaves formed a canopy gilded by a phosphorescent light. Soft streams of music floated around, gently awakening the spirits to their nocturnal revels. Suddenly the lights fell on a patch of green cactus, revealing the gay form of Prince Jarpeado exposed to the witchery of the fairy queen and her gorgeous attendants, robed in costumes so aërial as to disclose the full charms of their lovely forms. Phantom-Crickets sang love-ditties in the daintiest retreats, while a choir of winged musicians chanted the praises of the prince, who stood unmoved by the seductive art of this witching band. The passion-imbued glance of the queen fell, shivered against the armour of Jarpeado's true heart, where, enshrined in all its artless purity, he treasured the image of the fair Anna. The music ceased, and in a silvery voice the queen, radiant with an unearthly beauty, exclaimed—

"Jarpeado! Jarpeado! receive the homage of the fairy queen whose heart thou hast won."

The moment was enchanting. The perfumed breeze wooed the flushed cheek of the prince, and whispered love. Jarpeado stood irresolute. It was but for an instant, when rousing himself from the subtle influences that were kindling a fire of unworthy passion in his breast, he replied—

"Fair spirit, whose unearthly radiance lays siege to a true heart, and who with cunning and skill have sought out the weak points of my armour, all thine arts, wiles, and hellish tricks can never quench my love for the fair Anna."

Scarcely had the last word escaped his lips, when the weird scene was blotted out from his gaze, and a ghastly green light disclosed a slimy waste alive with crawling monads, and all the simplest forms of life. The balmy air was chilled and its fragrance replaced by the noxious breath of animal decay. A flash of lightning and peal of thunder heralded the approach of a monster with mouth wide open, dark and deep as the bottomless pit, his horns erect, his tail fiercely sweeping the waste; onward he came, spreading terror around, and leaving death in his train.

This was the Valvos, which preyed like cholera on the people, but the prince escaped, saved by a fair maiden.

"Daughter of my country!" he exclaimed, "my deliverer, cruel destiny stands between us; I cannot wed thee."

The scene changed, and Anna was transported unseen to the attic of her lover, the poor pupil of Granarius. Bent over his books, for a moment he raised his head, crying out—

"Oh! if Anna would only wait for me; in three years I shall have the cross of the Legion of Honour. I feel, I know, I shall solve this entomological problem, and succeed in transporting to Algeria the culture of the *Cocus Cacti*. Good heavens! that would be a conquest."

Anna awoke and found herself in bed, she had dreamed a dream. But who was this Jarpeado of whom her father constantly spoke? She hastened to ask the old professor. It was necessary to be careful, she must watch, and after breakfast seize one of his lucid intervals; for in his normal condition, her father's mind was absent exploring the fathomless depths of science. Seated at the breakfast table she exclaimed—

"Father!"—just as the professor was putting a spoonful of salt into his coffee—"what are you thinking about?"

"Well, Anna, dear, I was investigating the subject of monads, or rather the nature of these simple inorganic forms, twelve months before birth, and I come to the conclusion that"——

"That my dear father, if you succeed in introducing one of these ridiculous creatures to the scientists of Paris, you will both be decorated. But who, tell me, is this Prince Jarpeado?"

"Prince Jarpeado is the last of the dynasty of the Cactriane," replied the worthy professor, who employed allegory in addressing his daughter, forgetful that her mind had matured, and she had ceased to play with dolls; "a large country, basking in the sun's rays, and

having a longitude and latitude—matters these you do not comprehend. The country is populous as China, and like that unhappy land, subject to periodical inundations, not of cold water, but of hot water, let loose by the hand of man. This depopulates the land, but nature has so provided that a single prince may alone repair the damage. This reminds me of something I discovered ten years ago in connection with Infusoria, the Rotafera of Cuvier, they "——

" Yes. But the prince, the prince!" cried Anna, fearing lest her father should fall into a reverie and she would hear nothing more.

"The prince," replied the old professor, giving a touch to his wig, "escaped—thanks to the French Government—from the destroying flood, and he has been brought up without consulting his future, away from his fair realm. He was transported in his undeveloped form to my illustrious predecessor Sacrampe—the inventor of Ducks.

" Jarpeado came here at the request of the Government on a bed of dust, made up of millions of his father's subjects, embalmed by the Indians of Gualaca, not one of the nymphs of Rubens, not one of Miéris' pretty girls has been able to dispense with the mummies of this race. Yes, my child, whole populations deck the lips which smile upon or defy you from each canvas. How would you like the freak of some giant painter who would take generations of human beings on his palette, crushing them to produce the colours of an immense fresco? Heaven forbid that it should be so!" Here the professor fell into a profound reverie as was his wont after uttering the word heaven.

The pupil of Granarius, Jules Sauval, entered. If you have ever met one of those modest young fellows devoted to science, knowing much, yet possessing a certain simplicity, which, although charming, does not prevent him from being the most ambitious creature in the world, an innocent who would turn the earth upside down about a hyoïde bone, or a univalve shell. If you have seen a youth of this type, then you know Jules Sauval. He was as candid as he was poor—candour goes when fortune comes.—He venerated Professor Granarius as a father, and admired in him the disciple of the great Geoffroy St. Hilaire. Blessed be science, Jules Sauval would have just been the same, even supposing the professor had no pretty daughter Anna. He was a second Jarpeado alive among the dry bones and débris of antiquity. Just as the *Coccus cacti*—the subjects of Jarpeado—had been crushed to lend a glow of life to the finest works of art, so the young student identified himself with defunct organisms in order that science might all the more faithfully picture the forms and colours of pre-historic life. Like Jarpeado, Jules Sauval had his loves, he admired the fair Anna as a perfect type of a highly-organised sensitive animal—so he said.

In common with the professor he was intent upon uniting this red prince to some analagous creature. The men of science had come down to the level of the members of the Chamber of Deputies, and talked them into erecting a spacious hothouse to contain the finest plants of the tropics. Within its glass walls the illustrious professor has found a solitary living specimen of the *Coccus cacti*—Cochineal—Jarpeado, whose habits they had studied so profoundly as to discover that the prince was endowed with pride of race, and passion of sentiment, opposed to his union with any partner saving a princess of his own vermilion blood.

"Alas! Professor," exclaimed Jules, "I have just left the glass-house, and all is lost! There is no possibility of uniting Jarpeado to any living creature, he refused the *Coccus ficus caricæ*. I had them under our best microscope."

"Ah, you horrid creature!" cried Anna. "This is then a prince of the insect world, and yet his history is interesting. I might have known he was no human being, since you say he will die faithful to his first love."

"Hush, child," said Granarius, "I fail to note the difference between dying faithful and unfaithful, when it is a question of dying."

"You will never understand me, sir," said Anna, in a tone which startled the mild professor, "and as for you, Mr. Jules, all your science and all your charms will never tempt the prince to prove unfaithful. You, sir, shall never be capable of love such as his. A little less science and a trifle more common sense would have suggested keeping him among the dust of his defunct ancestors, where, perchance, he left his living partner, or will find another of red-royal blood.

The professor and his pupil elated by this marvellous suggestion hastened to replace Jarpeado in the dust from which he had been taken.

Alas! sighed Anna, Jules loves me not, else he would have lingered with me to tell his love. I made the path clear for him. Yet he perceived it not, but has gone with my father to speculate on the introduction of this scarlet *Coccus cacti* dynasty into Algeria. Following them to the large hothouse in the Jardin des Plantes, Anna

observed her father consigning the small paper of *Coccus cacti* dust into the centre of the first nopal that had flowered.

A jealous Englishman, witness of this scientific operation, remarked in passing, "This old fool uses the plant as a portfolio !"

"Heat the house well," cried Granarius, as he fell into a profound reverie, leaving his daughter and Jules to talk of love, or science.

"So, Mr. Jules, you have ceased to love me," said Anna.

"Nay," replied Jules, "I do not think you do me justice, but I have come to the conclusion that sentiment, or passion, in all animals, follows a fixed natural law, and being divided between two creatures ought to form a perfect equation."

"Oh, infernal science! thus to bamboozle a poor brain. Probably your sentiments are established on the equation of dowry, and you have yet to learn what love is, Mr. Jules. If you do not take care, science will claim possession, not only of your soul, but of your body, and you will become a beast like Nebuchadnezzar. History relates that he assumed this form because he devoted seven years to zoology in classing the different species, without once pausing to trim his beard. Six hundred years hence it will be said of certain zoologists that they were advanced types of the Orang-outang who stuck up for their race, and for themselves as examples of progression."

Jules was called away by the professor, while Anna, turning to a huge microscope, beheld a new world of creatures, invisible to the naked eye. There she saw the Volvoce engaged in a steeple-chase, mounted on an animal making for the winning post. Many elegant Cercairæ were on the course, the prize being infinitely superior to that of the Derby; for the winner was to feast on the Vorticella, at once animals and flowers. Neither Bory, Saint Vincent, nor Müller—that immortal Dame—have taken it upon themselves to decide whether the Vorticella is more plant than animal; had they been bolder they might have drawn valuable conclusions from the man vegetable known to coachmen as *melon*.

Anna was soon drawn from the contemplation of this little world to the fortunes of Jarpeado, who, in her vivid imagination, had become the hero of a fairy tale. He had at last discovered the object of his affections in a nursling of his tribe, over whom he watched as she lay in state beneath a perfumed pavilion, awaiting the incarnation common alike to heathen deities and zoological creatures. They were the Paul and Virginia of insect life. The pavilion was guarded by soldiers

attired in madder. The prince proved himself a wise general, as well as ardent lover, for in order to protect his domain against a powerful-

winged foe called the Muscicapa, he ordered all his intelligent subjects to throw themselves in such numbers on the monster, as to choke him, or else satisfy his hunger. For this service he promised decorations and titles ; that was all he had to offer. The breast of Anna was filled with admiration of these cheap and valuable political inventions.

Invisible nuns shrouded the little princess in grey veils, so that nothing but her head was seen as she lay in state, awaiting her new winged life. Anna witnessed the joy of Paul, when, like Venus rising from the waves, Virginia quitted her winding sheet, and like Milton's Eve—who is a real English Eve—smiled on the light, and looking at Paul, exclaimed, "Oh !"—this superlative of English astonishment. The prince, with a slave's submission, offered to show the fair one the path of life, across the hills and dales of his empire.

Virginia, growing in loveliness and in the prince's affections, returned his care with caresses, while Paul ministered to her wants, bringing the ripest fruits for her food; and they at last embarked in a little skiff, on a lake bright as a diamond, and hardly larger than a drop of water. Virginia was arrayed in a bridal robe of brilliant stripes and great richness, her appearance recalling the famous Esmeralda, celebrated by Victor Hugo, only Esmeralda was a woman, and Virginia an angel who would not for all the world have loved a Marshal of the court, far less a Colonel. Her whole affections were consecrated to Jarpeado. Happy pair, thought Anna, but alas ! what came of it all ? After the wedding came family cares, and a brood destined to make the fame and fortune of her much-loved, but faithless Jules.

A few evenings later, Anna was frowning on her father, and saying to Jules—

"You are no longer faithful to the palm-house, so much gazing on the Cochineal has affected your taste. You are about to marry a red-haired girl, with large feet, without any figure, devoid alike of ideas and manners, freckled. She wears dyed dresses, and will wound your pride twenty times a day, and your ears with her sonatas."

She opened her piano and began to play with such feeling, that the Spiders remained pensive in their webs on Granarius' ceiling, and the flowers put their heads in at the window to listen.

" Ah me !" said Anna, " animals have more sense than the wise men who preserve them in glass-cases."

Jules left the room, sad at heart, for the talent, beauty, and brightness of this good soul was struggling with the concert of vulgar coins which his red-haired bride was bringing to his door.

"Ah!" exclaimed Professor Granarius, "what have we here in the papers? Listen, Anna.

"'Thanks to the efforts of the learned Professor Granarius, assisted by his clever pupil Jules Sauval, ten grains of cochineal have been obtained on the Nopal in the great palm-house. Doubtless this culture will flourish in our African possessions, and will free us from the tribute we pay to the new world. Thus the expense of the great palm-house has been justified—against which opposition was not slow to make itself heard—but the costly structure will yet render many valuable services to French commerce and agriculture. M. J. Sauval is named Chevalier of the Legion of Honour.'"

"M. Jules behaves badly to us," said Anna, "for you have commenced the history of the *Coccus cacti*, and he has impudently taken up"——

"Bah!" said the professor, "he is my pupil."

Love Adventures of a French Cat.

MINETTE TO BÉBÉ.

FIRST LETTER.

"What will you say, my dear Bébé, on receiving this letter from your sister supposed to be dead, for whom you have doubtless wept, as one who is almost forgotten.

"Forgive me, my sister, for supposing that you can ever forget me, although we live in a world where many more than the dead are forgotten.

"First of all I write to tell you I am not dead, that my love for you is as strong as ever, and that I am still animated by the hope of one day rejoining you, alas! my sister, that day may be far distant.

"This evening I thought about our good mother, who was always so kind and careful of our toilet, whose delight it was to watch the flicker of the fire-light on our glossy, silken coats, and to train us in the paths of domestic peace, virtue, and sobriety. I was touchingly reminded of our simple family-life, with its happy days, and innocent frolic, all hallowed by the light of love. Yet the brightness of that light of true hearts casts many dark shadows across my path, shadows of regret for neglected ministries of tenderness to my mother who is now perhaps no more. Above the sentiment that prompts me to write, is the desire to make a regretful confession of the circumstances which separated me from the dear ones at home.

"Silently I took up the pen, and the result is before you. I am bending over my task by the dim light of an alabaster lamp, carefully shaded from the eyes of my sleeping mistress.

"Although I am rich, Bébé, I would rather be poor and happy! Oh, my mistress is waking. I must quickly say good-bye. I have barely time to roll up my letter and push it under the cover of a chair, where it must remain till daybreak. When it is finished I will forward it by one of our attendants who is now waiting on the terrace. He will bring me your reply.

"My mother! my mother! tell me all about her.

"Your Sister."

"P.S.—Place confidence in my messenger, he is neither young nor handsome, neither a Spanish Grandee nor a rich Angora, but he is devoted and discreet. He found out your address. He loves me and would do anything for me, so he has become my courier. He is a slave! Do not pity him; the chains of love are his fetters.

"You must address your letters to Madam Rosa Mika, that is the name I am known under here.

"My mistress is certainly waking up, she sleeps badly, and I dread discovery.

"Again, adieu! In all this scribbling you will recognise more of the heart than the hand of your sister."

BÉBÉ TO MINETTE.

SECOND LETTER.

"MY DEAR MINETTE,—I thought I should go mad on reading your letter, my joy knew no bounds, and indeed it was shared by all. One would willingly see all one's relations die, if they all came to life again like you. Ah, Minette, your departure caused us great grief. Were you forced to leave us so long in doubt? If you only knew how everything is changed here since you left. To begin, your mother is deaf and blind, and the poor old creature passes her days at the door, without ever uttering a complaint. When I wished to tell her you were still alive, I could not make her understand, and she could neither read nor see your letter. Her many troubles have told sadly upon her. After you left, she searched everywhere in vain for you, and the loss seems to have undermined her health and left her the wreck I describe.

"Do not grieve too much, old age no doubt must take the lion's share of blame. Besides, she sleeps, drinks, and eats well; and there is always plenty in the cupboard, as I would rather starve than let her want.

"Our young mistress has lost her mother, so she is more unfortunate than we are, as she has lost everything, except her pretty figure, which does not change.

"It was necessary to leave the little shop in Murais; to give up the ground floor, and all at once mount to the attic, and to work from morning to night, and from night till morning sometimes. But, thank heaven, I have a sure foot, good eye, and am a capital hunter.

"You touchingly remark that you are rich, and would rather sacrifice wealth for happiness. I do not clearly see how I can complain of being poor. How funny you are! you dine at a polished board, off gilded plates, and goodly fare. One would think from your way of putting it, that by stinting one's self of food, one gets what riches cannot buy. Some wise cat will no doubt prove before long, that poverty is the cure for all evils. Seriously, do you believe that fortune impairs happiness? If that is your creed, become poor at once, ruin yourself! Nothing is easier than that, live by your teeth if you can. Tell me what you think of it. Complain of being unhappy, but not of being rich, for we who are poor are no strangers to misery. I scold you as your elder sister ought to do, so forgive me.

"Do you not know that Bébé would only be too happy to be of some use to you? Do not keep me waiting for another letter. I begin to fear you have been seeking happiness where it can never be found. Of course you will hide nothing from me. Ease your heart and write down your griefs on your perfumed paper, as you proposed. Adieu, Minette, adieu! This is enough, it is the hour for our mother's meal, and it is yet running about in the loft. Things are not going on well there, the mice are clever, and every day seems to develop new instincts of cunning. We have feasted so long on them, they begin to notice it. My neighbour is a cat, not a bad specimen, were he not so original. He dotes on the mice, and pretends that some day there will be a revolution when mice will be able to hold their own against cats.

"You see I am right in profiting by the peace we now enjoy, hunting at will in their grounds. But do not let us talk politics!

"Adieu, Minette.

"Your messenger is waiting. He refuses to disclose your address. Shall we soon meet each other?

"Your sister till death,

"Bébé."

"*P.S.*—I own your old courier is very ugly. For all that, when I saw what he brought, I kissed him with all my heart. You should have seen him bow when he presented the letter from Madam Rosa Mika. Were you out of your mind Minette when you adopted such a name? Was Minette not a charming name for a cat so white as yourself? As I have no more paper, I conclude."

A Starling had the misfortune of upsetting a bottle of ink over Minette's reply to Bébé, so that several pages of the letter are illegible. The loss of these passages, however, does not interfere with the narrative. The missing matter is indicated by dotted lines.

MINETTE TO BÉBÉ.

THIRD LETTER.

. . . . "Do you remember the doll given to us by our mistress, which soon became a subject of discord. How you used to scratch me. Oh dear! I almost feel my back bleeding when I think of it. How I used to complain of you, to my mother when you so persistently called

me a story-teller, but I got no satisfaction. It is from this point, this little wrong, that all my miseries sprang? Indignant at repeated miscarriages of justice, I resolved to fly from you and seek a happier home. Ascending to the roof, the heaven of cats, I viewed the distant horizon, and determined to wander to its furthest limit. The prospect

for a kitten so young was not tempting. I foresaw many dangers to which I would be exposed in making my way into strange lands. I remember .... I seemed to hear choirs of voices in the air—

"'Do not cry, Minette,' whispered a voice—no doubt that of my evil genius—'the hour of your deliverance approaches. This humble dwelling is an unworthy shelter for one born by nature to adorn the halls of a palace!'

"'Alas,' replied a voice softer and more musical—that of my conscience—'You mock me, sir, I am a lowly maiden, a palace is no place for me!'

"'Beauty is queen of the world,' continued the first. 'You are extremely beautiful, therefore you are queen! What robe is whiter, what eyes brighter than yours!'

"'Think of your mother,' said the pleading voice. 'Can you forget her? Can you forget your sister Bébé?'

"'Bébé makes you her slave, and your mother does not love you. You are a child of misfortune. You have been reared by chance. Chance is your foster-mother. You are alone indebted to chance. Come, Minette, come, the world is before you. Here is misery and obscurity, yonder, riches and fame!'

"My good angel in vain tried to picture a future of darkness and despair. The love of finery took possession of my heart and sealed my doom!

"The voice became more and more irresistible, and I blindly followed its commands.

"I had fallen into a faint, but when I became conscious, judge my surprise to find that my charmer was no illusion. Before me stood a young cat gazing tenderly down on me.

"Ah, Bébé, he was handsome! and his eyes sparkled with the flame of kindling love. He was the ideal cat of whom we sing when gazing on the moon veiled by the city smoke. At last, in a high-pitched rapturous voice, he exclaimed, 'Divine Minette, I adore thee.' I felt my tail expand at his audacity, but my heart expanded as if in unison, for I already felt that he was mine. Soon he settled down, his gaze riveted upon my face. You ought to have seen how humbly he begged for a single glance from me. How could I refuse his request, he who, perhaps, had rescued me from the terrible death of a fall from the tiles.

"If you had only heard his eloquence, Bébé. I confess I felt flattered and puffed up with pride, and saw myself prospectively arrayed in all the finery he promised to lay at my feet; lace, collars, jewels, and a superb ermine muff. This last gift brought me into great trouble.

"I was naturally indolent—he pictured to me a life of ease, with its soft carpets, velvet and brocade cushions, arm-chairs, sofas, and all sorts of fine furniture. He assured me that his mistress—an ambassador's wife—would be delighted to receive me whenever I cared to visit her, and that all the collection which made her apartments a magazine of curiosities was at my disposal.

"Oh, it was delightful to dream of being waited on so; I would have a maid, and my noble mistress would serve me.

"'We are called domestic animals,' he said, why, it is impossible to say. What position do we fill in a house? Whom do we serve and who serves us, if not our masters? He assured me I was simply perfect, in tones so musical, that I heard the old landlady below screaming with delight. I said I felt lonely, and he swore eternal fidelity—Oh! how he did swear—and promised a life of cloudless joy. In a word I was to become his wife, and the ambassador's titled cat.

"What more need I add. I followed him and thus became Madame de Brisquet.

FROM THE SAME TO THE SAME.

FOURTH LETTER.

"Yes, Bébé, Madam de Brisquet.

"Pity me, Bébé, when I write this name it seems to me to contain the whole story of my misery, condensed and sublimated, yet I have imagined myself happy in the possession of wealth, honour, and his affection. Our entrance into the hotel was a real triumph, even the ambassador opened his window to receive us. The lady pronounced me the most beautiful creature she had ever seen, and after exhausting her store of agreeable flatteries, she rang for her people, told them all to respect me, and committed me to the care of her lady-in-waiting. I was at once named the queen of cats, the fashionable beauty, by all the most renowned Angoras in Paris. My husband was proud of my success, and I looked forward to a lifetime of happiness.

"O Bébé, when I recall all this, I often ask myself how it is I have any heart left.

T

"My honeymoon lasted fifteen days, after which I discovered that Brisquet had no real love for me. In vain were his assurances that his affection had not changed—I was not to be deceived. But love desires what is impossible, and is after all satisfied with very little. Even when all tokens of affection were at an end, I felt I still loved him, and would not believe that love so sincere awakened no kindred flame in his heart.

"Remember this, Bébé, there is nothing more transient than the love of cats. Far from being pleased at my constancy, Brisquet became impatient with me.

"'I cannot understand,' he exclaimed angrily, 'why love, the most gay and agreeable pastime of youth, should become the most serious, absurd, and bothering business of our maturer years.'

"I abandoned my mother and sister, because I loved you! I, I—— wept!

"My grief only hardened his heart, he became cruel, even brutal, and I, who had rebelled against my poor mother's neglect, bent under his oppression, and waited, hoping for brighter days. But time is a pitiless monster, and teaches us many a hard lesson we would rather not learn. Time may also be likened to a good physician, who, after many days heals the deepest wounds. I became calm, feeling that the last ember of my unrequited love had been rudely stamped out; and I forgave him.

"Brisquet was one of those who love themselves better than all the world, and who are easily elated by anything that flatters their vanity. He was a true disciple of the school of gallantry, whose doctrines are framed to please, without the troublesome sentiment of love. Their hearts have two doors which open almost simultaneously, the one to let you in, the other to kick you out. Naturally, Brisquet while ceasing to care for me, had found another dupe. Fortune had furnished a singular rival, a Chinese creature from the province of Peichihli, who, soon after she had landed, set all the cats in Paris in a ferment. This gay intriguer had been imported by the manager of a theatre, who wisely foresaw that a Chinese cat would create a tremendous sensation among the Parisians.

"The novelty of this last conquest pricked the self-love of Brisquet, while the drooping ears of the foreigner did the rest. Not long after he announced his intention of leaving me.

"'I found you poor, I leave you rich. You were despairing and knew nothing of the world, now, your instinct has been sharpened by experience. You owe all to me; thank me, and let me go.'

"'Go,' I said, 'I ought never to have loved you,' and he left me.

"His departure lifted a load from my heart. I no longer cared for him. O Bébé, if I could only have forgotten all, and become a kitten again.

"It was about the time of Brisquet's disappearance that I renounced the world, and refused to quit my apartments. Under the able tuition of my mistress, I soon perceived that there was more probability in the fable of the cat transformed into a woman, than one would suppose. In order, therefore, to wile away the time, I took to the study of human nature from our point of view. I resolved to put together my observations in the form of a little treatise, entitled, 'History of a Woman, as a Caution to Cats; by a Votary of Fashion.'

"Should I find an editor, this important work will soon see the light. Bébé, I have no heart to write more. Oh, that I had, like you, remained poor, and never known the pain of luxurious misery. Bébé, I have decided to return to the loft to rejoin you and my dear mother, who, perhaps, after some time may know me again. Do not deter me, I will work, I will forget all the pomp and vanity of riches. Adieu! I hope to leave for home to-morrow."

BÉBÉ TO MINETTE.

FIFTH LETTER.

"As I have just received and perused your long, sad letter, I can only say, that I am ready to welcome you home. Your story was read through a mist of tears. Although, as I say, I am ready to receive you, for your own sake, I entreat you to remain where you are. Think well before plunging into poverty, and exchanging the sentimental misery of your position for the real woes of want. Remain where you are, for beneath the richly-laden boards of the great, you can never feel privation. You can never feel the savage instinct that causes your poor relations at home to fight for the foulest refuse.

"Mark well my words, Minette. There is only one overwhelming type of misery in the world, and that is, born of poverty. I need say nothing to prove that our lot is a sad one. The masons have just left the loft, where they stopped up every mouse-hole, and transformed our happy hunting-grounds into howling wastes of bare timber and plaster.

My mother, who knows nothing of all this, is dying for a meal. I have nothing to give her, and I have tasted nothing for days.   BÉBÉ."

"*P.S.*—I was begging the privilege of hunting in the neighbours' preserves, and have been driven from their roofs and spouts. Keep your sorrows, you have leisure to weep over them, and over the sad lot of your poor sister and mother.

"It is said no one dies of hunger in Paris—we shall see!"

FROM BÉBÉ TO MINETTE.
SIXTH LETTER.

"We are saved! a generous cat has come to our aid. Ah, Minette, how joyous it is to come to life again!   BÉBÉ."

FROM THE SAME TO THE SAME.
SEVENTH LETTER.

"You do not reply, Minette. What is the reason? Ought I to excuse you? I have great news, I am going to be married. I have consented to wed our deliverer. He is elderly and fat, but very good. I feel certain you will approve of the step. His name is Pompon, a nice name which suits him well. It is, besides, a good match, he is a well-fed cat. You see my education has led me to view this union in a plain practical way. Write soon, lazy one!   BÉBÉ."

FROM MINETTE TO BÉBÉ.
EIGHTH LETTER (*written in pencil*).

"While I write to you, Bébé, my maid—the one kept for me by my mistress—is engaged in making a linen bag, when finished I will be thrust into it, it will be sewn up, and I shall be carried off by the footman and thrown into the river.

"This is to be my fate.

"Do you know why, Bébé. It is because I am sick, and my mistress, who has the most superfine feelings, dreads the sight of suffering and death. 'Poor Rosa Mika,' she said, 'how she is changed!' and in a sad voice gave the fatal order, 'Be sure to drown her well, do not have her suffer pain.'

"Ah, Bébé, what do you say now? Do you still envy my miseries? My illness prevented me from writing. Adieu.

"Bébé, in a few minutes all will be over.   MINETTE."

You know the history of my married life, would you wish me to begin again?

As for Bébé, her lot in life was a happy one, only marred by the death of her mother, who expired in her arms while blessing her daughter.

Pompon proved a devoted husband and father, for Bébé soon became the mother of a numerous family of little Pompons and Minettes.

Epilogue.

CHIEF EDITOR'S NOTE.

"We are happy to say that poor Minette is not dead, a telegram has just been handed to us intimating that she escaped as if by a miracle the sad end which menaced her.

"Both mistress and maid died suddenly before the fatal bag was finished. Their death is an event most unaccountable, unless it was brought about to meet the exigency of this romantic tale. Minette, by means best known to the author of this faithful history, soon recovered, and was restored to her sister, with whom she lived happily for many years, enjoying neither riches nor poverty. Minette's tranquillity was broken for a time by the news that Brisquet had first associated himself with a desperate gang of nocturnal serenaders, and ended his midnight exploits and his life by falling from a roof into the street. Bébé seeing Minette a lonely widow, was filled with compassion, and tried to persuade her to wed one of the friends of Pompon. All her efforts were vain. Minette remained unmoved, saying, 'One only loves once. There are those for whom I might die, but with whom I must refuse to live. Besides, my resolution is taken—I shall end my days in widowhood.'"

THE FATAL FALL.

CELEBRATED TRIALS.

AM an old Crow, a member of the Bar of the animal kingdom. At the urgent request of my friends and a wide circle of admirers, and owing to the shortcomings of law reporters, I have resolved to set before you a succinct account of the last assizes. They created a great sensation; it could hardly be otherwise, since the happy thought had suggested itself of selecting most of the judges and jurymen from members of my own tribe, and these, by their grave solemnity of countenance, and by their black attire, presented an imposing spectacle to the crowd, for it was but natural to infer that creatures so skilled in ransacking dead bodies would be peculiarly apt in drawing conclusions as to the moral decomposition of prisoners.

A Stork was appointed President, his cold-blooded patience and stolidity rendering him not unworthy of that honour. Perched motionless on his chair with his eyes half shut, his breast puffed out, his head thrown back, he carefully watched for any contradictory statements made by the accused, and looked as if in ambush on the borders of some swamp. The post of Attorney-General had fallen to a wry-necked Vulture. This personage, if he ever possessed any sensibility, had long forgotten its influence. Ardent and pitiless, his only thought was to obtain success, or in other words conviction; his claws and beak were ever ready to attack but never to defend. The court of assizes was a field of battle, and the prisoner a foe who must be subdued at any price. He proceeded to a criminal trial like a soldier to an assault, throwing himself into the case like a gladiator into the arena. In short, the Vulture makes an admirable Attorney-General.

The inhabitants of the holes, nests, copses, molehills, and neighbour-

ing marshes flocked in crowds to attend these judicial ceremonies, while Geese, Bitterns, Buzzards, and Magpies swelled the throng.

This is the way of the world. Seats were reserved for the representatives of the press—Ducks and Parrots most of them. With what eagerness these gentry hurried to their places! A reporter pounces upon a horrible trial as if it were his lawful prey. When such an occasion presents itself, the regular staff find themselves no longer obliged to task their imaginations, to cudgel their well-worn brains. Copy is supplied to them ready-made, needing no fresh spice to suit the public taste, but rather abounding in dramatic incidents, such as the journalists could never have invented themselves; so the editor can proudly cry out to his printer, "Strike off 10,000 additional sheets!"

It is needless to describe in detail the whole business of the session. We will set aside the proceedings against a jolly Dog, who in a moment of excitement bit the tail off a rival in front of a tavern; against a Peacock for assuming an aristocratic title not his own, a Magpie for theft, a Cat for unlawful trespass on private tiles, a French Cock for stirring up hatred against the constituted government, a Fox for fraudulent bankruptcy. We will content ourselves by noticing the two leading trials, saying with a Rat of our acquaintance, who had gnawed his knowledge out of a book-worm's library, *Musa mehi causus memora.*

In a recent issue of "The Microcosm," a journal much patronised by the Ducks, one might have read the following words:—

"A crime has just been committed of a nature so diabolical as to rouse the indignation of the whole country. It is deeply to be regretted that at the moment when the confederated animals had sworn to maintain eternal friendship and peace, a Toad should be found foully poisoned in a field. Justice is making investigation; she investigated to such good purpose that two Sheep, three Snails, and four Lizards, all equally guiltless, were arrested on suspicion, and not released until they had been detained for ninety days in precautionary imprisonment. May Providence protect you, my friends, from having any idle charge ever laid at your doors. The first thing to be done will be to lock you up in a cell; there you will be detained in custody, that you may be interrogated, and even cross-questioned, about family antecedents and occupation, your mode of spending your leisure, and how you have been employed on certain days, at certain hours, for some months past. After it has been duly established that you are innocent, you will be politely requested to go back to your domicile. During all this time your affairs have languished and fallen into disorder, creditors have become furious, debtors have flown, your family has been injured, and calumnies of all sorts have been kindly set afloat concerning you, for we may always find plenty of animals who will say, 'Where there's smoke there must be fire.'"

Those who were arrested on suspicion in this instance were found to exhibit no traces of guilt. The inquiry was pushed with the greatest energy and activity under the direction of a pair of Tortoises, but the longer their examination continued, the more profound became the darkness and mystery which shrouded the Toad's death. At last a Mole came tumbling up from under his hill, and stated that he had seen an enormous Viper—*monstrum horrendum*, as my friend the Rat would say—darting at the Toad. When brought face to face with the remains of the deceased, he swore positively to its identity. The Bull-dogs were instantly despatched in search of the Viper, and falling valiantly upon him during his sleep, brought him before the judges.

The court is opened; the indictment is read; the Ant, a distinguished analyst, who had been ordered to examine the contents of the stomach, proceeds to read his analysis—marked attention.

"Gentlemen, our duty has been to examine the body and intestines of the unfortunate Toad, and to ascertain beyond doubt whether they contained traces of the poisonous matter distilled in the fangs of the Viper, called by the learned *Viperium*.

"This substance, combined with diverse oxides, acids, and simple bodies, forms variously *Viperates*, *Viperites*, or *Viperures*.

"We have analysed, with the greatest care, the stomach, the liver, the lungs, and the encephalic mass of the victim, using a variety of reagents pilfered from a homœopathic chemist who carried his medicine-chest in his pocket. After heating and evaporating to dryness the pancreatic juice and other substances contained in the stomach, we obtained a sweet solid body, which we treated with two milligrammes of distilled water; by placing the whole in a glass retort, and submitting it to ebullition for two hours and twenty-five minutes, we obtained no result. But this same substance treated successively with acetates, sulphates, nitrates, prussiates, and chlorates, yielded a liquid of a blue apple-green colour which, when combined with certain powerful reagents, deposited a powder of an indefinite but most characteristic colour. This powder can be nothing but *Viperium* in its pure state."

Such a lucid and conclusive report deeply impressed the audience.

This trial, which ended in the conviction of the Viper, would doubtless have excited greater interest had not public attention been drawn away by important political matters, and by the account of a still greater trial which took place about the same time.

The announcement of this affair appeared in the page of "The Microcosm" consecrated to the horrible, headed, as usual, "Another dreadful Tragedy."

"A Ewe and her Lamb, setting a noble example to other domesticated animals, had escaped from their fold. Both were at once placed under the special protection of the Free Confederation of Animals, in spite of which they have been basely murdered."

"A wolf, believed by all to be the true assassin, has been arrested, thanks to the zeal and energy of the commander of the Bulldogs."

The point of importance was to ascertain how the Sheep came by its death. Accordingly, to place this question beyond doubt, a Turkey was appointed to hold a *post-mortem* examination. Now this Turkey was among the most learned of birds. He had won a title by his marvellous skill, and had gained a well-deserved reputation by researches—unhappily inconclusive—into that important problem *Quare opium facit dormire.*

This eminent practitioner stated that the Sheep had certainly not succumbed to an attack of cholera as some had falsely reported, but from a wound six inches in length having been made in her neck, nearly severing the head from the trunk.

The trial was impatiently awaited, and at last came on for hearing. From break of day an immense multitude besieged the entrance to the court, but the authorities had taken measures to prevent disorder. At ten o'clock the accused is brought in; he looks pale, his dark eyes have lost their lustre, his attire though decent has nothing *recherche* about it. One can scarcely make out his features, which seem to shun the curious gaze of the public. An old Crow, who out of twenty applicants obtained the honour of defending the prisoner, was in his place in his professional robes prepared to enter upon his task. At length the examination commenced.

Q. "Prisoner, stand up! Your name and surname?"

Ans. "Canis Lupus."

Q. "Your age?"

Ans. "Twelve years."

Q. " Your profession ? "
Ans. " Botanist."
Q. " Your dwelling ? "
Ans. " The woods."
" The charges against you, Canis Lupus, will be read over."
The indictment was read amid profound silence, after which the presiding judge resumed examination of the prisoner.
Q. "Canis Lupus, what have you to say in your defence ? "
Ans. " I am innocent of the crime laid to my charge. I own, my lord, for a long time I was accustomed to destroy Sheep, but in so doing I consulted less my inclination than my hatred for man. If the death of a Sheep or Lamb gave me pleasure, it was simply because I knew that I thus carried off from my oppressors a portion of their daily food.

"For some time past I have looked upon Sheep with the tenderest solicitude, without in any way permitting this sentiment to interfere with my hatred for mankind. Picture my horror, my indignation, when a few days back I beheld the innocents of whose death I am accused, pursued by a butcher who struck them down without pity. I flew to their aid, the infamous executioner taking to his heels in terror. Just at that moment when I was preparing to bind up the wounds, the officers of the court apprehended me as if I were a vulgar assassin! Hereafter I propose to sue for false imprisonment and damages."

The prisoner resumed his seat, placing his paw on his eyes. His address awakened the sympathies of the audience, especially of the fair sex.

" How well he spoke ! " said a Crane.

" What wonderful grace and eloquence ! " exclaimed a speckled Magpie.

" It is a thousand pities that a youth so handsome should be condemned," said a Woodcock, sighing, " Ah me ! ah me ! "

It would almost seem that in order to please some ladies one must be a villain, but if one wishes to touch their hearts, hypocrisy must be called in to add attractiveness to crime. Let us, however, return to our mutton.

The judge replied—

" Prisoner, your version of the occurrence is full of contradictions and must be set aside as utterly false. It is opposed to the sworn testimony of the witnesses we are about to examine. Let us assure you, once for all, you will never be able to persuade your fellow-brutes that you are capable of one spark of generosity. Your antecedents are deplorable."

Prisoner. "Alas! I have always been the victim of calumny."

"You appear to have been reared in a hotbed of crime. At two years old you bit the mother who nursed you."

Prisoner. "She bit me first."

"Later in life you fell a-quarrelling with one of your neighbours and called him a Toad!"

Prisoner. "He had called me an Alligator."

"Three years ago you were seen prowling round the royal rabbit warren, a place which no animal of your species is permitted to enter."

Prisoner. "My lord, I never set foot inside it."

"Perhaps not, but you intended to get in there, and to create a disturbance inside. The gentlemen of the jury will know how to take all these circumstances into account."

The hearing of the witnesses followed, the Wolf cross-examining each with great ability—calm with some, ardent, jocular, or sarcastic with others, always ready with a reply to any damaging statement. Little by little, nevertheless, his strength failed him; to the strain of overexcitement there succeeded a sudden prostration, and at last he fainted away.

The trial had to be adjourned till the following week. For some days the Wolf was too feeble to appear. Never has an illustrious animal, the head of a family or a prince adored by his people—as official proclamations assure us—excited so keen a public interest during sickness as did this unlucky Wolf. The *habitues* of the court feared lest a sensational prosecution should be lost to them. The judge's heart bled lest this important and popular trial should come to an end, depriving him of the opportunity of summing up, and so dealing with the evidence as to present to the jury the distorted form of justice seen through the illusive medium of the law. The executioner, his keen blade athirst for a victim, trembled lest it should be robbed of its proper prey. The Vulture general dreaded lest his eloquent speech should have to be shelved, again undelivered—a speech that had cost him three weeks of close study.

Every morning the press published a bulletin of the Wolf's condition.

"The accused suffers dreadfully, and is closely confined to bed. He has always a number of Leeches near him; nevertheless he seems calm and resigned."

"The prisoner had a bad night. Several Geese of the aristocracy have sent to the prison to inquire after his health."

"The accused recovers slowly, he devotes his hours of convalescence to reading and writing. The chief subject of his study is the 'Proverbial Philosophy of Martin Tupper.' He has used during his captivity two thousand nine hundred and twenty-one sheets of paper. He is composing a drama in seventeen acts, entitled 'Virtue's Triumph,' also a philosophical treatise on the desirability of abolishing capital punishment."

The following verses were penned by the prisoner, and will doubtless be read with the interest they deserve:—

I.

" Ah, hapless is the prisoner's fate in convict cell condemned to pine,
While birds abroad their songs uplift, and fields in summer's glory shine.
If breeze-borne from the far-off flock, the fitful tinkling bells are heard,
If corn-fields wave their nodding ears, by wanton zephyrs lightly stirred,
All these the wretch's sorrows swell, he scents but may not see the flowers,
And darker grows the lonely gloom which broods o'er all his friendless hours.

II.

" Soft coos the plaintive dove, the waves in whispering throbs their music pour,
Each after each in cadence breaks, and dies in rippling on the shore;
The woods and winds their voices blend, no heed the cheerless captive pays;
No joy to him the sunbeam brings, which o'er the smiling meadow plays.
Unhappy outcast! not for thee does universal gladness reign,
These joys were all in mockery sent to wring thy breast with deadlier pain.

III.

" The world outside, the busy world, its dear familiar rounds may tread,
But vain are dreams of pleasant life, when life's long-lingering hope has fled.
Then, prisoner, cease to shake thy bars : no mercy cold mute iron shows ;
In torments, terrors, threats, and tears, thy few remaining days must close.
Thy doom is sealed; the gaolers stern may never more their grip relax,
Until the headsman comes to claim thee for his hungry axe."

I avow, ye gentlemen of the press, that the sort of enthusiasm of which this miserable Wolf became the object, inspired me with sad reflections. I have heard of unfortunate Nightingales, who for long years together have poured forth the most sublime songs without ever rising from obscurity, or obtaining a wider fame than that embraced in their native woodland shade, and yet this Wolf, because he has committed a foul crime, saw his clumsy doggerel rapturously applauded. I know of some good animals who, though they have proved themselves heroes of virtue, have never got a single line from the public press. Nevertheless the minutest sayings and doings of this condemned wretch have been chronicled to please the public craving. Mammas who would have thought twice before placing the fables of Florian in the hands of their daughters—mammas strict even in the choice of their own reading, have in the family circle freely discussed details which initiated their children into all the refinements of crime and depravity. Without ignoring evil, could not the reports of crime be so framed as to avoid the ghastly pomp and morbid parade with which they appear in the newspapers?

If an editor were to confine himself exclusively to the relation of good actions, he would frequently have to supply blank sheets to his readers.

As soon as the prisoner was able to appear at the bar, the proceedings began anew, and continued eight days. Twenty-eight witnesses were heard for and against the Wolf, while judges, jurymen, counsel, and defendants poured out their questions, interruptions, and observations in a never-ceasing flood. The result was that the whole affair, clear and simple as it had been at first, became gradually so confused as to be almost incomprehensible.

Most lawsuits are like the water of a fountain—the more it is stirred up, the muddier it grows.

The prisoner had used so many subterfuges to rivet attention, he became so thoroughly the lion of the day, that a profound feeling of sympathetic emotion prevailed when the Vulture delivered himself of the concluding speech for the prosecution.

"Gentlemen of the jury," he said, "before I enter upon the details already submitted to your intelligent consideration, my duty commands me imperiously to put to you a question as grave as it is important. I ask you with feelings of the deepest grief and bitterest pain—I ask you, what is society coming to? In truth, gentlemen, turn where we will, look in which direction we may, we discover nothing but disorder—disorder, gentlemen, among quadrupeds, among bipeds, among geese, though they may use but one leg at a time. What we see is neither more nor less than symptoms of disorganisation, from bottom to top, from root to core. Yes, gentlemen, the social fabric is being undermined, the social body is corrupting; it totters to its fall, and fall it will, gentlemen, unless you are able to rear up a barrier which shall arrest its dreadful downward progress towards moral dissolution."

The orator proceeded to view the crime in every possible light, showing how such atrocities were committed in ancient times, how they might be committed at any time by anybody, and how the guilt of this particular crime had been clearly brought home to the prisoner.

The counsel for the defence replied in an effective series of vigorous croaks, having first declared that in his opinion the finest spectacle on earth was that of innocence overtaken by misfortune.

At half-past twelve the jurors retired to a silent copse to deliberate, and soon returning, found the culprit guilty on all the charges of the indictment.

The judge touchingly inquired of the felon whether he had any objection to the sentence of death being passed upon him, to which the prisoner replied with a feeble grin.

"The Wolf is condemned to be hanged."

The immense crowd remained gloomy and speechless, not a word, not even a bleat disturbed the scene, not a tail gave an involuntary wag. One would have imagined, when viewing all eyes bent on the Wolf, and all beaks hushed and dumb, that the assembly had been suddenly turned to stone, or that an electric shock had struck them all motionless for ever.

The Wolf was hanged this morning, gentlemen, and some zoophytes took good care to avail themselves of the opportunity for a demonstration in favour of the abolition of capital punishment. I confess that their arguments have little effect on me. I cannot conceive why they made so much fuss to save a wretch who destroyed his brother. It is to punish him more severely, they say, that they would permit him to live! How they deceive themselves! The convict always cherishes the consoling hope of being one day able to escape. It may be he will settle down contentedly to the undisturbed round of prison life. From a wretched outcast who gained a precarious subsistence by crime, he comes to take pleasure in his banishment. The burden of care has been lifted from his back. His wants are provided for by the State, and he need no longer dread the horrors of dying from hunger. The punishment inflicted has given him at last a recognised position in society.

If the penalty of death is to cease to be carried into effect, the nations

U

of Europe, and the world at large, must commence by the abolition of war, for on the field of battle thousands of innocent lives are sacrificed as the penalty of the guilt or misgovernment of a single individual.

Let kings and emperors so raise the moral tone of their statesmen and subjects as to enable them practically to carry out the Divine command, "Thou shalt not kill."

Twenty-two different portraits of the Wolf were issued, no one of them resembling another, yet all guaranteed likenesses.

The complete account of the trial, drawn up by a clever shorthand writer, was sold by thousands. The memory of the Wolf was also enshrined in verse and recited in the streets.

I.

" Give ear, Jays, Hawks, and Magpies,
Attend, all Kites and Crows,

A story we shall now unfold
More black than ye suppose.

II.

"The story of a guilty deed,
　For harpies vile befitted,
Which cunning Wolf with crafty tongue
　And keen-edged tooth committed.

III.

"A tender Lamb one joyous morn
　Beside its mother played,
The Wolf came creeping up
　And friendliest greeting made.

IV.

"The Ewe responsive welcome gave,
　The Wolf lay down to sleep,
But soon he started up again
　And slew that trustful Sheep.

V.

"'Help, mother dear!' the Lambkin cried,
　But oh! its cry was vain,
With cruel fangs the unsparing Wolf
　Straight clove its neck in twain.

VI.

"But never while misdeeds abound
　Shall wakeful vengeance fail,
Two Watch-Dogs bold, who guard the fold,
　That guilty Wolf assail.

VII.

"'Now, comrades,' cries the wily Wolf,
　'Some healing balm obtain,
In yonder cave 'tis stored;' but soon
　He found such tricks were vain.

VIII.

"For up and spake each trusty Hound,
　'Thou felon Wolf, say true,
Who bade thee slay this blameless Lamb,
　And kill its mother too!'

IX.

"'I cure, not kill,' the Wolf replied,
　'Vex not a poor physician;
Such lies, base curs, would place my name
　In quite a false position.'

X.

"The Watch-Dogs drag the prisoner off,
　The courts his death decree,
Now hanged in chains his body swings
　On yonder gallows-tree.

MORAL.

"Whene'er your steps incline to stray
　Along the sinner's wicked way,
A warning from this story take,.
　And know that truth sublime—
Each creature is a criminal.
　When he commits a crime."

The Bear; or, A Letter from the Mountains.

"When introduced to the world, I brought with me a craving for solitude, doubtless bestowed for some wise purpose. But instead of directing my faculties to an end which answered my vocation in the harmony of beings, like most gifted natures, I followed my own inclinations.

"Soon after the event which brought me to light, a fall from a lofty tree lamed me for life, and contributed not a little to render me a prey to fits of melancholy.

"Our den was the favourite resort of Bears of the surrounding district. My father was a splendid hunter, and entertained his convives sumptuously with the produce of the chase. Life in those days seemed to be one endless round of dancing, gaiety, and feasting. As for myself, I remained a stranger to my father's guests, whose visits bothered me. Although the good cheer was not wholly distasteful, the frequent and vulgar eating, drinking, and roaring bouts were odious to my nature. This repugnance was not to be attributed to a finely-strung organisation, although modern philosophy points to our organisation as the source and cause of our positive and negative affections.

Note.—This letter was meant for private circulation only; the young Bear from whom it was received thought he might venture, without offence, to divulge the secrets of friendship—more especially as the writer had died, leaving this, among other manuscripts, to his care. A dead Bear is not likely to complain of ingratitude. —Ed.

"My love of silence and solitude at last settled into the gloomy moroseness of a *misunderstood Bear*, which has always passed as the token of incomprehensible genius, or of virtue too pure for the world. Years of self-examination, added to a growing feeling of dissatisfaction, convinced me at last that pride was the parent of my brood of sickly imaginings, whose ghostly food was the moonbeams, and the sighing of the mountains, as they whispered about me to the passing wind. Before resipiscence, it was needful I should suffer misfortune.

"My parents were grieved by my monomania. I had indeed determined to leave them, and seek some distant secluded spot in which I might remain undisturbed and alone. Conscience smote me in vain; my project was at last confided to a friend of the family, who after I had left broke the news to my parents, telling them I had voluntarily renounced the world. Never shall I forget stealing like a thief from the home of my childhood. The morning mist rose over the mountain from the valleys in blinding masses. Soon settling into clouds, one of pearly whiteness, fringed with the golden light of dawn, floated like a curtain in front of my old home.

"It was a glorious scene; I could dimly descry my father returning from the chase laden with a store of game. Snow mantled the heights, and an icy wind rising with the sun shook the dark pines. The violence of the wind increased, the clouds were driven, torn into shreds, against the jagged rocks, and scattered like flames of living fire flying over the pine forests. The wind, after a fearful blast and deep-drawn sigh, paused as if to view the sport, then rising suddenly, lifted the vapour from the hollows, chasing it from its warm bed up the snowy steeps, and spreading it out in a dark veil across the sun. In the deep gloom the voices of a thousand fiends seemed to rise from vale and crag. The caverns and gorges were filled with the spirits of a gathering storm, shrieking and clamouring like a crowd at the gates of hell, impatient to be let loose to lay waste the land. At last they burst forth; onward they came, guided by a sword of lightning that shivered a great rock close to my feet, and pierced the heart of my favourite tree. I rolled over in a faint of panic fear, and awoke to see the wreck of many a green sapling, the pathways strewn with leaves, branches, and the trunks of giant pines. The storm had abated, and in its track left angry torrents leaping from the once dry rocks, gathering force and roaring in brown torrents down through the chasms, to flood and wreck the smiling plains beneath. This is not all, for a sentimental Bear is a great observer.

"The sun again shone upon the scene with the brightness of hope to the torn breast of Nature, for every green thing took heart and expanded beneath its welcome rays. As for me, nothing daunted, I started and pursued my way until I found a spot inaccessible to everything but sweet solitude and myself.

"During five years my only visitor was an Eagle who perched on a stunted tree not far off. No other living creature had ventured to invade my horizon.

"My occupations were very simple. At dawn I sat on a ledge of rock watching sunrise. The freshness of the morning filled me with a sense of newness of life, and a vividness of imagination whose fruit was a palingenesian poem, in which I meant to express all the griefs of those who had raised the cup of happiness to their lips, only to find it empty and polluted.

"During the day I studied the healing properties of plants, while my evenings were devoted to watching the stars appear one by one in the sky. My heart expanded when gazing on the moon and the sweet planet Venus, and I even at times imagined I must have had some hand in creating the stars and moon, in order that they might shine for my special benefit. Five years were passed in dreaming, after which my eyes opened to behold the vanity of a Bear. My illusions vanished, and objects appeared in their true colours. A sense of loneliness took hold of me, the stars lost their lustre, the flowers and grasses their ethereal fragrance and heavenly hues. I considered my limbs, my claws, my coat, and behold they were made for climbing, crawling, clutching, and covering my nakedness. I found I could neither climb to high heaven nor clutch the stars; on the contrary, my attributes were practical, brutish, and earthly. These mortifying but useful discoveries compelled me to seek other scenes—to return, in fact, to the world and rejoin my fellows.

"Back I accordingly made my way, and, all unused to the craft of wise Bears, became a prey to the cunning of men.

"I started one morning early to carry out my resolution, and had not proceeded far when strange sounds smote my ear, voices shouting, 'A Bear! a Bear!!!' Pausing to listen where the sounds came from, I was suddenly struck and stunned by an invisible weapon which sent me rolling over on the ground, where I was immediately surrounded by four savage Dogs, followed by three more savage men. In spite of the pain of my wound I struggled bravely, but was at last overpowered, and fainted from loss of blood.

"Upon recovering I found myself tied to a tree with a rope fastened to a ring in my nose. To this day I have never been able to make out how that solid metal ring was spirited into my nose. Verily the skill of man passeth the knowledge of Bears! Homer says the man who has lost his liberty has lost half his soul. I had sustained that loss, and had gained a permanent ornament, so fixed that to regain my liberty I must sacrifice my snout. There was no help for it, I had been rudely pulled up to survey my changed position. Wherein did the change consist? Sun, moon, and stars were still above me, but they had no longer the same interest for me; they were simply sun, moon, stars, and nothing more—heavenly bodies having their own affairs to look after, while I had mine, which proved all-absorbing. Formerly the beautiful in nature was my constant feast; there it was still around me, but it had lost its old fascination and power of feasting the senses.

"The truth is, I had never really renounced the world. For a time I was the slave of morbid fancies, and had no more given up the flesh-and-blood interest in life, than does the Buddhist bonze, who, while he courts seclusion and broods over the ethics of his creed, is careful to nourish and cherish the material part of his being.

"Here I was, by a mere fluke of misfortune, brought face to face with my real self, a heavy-footed, full-grown, and withal sentimental Bear. Many days passed in a sort of stupor of despair, followed by the sweet inward confession of my sins, which brought resignation and a calm I had never before experienced. If anything could replace the loss of liberty, it was the repose of my new life, for my master showed me uniform kindness. I was commensal of his house by day, and by night was consigned to a stable with some other socially-disposed animals.

"Soon after daybreak I was taken to the doorway, where, seated beneath a plane-tree, the hours passed pleasantly in playing with my master's children, who showed me much affection, while the thoroughfare along the highroad procured endless amusement.

"On fête-days the rustics came to dance under the tree; for my master was an innkeeper, and his house a favourite resort.

"There the noise of jingling glasses and songs of gay spirits sounded from dawn to sunset. I had always a formal invitation to the dances, which commenced after the evening repast, and were kept up far into the night. Usually I had the good fortune to open the ball with the prettiest girl of the crowd, by a dance similar to the one in vogue a Crete, invented for the amiable Ariadne. Since then I have been enabled to study the private life of men of rank, those on the upper range of the social ladder, and give it as my conviction that the poor mountaineers have a happier lot in life than those regarded by the world as the highly-favoured ones. The conclusion forces itself upon me, that men are happy just in proportion as they are ignorant. It is sad it should be so, as it brings them down to the level of the beast, and tempts some to regard even the Bear, owing to the simplicity of his nature and habits, as an infinitely happier animal than man. My rustic life lasted six months, during which time I followed the example of Apollo, deprived of his glory, guarding the flock of Admetus.

"One day, while I was seated as usual beneath the tree, a postchaise drawn by four horses stopped at the door, and I learned that its occupant, who had the air of a travelling aristocrat, was a poet of noble birth and European fame, who had been voyaging in search of adventure. This personage left the carriage to take some refreshment, and during his stay I seemed to be the subject of a conversation which ended in the stranger placing some pieces of gold in the hand of my master, who undid my chain and consigned me to the vehicle.

"The peaceful valley where I had spent so many happy days was leagues off before I recovered from my surprise. It is needless to remark that any change in my mode of life caused me much pain and anxiety. Believe me, dear reader, happiness is only to be found in the monotony of an uneventful life.

"As the scenes of my youth faded in the distance, sorrow took possession of my heart, and at last I bade adieu to my dear mountains. I felt for the first time that loss of one's country is immortal, and that travels only produce fatigue of body and mind. Now I was enabled to comprehend how Calypso, arrayed in all her charms, could not tempt Ulysses to abandon his poor but much-loved Ithaca, or to relinquish the noble ambition which induced him to return and behold once more the smoke rising from his chimney.

"'Vivite felices, quibus est fortuna peracta!
Vobis parta quies, nobis maris æquor araudum.'

"We embarked at Bayonne on board a ship setting sail for the British Isles, where I afterwards passed two years with my master in a Scottish castle. This gifted man was to me a most interesting study; at once poet and misanthrope, his example sealed my fate for life, thoroughly curing me of the monomania which had forced me into seclusion. I had at the same time contracted a depraved habit of composing verses or rhymes, which I could not shake off, never fully realising that only a few gifted poets have been enabled to win fame by placing their sentiments on record. Like most half-fledged misunderstood poets, I suffered acutely, being no favourite either of the Muses or the public. Inspiration would not come, in spite of great agony and superbearish effort. It was in vain I lay on my back or rolled on my belly—rhythm, rhyme, and romance proved my severest taskmasters. I walked fast in the dark lanes of the garden, as Pope used to do, scaring the birds by the deep growlings that escaped my breast.

"Who would believe it? My poetic breakdown stirred the worst passions of my nature, and drove me to hate every successful songster—to hate past, present, and future—to hate every one and everything saving my own soured self.

"Since Solomon's time many books have been written, but the book which shall faithfully picture the miseries of a literary life has yet to be penned. My master himself, with his acknowledged genius and inordinate—— I must not retail his troubles, as most worthy recipients of his kindness might be tempted to do. I shall content myself, as a faithful servant, by merely raising the corner of the veil. The Muses were his true loves, to whom he was fain to prove unfaithful when he sought the joys of domestic life, to lay the storms of his heart in the haven of home. But it was all too late, the experiment failed, and he fled to end his accumulated woes on a foreign shore.

"Here was a lofty example for me, an unfortunate poetaster, proving as it did that poetic genius, just in proportion to its intensity, dries up the font of social happiness and plays fearful havoc with common sense.

"Fortunately for me, as it gave me my liberty, whatever it may have done for himself, my gifted master, at the sound of the strife of Grecian insurrection, determined to leave England, resolved to seek a brilliant tomb. Some days before his departure, wishing to make a last appearance in London, he profited by the representation of Hamlet, one of his favourite plays, to show himself once more to the British public. We drove to the theatre in an open carriage, and found the place crowded as we seated ourselves in a stage-box. Our appearance created a tremendous sensation, all eyes and eyeglasses were turned towards us; the ladies, bending over the balconies, recalled lovely flowers peeping out from rocky clefts. All were eager to get a glimpse of the great poet; so worshipful indeed was this well-dressed crowd, that the play was totally disregarded till the ghost of the prince stalked across the stage, and as a tribute to Shakespeare, the great character of the phantom was received with profound respect. The details of the tragedy appeared to be of a nature to familiarise the spectators with our presence, like the appropriate music which introduces and accompanies the hero in an opera. But the ghost was too signal an evidence of creative genius to be lightly passed over. This wonderful performance supplied all the metropolitan journals with a glowing leader. It is to these papers, for the past twenty years, we have been indebted for all the political, philosophical, religious, and literary achievements of learned Europe.

"Next day we embarked for France, and as good-luck would have it, my master made a roundabout journey to visit some ruins.

"One evening when he was seated at the foot of an old tower, I profited by the reverie in which he was plunged to make my escape. For four days and nights, I fled from mountain to mountain without once looking behind. At last, on the evening of the fifth day, I again found myself in the Pyrenees. In an excess of joy I knelt down and kissed my native soil, after which I made for the cavern where I first breathed the air. It was inhabited by an old friend of the family, who told me that my parents were dead. After shedding a few tears to their memory, I took up my abode on Mount Perdu, and made myself a happy home.

"Although I am a poet in a small way, I love my wife, and find my children perfect; they are moulded very much after their father's image. We do not see much company, almost none, save one or two desperate duns, who thought so well of me as to come over here all the way from London to "look me up," as they say. Their excuse for intruding on my privacy is that they frequently pass my way, and it suddenly occurs to them they have each a trifling bill for Mr. Bear. These scraps of paper are the tender links which bind me to the past, and recall the licence of poetic inspiration. Happy is he who dwells at home, and who has never drifted into doggerel!

"All I now require is to be left alone to the use of my natural instincts, which have ripened under affliction, and to the enjoyment of the attributes with which nature has endowed me. I have been long in discovering my true self. Now that I have found the rascal, I will keep watch over him, and prove to the world that my wandering life has not been wholly spent in pursuits of vanity.

"What more do I require? Does not the naïad of the rock distil from the elements an exhaustless store of water to quench my thirst?

The beloved tree of Cybele, does it not shelter my dwelling with its evergreen boughs? Above all, when the day's toil is ended and I return laden with the trophies of the chase, have I not a devoted partner to welcome me home?

"I have now no ambition save one, and that is to make the acquaintance of that heavenly constellation which bears our noble name."

THE SEVENTH HEAVEN.

VOYAGE ABOVE THE CLOUDS.

CHAPTER OF DREAMS.

I.

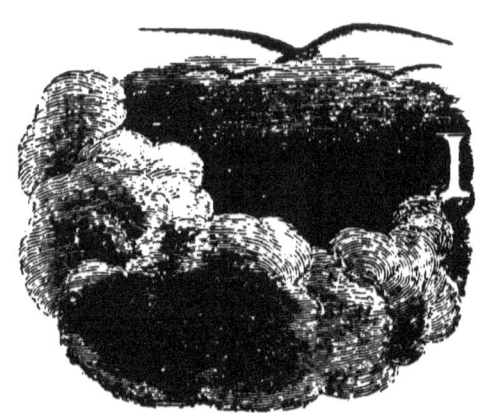

WAS dead. Dead as one perhaps dies when uncertain whether it is better to live or to die; dead without knowing when or how. I had indeed died painlessly, pleasantly, and mysteriously.

So easily had my life left my body, so little had it suffered in quitting the form of clay, that at first my body did not perceive the change.

Of the precise moment when from a living Turtle-dove I became a corpse, I remember nothing, unless it be that before death the moon shone brightly in a cloudless sky; and when my astonished spirit made out that it had fulfilled its duty on earth, the moon had not ceased to shine, and the sky was still cloudless. Probably my death, far from quenching the light of the moon, or sending the sky into mourning, had made no visible change in earth or heaven. What can it matter to fruitful nature whether a creature like me lives or dies? Yet after all, we are assured that a Sparrow shall not fall to the ground without its heavenly Father.

II.

I have no doubt my spirit rejoiced at finding itself free, since it could have no real love for a body so impotent to respond to its lofty aspirations. In truth, many times in the days of their union my poor flesh had been almost left alone to look after itself, while my spirit dreamt at ease of some peculiar mythical world. Is it not possible during dreams that the body is quietly left to slumber while the spirit roams about in ethereal realms of its own? First it carefully lays a telegraphic line from its slumbering solid dwelling on earth, and in an instant traverses space, sending back to the living brain flashes of strange intelligence from other spheres.

III.

Yet the spirit mourned, seeing its old tenement, whose strength and weakness, beauty and deformity, were all so familiar, falling into decay, marking the dissolution that had already set in, and would before long yield up the materials to the four winds of heaven and to the earth that supplied them. The spirit exclaimed, "Why was I thus released without a moment's warning? The light has left the bright eye, nor will the wings respond to my wish. I cannot bear this parting! Awake, mute form! awake! cast a loving glance across the bright scene! Wake, and tell me our union was not a dream! Alas! then it must be farewell."

IV.

For the first time the appeal of the spirit remained unanswered. Why love that which must die? Since we cannot enjoy the hope of eternity, let us part!

Of men alone it is written that their spirits after death shall at some future time reunite with the body, when the soul shall recognise and reanimate its ancient dust. Nevertheless, I have dreamt that the Dove shall again rise from the dead.

V.

The silence of night was alone disturbed by the falling leaves—for they too must die—and by the distant approach of a bird of prey.

Tender flowers, green leaves that once sheltered my poor frame, bend over it now and screen its beauty from the impious Vulture. Alas! the dread sound came nearer and yet nearer, and the deep shadow of the bird of doom fell on the peaceful remains.

VI.

A musical voice hailed me from the air and bade me follow. Instinctively I floated upward with my spirit guide, who seemed to bear me on invisible wings far beyond the range of earth.

VII.

In a moment the past was severed from the future, all memory of my former being vanished. I soared through space without an effort, obeying my new condition implicitly, just as on earth one loves and thinks without knowing why one does so, or how thought and love have come to form so important a part of our earthly lives.

VIII.

I had floated away so far from the world that it seemed nothing more than a bright speck in an ocean of immensity. For a moment I recalled my loss, the body I had left behind, and exclaimed, "Shall the joys of my future banish regret, or is sorrow also eternal?"

IX.

Is there no link in heaven to bind one to what is dear on earth? Has my life among mortals been a dream? Still I was wafted upward and onward to a region full of stars, where I passed from one orb to another. Bright stars, whither am I going? But the stars, yielding no response, noiselessly ranged themselves to light me on my way.

X.

I was floating in a realm of light. Space spread out before me like an azure veil studded with diamonds. But the light of the stars was eclipsed by a greater refulgence. Filled with awe, I paused, and the voice—more silvery than the sweetest tones of earth—whispered, "Follow me, we shall only stop in a blissful region. You are at the gates of paradise. Follow me and fear not, doubt not. Doubt is born of the devil, faith is an attribute of heaven.

XI.

The speaker was a purified immortal, the spirit of a snow-white Dove that death had taken in all the beauty of its youth, unsullied by the sight of human misery. Its mission was to receive and guide liberated spirits on their way to the new world.

XII.

I then saw—what I had not been able to perceive before, owing to the imperfection of my sight—many disembodied spirits, each, like myself, floating towards some resting-place. My first sensation on finding myself in such company was fear mingled with a vague hope which impelled me onwards. "Sweet spirit," I said to my guide, "the Turtle-dove's paradise, is it far?"

"See," he replied, smiling at my impatience—"see yonder orb alone. There is the seventh heaven, where our arrival is awaited."

Who can want me there? I thought. Is it still alive?

XIII.

Ascending beyond worlds and spheres without number, we alighted at a gate whence shone the most dazzling light, eclipsing the sun in brightness. Above the portal was inscribed in letters of fire, "Here is the abode of undying love;" and beneath, "Here is no change save that of ever-growing love." The door flew open, but what can I say of the sight revealed to my gaze? No words of mine can picture the glorious light which, without pain or strain of vision, revealed everything so clearly that the minutest details of the picture could be seen and understood.

XIV.

"I now leave you," said my guide, "at the threshold of your new home." The words still lingered in my ears when I beheld a pearly cloud in the sky; it was my treasure, my Turtle-dove, winging its flight towards me.

"Ah!" I cried, "pure spirit of my sister, do I indeed behold you, my sister?" She came, and our hearts were filled with a sacred joy, for she knew me and loved me still.

She had not changed; yet she seemed brighter, whiter, more beautiful, and as I looked, her beauty, like the beauty of a great painting, only increased. "Ah! my well-beloved and long-lost sister, this is indeed a joyous meeting. When I heard of your death the pain preyed upon me, and I soon followed you, for grief broke my heart." Who dares to disbelieve in happiness? Alas! is it not a dream?

XV.

Alas! it was a dream. . . .

But why awake from such a dream? This dream that had carried me through space and filled me with unmixed joy, had been of so short duration that I awoke to find nothing had changed on earth. The moon still shone in the clear sky. Nothing, indeed, proved real save the bird of prey circling through the air near my nest.

NOTES ON THE LIFE OF THE AUTHOR OF THIS CURIOUS FRAGMENT.

We deem it our duty to place before our readers some biographical details concerning the author of the foregoing fragment, handed to us by the governor of a lunatic asylum.

"The author of these strange imaginings was early left an orphan. His parents without warning, without even leaving their future address, left him one morning while his young beak was deep in slumber, buried in his callow down. Yet these good birds, owing to the gentleness and simplicity of their habits, left a doubtful reputation behind them, the only inheritance of our young hero. A sympathetic circle of friends agreed that they had come to an untimely end, nothing short of death could have caused them to abandon their child. One or two old Magpies there were, who, putting their heads together, whispered among themselves that Parisian Doves were not so good as they looked, and that they had purposely deserted the youngster, who interfered with the pursuit of their own pleasure.

"Be that as it may, the parents were never again seen or heard of, and the little one struggled on wonderfully, being greatly indebted to the good offices of some poor but true-hearted thrifty friends. As soon as the orphan could leave the deserted home and trust himself to his

wings, he commenced a search which only ended in disappointment, for the lost ones were nowhere to be found. For all that, day after day he persevered in his vain efforts, saying, 'I must find my parents, or perish in the attempt!'

"In one of his journeys he fell in with a young Ringdove, who at once won his heart, first attracted by her guileless beauty and then conquered by her sympathy. But being an honest bird, this new sentiment in his breast could not tempt him from the path of duty; on the contrary, it only stimulated him to greater exertion, and he winged his flight anew. 'I will return,' he said; 'my true love will wait for me.' So he left, and she waited till her patience was worn out by waiting, and then wedded another.

"After many days of fruitless search our Dove returned to seek his bride, and found her surrounded by the family of his rival. The blow was too much for him, it broke his heart and drove him mad.

"Perhaps the Ringdove might have waited his return, had not his rival poisoned the ear of his mistress by whispering strange rumours about infidelity. When her first love returned she was seized with remorse and despair. What could she do? Like a sensible Ringdove, she continued to be a good mother, redoubling her care for her little ones, and doing her duty towards her husband, while her sorrows were buried deep in her own breast. No one knew her secret, even her most intimate friends, looking on her snug home, said, 'How happy she must be!' The same remark is made of a great many who have never known what happiness is.

"As for the poor Turtle-dove, he was perfectly harmless in his insanity, betaking himself constantly to the top of a mountain, where he dreamed away his days. That for which he had sought in vain in the solid realities of earth, perchance he found in dreamland, where at times even the wise ones of the world would like to abide. But, alas! they too must awake and be recalled to the rude realities of life.

"After his death, beneath a heap of leaves was found a manuscript entitled 'Memoirs of a Madman,' 'Happiness is made of Dreams.' It was really a poem in prose, written straight from the heart, free from the fetters of rhyme."

Some feathered wits may be disposed to smile at the poor Turtle-dove, his misfortunes and writings. All we need say to such gaily-disposed critics is, that they have none of the gentle attributes of our loving but weak Ringdove.

326 PUBLIC AND PRIVATE LIFE OF ANIMALS.

P.S.—Out of consideration for those who dislike anything obscure in a story, we may add that the Ringdove, having reared her brood, when she heard of the fate of her first love, died of a broken heart.

Practical-minded Sparrows, and other common members of the feathered tribe, may think that the story would have been better as a whole had the lovers wedded and lived happily together. All we can say to this, as faithful narrators, is, "Truth is stranger than fiction."

Letters from a Swallow to a Canary Reared in a Convent.

THE SWALLOW'S FIRST LETTER.

At last, dear friend, I am free and flying with my own wings. Far behind me I can still descry the horrible barrier of Mount Parnassus, and the equally dreary plateau of social conformity, which I had already crossed. In the air which I breathe, and in my freedom of flight, there is truly an intoxicating charm. On starting I cast a scornful glance on my companions, the Swallows who prefer the solitude and obscurity of their deplorable existence to all the world and all its joys. You may think me puffed up with vanity, one of the meanest of vices, when I tell you that nature never intended me to do the work of a builder, for which all the wretched females of our race seem to have an aptitude. Let them spend their youth in building, in polishing with beak and wing the inside and outside of their dwellings. Let them, I say, continue to construct their homes with as great toil as if the frail tenements in which they rear families were to last for ever. My efforts to enlighten them have been fruitless, and I leave all those to their fate who fail to profit by the experience contained in the following account of my travels. I perhaps ought to congratulate myself on having no travelling companion, and never being tempted wholly to give up my heart and independence to another. You have often told me in a tone of friendly severity that, constituted as I am, I could never submit to the guidance of another, however much, by reason of youth and inexperience, I was incapable of guiding myself. For all that, I have followed my own course in spite of your sage advice, and I am proud of it. You have cursed my craving for seeing the world, which has carried me far from yourself and your wise counsels. It is true I greatly esteem your friendship and value your advice. The one has often lightened my sad heart, while the other, although good, has rarely been followed by me. I have fully understood your dread of adventure, but it has never influenced my pursuits. Our lives and our ways have nothing in common, and our meeting only shows all the more clearly the divergence of our courses in the world. Our thoughts do not harmonize, and our hopes do not point to the same end.

You first beheld the day through the bars of a prison in which you must live and die a captive, and the notion that beyond these bars lie a boundless horizon and liberty has never entered your head. Doubtless had such a thought crossed your mind, you would have crushed it as men are said to stifle the whisperings of the devil.

I was brought forth beneath the roof of an old deserted house in the corner of a wood. The first noise that fell upon my ears was the wind whistling through the trees. It was a sweet sound, the very thought of it wakes pleasant memories.

The first sight that met my eyes was that of my brothers poising themselves on the edge of the nest before flying away never to return. Soon I followed them.

While I was thus beginning my career, you had reached maturity, and your faint warblings had ripened into rich melody. Those who imprisoned you gave you food, and you blessed them for it. I should have cursed them, my gentle friend! When the sun shone brightly they placed your cage outside the window, never thinking that sunstroke might cut you off. No, you were their slave, so that all seemed for the best from your narrow point of view. As for myself, I followed the life of my nomadic tribe, sharing its toils and dangers, and gladly submitting to the privations experienced on our journeys. I became strong to suffer, and so long as I had free air, I forgot that there was little else in my lot worth having. To crown all, you readily accepted the husband provided for you, and implicitly obeyed his slightest wishes. It was of course necessary you should obey some one, and perhaps as well that your master should be your husband. You are now surrounded by a numerous family whom you love; you are a model wife and mother. My ambition does not extend so far. Were I surrounded by a bevy of little screamers such as yours, I should die. Your devoted and much-loved husband would also be a terrible bore. Love, alas! has torn my poor heart so deeply during the time it became its temporary abode, that I have barred the door for ever against the foolish passion.

I am aware of your cruel opposition to the recital of my griefs, and you were kind enough to attribute my fall to the slight importance I myself attached to the duration of a union you thought should be eternal. You are welcome to say whatever you like, but you need never hope to find the true clue to our misery in such unions.

Society is wrongly modelled from beginning to end, and so long as the dry-rot of conventionality is left to destroy its foundation there will be no happiness for superior beings or loving spirits. Not until the entire structure is levelled with the ground.

I entrust my letter to a bird of passage who will cross your latitude; the postman is so impatient to continue his course that I am compelled to postpone the details of my journey.

THE SWALLOW'S SECOND LETTER.

I have striven to beguile the days of absence by relating my experiences as they occur *en route*, knowing that loving hearts find a charm in incidents the most simple and the most indifferent to strangers. The weather favours my progress, and nature is arrayed in her gayest attire. It seems, indeed, as if the kindly sun shone her brightest to cheer me on my way.

I have made a multitude of new acquaintances, nevertheless you need neither feel jealous nor uneasy on my account. I have not the leisure, still less the desire, to make friends, although I am forced at times to halt and acknowledge courtesies, as my quality of stranger has opened the hearts and homes of many hospitable tribes. Notwithstanding the fact that pressing invitations pour in upon me, I studiously refuse to accept them, preferring as I do my wandering life, full of all that is unexpected and capricious, above the daintiest fare and the finest society.

You predicted ennui and disenchantment. I still happily await the advent of these foes, taking my amusements when and where I find them. Up to the present moment these last have come unbidden to my door.

This morning I breakfasted *tête-à-tête* with the most accomplished singer I have ever heard, a Nightingale, who, willingly yielding to my entreaties, at the close of our repast sang some of his favourite pieces.

It was not without a feeling of vanity that I thought of those who would have given anything to fill my place. All distinctions, you know, are flattering, and the one which made me the sole listener to harmony so divine, made me more important in my own eyes.

I was strongly impressed with the simplicity of the artist. Seeing him so *négligé* in his dress, so careless in his posture and manner, no one would have thought that he was a person so distinguished, at least I have still a strange illusion that prompts me to look for talent only beneath a grave and dignified exterior. I have discovered that this is simply an illusion, you will therefore admit I have made some progress.

This remarkable tenor informed me that he lives for his pleasure, the best mode of living one can adopt; so he said, but I doubted the soundness of the opinion, and was careful not to be led away by doctrine so heterodox.

A happy and useless existence is not what I dream of, I who have the faculties of feeling and understanding. My desire is to add one more stone to the edifice which is rising up in the shade on the ruins of a dying civilisation. I have thought for some time of entering upon a literary career—all my tastes lie in that direction—as it would enable me to carry out my schemes for the regeneration of females. This question has absorbed my attention from my earliest youth. I can picture you smiling at what you call my folly and ambition, let me tell you once for all, you can no more conceive the pure happiness to which I aspire than I can accept life in your style.

But what does it matter; although we differ in opinion, our friendship is true, lasting, and sincere. The charming sweetness of your character enables you to overlook my faults and my extreme vivacity, and in return I hope that my deep regard helps to render your captivity less galling and monotonous.

I have just left my amiable songster, and, strange as it may appear, without regret. My curiosity and thirst for knowledge increase daily since I have at last begun to see and learn. A Jay whom I met in the environs preceded me, and promised to warmly recommend me on her way. In short, I can never find space to name, far less to praise, all those who have received me with a fraternal welcome. Had I followed your timid advice, I should have been constantly on my guard against tokens of affection, in case they might be held out as snares to betray me. But when I reflect on the life you lead, I am not surprised to find you swayed by warped notions of the world and its winged tribes. You cannot form just impressions of objects seen through the bars of a cage, they must appear distorted and confused. It must be so. You have never left your retreat, and your little world is filled by five or six creatures, objects of affection; all this renders it impossible for you to give an intelligent account of things of which you know absolutely nothing, or to appreciate without error what you have never seen.

It is true your youth was passed in a spacious aviary, where you respectfully received the lessons and counsels of some old fellows reputed for their wisdom; even these venerable teachers never breathed the air of liberty, and the sort of experience of which they were proud they owed solely to their great age, and not to free and independent research. I feel certain that I shall learn all these sages knew, and more, in a single journey. Before, indeed, I can venture to advocate reform in any shape I must travel, and read the living books in birds of every feather. I must study the degrading positions into which females of many so-called civilised lands have drifted, and find out how best to befriend them. My heart is filled by immense projects, and I need not disguise the fact that I may not see you for many days.

Adieu, it is getting late; I continue my journey—always southwards.

THE CANARY TO THE SWALLOW.

Will this letter ever reach you, my child? It is impossible to say, as I am ignorant of the direction of your last flight. I scarcely venture to hope that one day your eyes will fall on these words of maternal solicitude. Yet should fortune favour me, you will find that my affection is still unchanged, although it manifests itself in grumbling fears for the safety of a spirit so adventurous.

I grieved to see you set out on your journey, nor could I conceal my apprehension for your safety. Unfortunately the union of our hearts does not extend to our ideas, accordingly I did not succeed in changing your plans. Far from regarding myself as infallible, I own my mistake in wishing only for the things attainable in my sphere of life. If this be an error, yours is surely a greater one—the ambition which aspires to everything beyond your reach. The false inspiration derived from books has led you into a dark road, along which your tutors, believe me, will never follow you. Your life has become an illusion, and the more complete the illusion, the more terrible will the disenchantment prove. When the hour of awakening does come, as come it will, I tremble for the result.

I know that I am a mere dotard, and you are right to complain of my persistency in heaping sermons upon your head. Complain if you will, but allow me still to preach.

I have been told that many of our sex use their feathers for writing, and I perceive with regret that you are yielding to the popular mania with which they are possessed. For myself I seek nothing but knowledge, and I should like to know what good end is served by soiling snow-white paper. Let us handle this subject freely. Either you have great talent, small talent, or no talent at all. I do not see it can be otherwise. If by fatality you are favoured with great talent, as are the males, who make laws for others and reputations for themselves, these very males, by reason of constitutional jealousy, will not permit you to rise superior to themselves. The highest fame has always been, and must always be, male-fame, ill begotten as it is at times. That being so, females are by law, and, as males say, by nature, unfitted to fill the loftiest posts of honour. They are essentially the potter's clay fashioned into humble vessels suited to adorn or to become useful in the household, whereas the males are the marble of which monuments are made.

Apart from the public life in which you are the slave of fame, you may wish to have a private domestic life hidden away from the world, to which you may betake yourself when weary of triumph and tinsel. But where will you find a partner vain or humble enough to share your lot, to joyfully wear the ridiculous livery inflicted on him by your success? Who would be the husband of a great female? Certainly no one you could respect and look up to for counsel and advice. You will remain, then, powerful and solitary. This is all very fine, but the position is trying, and high intelligence can better serve its God by dutifully lifting a small but compact circle to its own level of happiness than by striving to move the world. Fame brings many little cares of which I have not spoken; it has to bear hatred, envy, calumny—troubles these which seldom invade the quiet nest. On a column in sight of all, and in the full blaze of noonday light, the flaws and defects of the finest marbles are all observed and attacked by the critics. Let us descend from the column and come to the nicely-poised mind that would be so charming in some obscurer spots if only it could be schooled to perform its great feats in the shady nooks of the world. Here I lay my finger on the root of your malady. One makes a very good show among a circle of indulgent friends, but the public ought not to be disappointed, for they did not complain of the want of your special talent, and did not invite you to become their idol in the temple of fame. One must walk upwards to this shrine with timid step, for there are more thorns than roses by the way. When the foot grows bolder, one becomes used to the compliments that are lavished, as well as to the curses that are heaped, on one's head by those over whose prostrate forms one tramples. At last life loses its lustre, and you become the slave of a cold, cruel, callous mind, possessed by aspiring to a glory it can never attain. Critics, at first silent, grow tired and bite; they rudely signify to your astonished friends that after all you are no Eagle, but only a Swallow.

This dawn of opposition irritates you, and self-love seeks consolation in the rapid flatteries of supporters whose pride prompts them to sustain you at all hazards, and the clever head, which might have been a reasonable one, is turned and lost!

I will, with your leave, now pass on to the third point in my observations, glancing for a moment at the picture of a daughter, wife, or mother who, in addition to all the other virtues, cultivates literature. She must indeed be an amiable authoress who with one hand rocks the babe to sleep, while with the other she wields the pen that is to wake the world.

During periods of inspiration the children tear her manuscripts, and add to her finest pages a sort of illumination on which she had not reckoned. Here you have a faithful description of this fantastic being whose infants are reared on a mixture of milk and ink. It is not, however, into the ridiculous that I fear to see you fall. I know your tastes too well, and hope they will shield you from such depths of depravity.

What I dread most is the vanity which has led you to adopt a course so ridiculous as advocating the right of females. It may lead you into many grievous mistakes unless common sense comes to the rescue.

I have spoken thus freely in order that my advice may be of service to you. Had I loved you less, my letter would have been milder and more pleasant to read. You may find it a bitter pill to swallow, but it will cure your malady!

THIRD LETTER FROM THE SWALLOW.

A NEST OF ROBINS.

I have by the merest chance fallen in with a friend, a most obliging creature, who will wait for this letter and deliver it to you. He is the bearer of important despatches, and appears worthy of the trust placed in him. While he explores the environs of my present halting-place, I hastily take up the pen to let you know my whereabouts, and to recount the events of my journey. Happily they are few and far between.

As you do not seem to approve of female genius, I must make an effort to suppress the poetry that flows naturally from my pen. When I have finished a volume of inspired writing, you shall have a copy to study at leisure. Then, and not till then, shall I expect justice at your hands.

I should have delayed writing, had circumstances not forced me to remind you of my existence.

The day dawned under depressing auspices, which will account for the sad tone of this epistle. On arriving in this delightful neighbourhood, I made the acquaintance of a most agreeable family, consisting of a father, mother, and two little ones, the latter still under shelter of the maternal wings. As they had greeted my arrival with much grace and show of kindness, I thought it my duty, on waking this morning, to make a formal call at their nest. The manner in which I was received raised them tenfold in my estimation, but just as I had left them to return to my lodging, the air was suddenly filled with cries of distress. On wheeling round, I perceived that the situation was dreadful: one of the young brood had fallen to the ground in imprudently trying his wings; although the fall was not great, danger was none the less imminent. An enormous bird of prey, after swooping through the air in ominous circles, descended like a stone, straight to the scene of the disaster. The mother's resolution was soon taken; addressing a few words to her husband touching the care of those she was leaving behind, and casting a fond look on the loved ones, she descended to the ground. There, showing a bold front to the enemy, she covered her little one with her wings; but the dread foe kept slowly approaching, and at last quickened his pace, trusting to the immobility of his victim for an easy victory. The poor mother unflinchingly met her doom; for the fierce bird, with eyes of fire, pounced down upon her and carried her away, leaving the little one

unharmed on the ground. After a moment's silence, the father descended and bore from the sad spot all that had been left by the bird of prey. I laid the little one in the hollow of the nest and took the vacant place of the mother. My sympathy rendered me speechless, while the father was mute with grief, he whose breast but a moment before had been bursting with joyous song. Suddenly a dull noise sounded near, our heads turned to the quarter whence a new danger seemed to threaten us. Imagine our joy when, in place of danger, we beheld our oppressor felled to the earth by an unseen hand, and the lost one returning safe to the nest. The delight of thus meeting one whom we thought dead filled all our hearts, and caused us to feel as one in happiness.

Yet I feared the indiscretion of remaining too long to share their joy, and had just retired when a huge animal, one of the species inhabiting towns called Poacher, whistling gaily, approached the tree which sheltered the Robins. On his back he carried a bag, from which the head of their enemy hung out, and on his shoulder the instrument that delivered them. The poor mother could not restrain a cry of joy on recognising her dead foe. It was a cry that might have moved a heart of stone, but brutes, it is said, have no hearts.

"Oh! oh!" cried the Poacher, "you sing sweetly, your song is most agreeable, but I would prefer the sound of you roasting on the spit. The little ones would not be worth eating, still one must be careful not to separate what God has united."

After these words, he brought down my friends and consigned them to his bag. That is the reason of my sadness."

THE SWALLOW'S FOURTH LETTER.

MY DEAR FRIEND,—I have been suffering for some days past from the effects of a slight accident which befell me on the road and compelled me to rest. In spite of regrets and impatience, I see no prospect of moving out of my narrow uncomfortable abode. Yet I ought to feel thankful for shelter of any kind. Overtaken some distance from my resting-place by a great storm, the wind drove me with such violence against a wall as to fracture my leg. Nothing surprises me more than my inability to proceed, the injury seems so trifling. A tribe of Sparrows, who, with characteristic foresight, established themselves before the bad weather set in beneath the roof which shelters me, have shown me great kindness. Unfortunately for me the sun soon reappeared, and his first rays have carried off my good-hearted hosts; even my helplessness had no power to detain them. I therefore suffer all the more, as I had given them credit for pure disinterested charity. What little they have left in the shape of food will soon be exhausted, and I am still too weak to forage for myself.

It is at such a time as this, pressed by poverty and enfeebled by sickness, that all the true friendship I have enjoyed in life proves a real comfort to me. Now I feel the curse of solitude and the need of a partner's care and affection.

Although I might have weighed before starting the dangers of so long a journey, and accordingly felt neither surprise nor discouragement at this first mishap, I am certain that you, who dread everything which menaces the uniformity of your life, would have borne the affliction with greater patience and fortitude. You have accustomed yourself to abide contentedly in one spot, so that this enforced repose which galls me, had you been the sufferer, would have in no way ruffled the calm of your head and heart. We are differently constituted, so differently that this constraint will drive me mad if I have to endure it much longer.

Oh how it affects my temper, and tunes my ear to a painful pitch of perfection! There is not a bird within hearing that does not sing false. My nearest neighbour is a Magpie, the stepmother of two little warblers, to whom she is a perfect tyrant, holding them in complete slavery, and taking pleasure in corrupting their natural tastes by making them sing all day long contralto airs unsuited to their voices.

This female friend is a widow who receives no one, and who spends her days in scolding, an occupation which she varies by picking faults and feathers out of her step-children. I flatly refused the proposal she made through an old Crow, to replace her when she felt inclined to leave the nest in search of pleasure. This occurs chiefly in the evening. I think she is a person of very doubtful morality indeed. The offer was a tempting one, but I would rather starve than aid the dark schemes of this wicked female; for dark they must be, as she takes no

one into her confidence save a blackguard-looking Crow who, I am certain, lives by plunder.

So you see I not only have the misfortune to be, but to have made, a formidable enemy of this unscrupulous dame. I think I shall risk destroying my bad leg, and limp out of the dilemma into pastures new and an atmosphere more congenial.

You whose goodness once drew me out of a like scrape, will pity my misfortunes and sigh for me more profoundly than I deserve. Still the thought of your kind interest will strengthen me nearly as much as if you were here to lend me a helping wing. I seem to feel as it were your guardian spirit hovering over my head; so real does it appear that I shall implicitly trust to its guidance. This you will set down as a morbid fad of mine, as your spirit knows better than to trust itself into such latitudes. Be that as it may, your influence, if not your spirit, is ever with me.

THE SWALLOW'S FIFTH LETTER.

It is now a month since I left my last lonely retreat. A Linnet who was wandering about without any fixed purpose promised to help me. You may judge how eagerly I seized the proffered help, and the glorious prospect of quitting my disagreeable neighbour, and the still more disagreeable hole in which I had been cooped up so long. My foot is far from well, and, although my friend tries to persuade me to the contrary, I fear I shall be lame to the end of my days. I ought here to quote the fable of the "Two Pigeons," so often brought under my notice when you lectured me on my vagabond life.

Surrounded by strangers, enfeebled by suffering, my future seems to grow daily darker and more dim, while no opportunity offers for the ventilation of my peculiar views. The males here, as elsewhere, are our masters—one must own it if for no higher reason than to get one's share of the necessaries of life. The cause seems hopeless, unless one could hit upon some quinine or vaccine matter that would cure us of the weaknesses and vanities of female nature. As it is, the malady or weakness is there, and males, as of old, continue their endeavours to beat, kick, and govern it out of us; one day they will succeed, when one kick too many will make us their masters. As for myself, who have not come under this peculiar bondage, I would gladly give my life for the enfranchisement of our sex; but females will persist in religiously following in the beaten track, pleasantly taking the alternate love and kicks as they come, and retarding progress. They thus maintain a prodigious inert force, against which active energy is broken like the waves of the sea against a solid rock.

I shudder at the thought of our impotency, and know not what course to follow that my name may receive the blessing of generations yet unborn. I shall wait, like a true philosopher, for my good star to light the path of this noble ambition and lead me to my goal!

My Linnet, who has no ideas, and is not accustomed to reflect, will, I fear, soon grow weary of my company, and of the heavy task her heart has imposed on her. I am not a very agreeable companion, and I do not fail to notice that she endeavours to escape from the *tête-à-tête* of our daily life.

Although sincerely in the humour to see the world, she took me yesterday to a meeting which at any other time would have filled me with hope.

Our sex alone were admitted, and the end to which all my aspirations tend was the theme the young hearts were waiting to discuss with noble impatience. Several points as to the ways and means by which our rights were to be secured and guarded were dwelt upon by various speakers, after which, I am sorry to say, a number of ill-favoured females entertained the meeting by recounting their love-experiences, gossip, and scandal.

These absorbing topics found a patron in the mistress of the occasion, an old Ringdove, who amiably recalled the far-off love-adventures of her youth.

Tired and dispirited, I retired to rest, not to sleep, but to brood over the future, till at last, weary of thinking of the where-to-go and what-to-do of to-morrow, my eyes closed for the night.

THE SWALLOW'S SIXTH LETTER.

MY DEAR FRIEND,—After so many shattered hopes, so many vain endeavours, I determined to narrow my ambition and end my journey with the Linnet. Were you not a grave true-hearted Canary, you would smile at this consummation. I am completely at your mercy, and you are too good to abuse your advantage.

Although there is something supremely ridiculous in all the fuss with which I set out to reform society, when one considers the result, I claim the privilege of pointing out that my scheme is none the less sound and good because it has failed. I am not converted. Society is not ripe for such a measure of reform. I have pleaded, solicited, preached—to deaf ears—and urged the adoption of my views; the males listened and shrugged their shoulders, the females refused to listen and shrugged their shoulders, and in order to continue the struggle single-handed, I should require a stock of patience with which nature has not seen fit to endow me.

Above all, I am lame, and to undertake—no matter what in this world—even to promote a good cause, one must begin with personal attractions that will appeal to the eye. A lame Swallow has therefore not much chance of success in this fast age.

The spring will again find me in Paris, when I shall present my little companion, who I am sure will please you, notwithstanding her gaiety. She may even seem to you giddy. All I can say is, she is genuine and good-hearted. I must tell you she fell in love the other day with a young fop, with whom she would have decamped had I not caught her in time to arrest her fate. I gave her a page or two of my own early experience, which produced a deep and, let us hope, lasting impression.

She wants looking after, guiding, and controlling. Yet why should I speak thus in opposition to my doctrine of freedom for the female sex, and lay my plans for her guidance? Can it be that my principles are gradually changing? It cannot be! Soon you will see me, my friend, sad but submissive, having found the world bad, and being unwilling to force it to become better. You will find me, as you would say, disenchanted—as I would say, reasonable, although, to tell the truth, the two expressions may mean one and the same thing. I have travelled far in search of that wisdom which I might have obtained without going out of my way. In my narrow view of life I had only been willing to notice the shortcomings of what is, and the advantages of what is not.

These advantages are still manifest, so also is the danger of any change, even though it might bring a certain measure of amelioration. It seems, indeed, better to keep and improve a defective form of government than to change it for something new—however good—and untried.

My only ambition now is to end my days near you.

MEDICAL ANIMALS.

A VENERABLE Crow announces the approaching death of one of our colleagues; he flatters himself on being able to foretell the event. His prognostication is, we should say, certain to be verified, for at that moment the poor sufferer enters; he was a Dog—we say was, for he is now, alas! nothing more than the skeleton, the shadow of that long-suffering animal. We tenderly inquire how he feels.

"Ah," he replies, "my only feeling is pain; they tried to cure me—that is, my illness—and behold the result. Ah, my brothers, what have you done? what is the world coming to? You have provoked the animals to write, your counsels have been pushed too far, many of us poor brutes have been forced to think. That is not all, some even dream of poetry, painting, and science. These fools would have us believe that such mad courses raise us above ourselves and our sublime instincts. Nightingales imagine themselves birds of prey, Donkeys masters of song, while Cats conceive they discourse the sublimest, sweetest harmony. Civilisation does it all; it is a muddle, my friends, a fearful muddle. But the last notion is by far the most dreadful. Our brothers, weary of dying a natural death, have resolved to found chairs of medicine and surgery. Already they have begun their work; behold me, the result of their experiments—skin and bone, gentlemen! skin and bone! I have just been ordering myself crutches and a coffin. Dear me, how faint I feel!"

"Have a drink?" said the Fox.

"Most thankfully," replied the Dog, who had been a very jolly Dog in his day.

The Fox, preparing pen and ink, requests him to write down his mischances for the good of posterity. The Dog obeys—it is his nature to do so—only he requests the Fox to write at his dictation.

"Being honest," he commenced, "I have no desire to conceal anything. There have been for some time amongst men certain individuals called Veterinaries—most damaging rascals; one is no sooner in their clutches, than they bleed, purge, and put one to the direct straits, bestowing a diet not fit for a Cat. I object to this most strongly, to this last phase of their treatment. They imagine that disease has a craving for food, and determine to kill it by systematic starvation; the result is too often the death of the animal, and not the disease, which lives and spreads to others. I was one of those who proposed a commission to inquire into and state facts. You would hardly conceive, gentlemen, on what fools—pardon—I mean on what creatures the choice fell; on Linnets and Moles—the one for clear sight, the other for seeing in the dark. The commission set to work, taking it for granted that the poor never complain without cause, and examined everybody as they would convicted felons. I do not know what happened, but soon a majority of the enlightened commissioners, who had discovered nothing, decided that the affair was understood. A compiler produced a work for which, in common with all the other members of the commission, he was handsomely rewarded, and that was all. As for me, I barked, howled, and manifested my disapproval; many of my friends thinking they ought to do the same, the agitation became general."

"Let that pass, my friend, let that pass," said the Fox; "everything has an end. Prudence and generosity forbid our dwelling on this subject."

"In short," replied Médor, somewhat crest-fallen (Médor was our hero's name), "we agreed to form schools of secret medicine, and faculties of clandestine surgery, under the presidency of the Cock of Æsculapius and the Serpent of Hippocrates.

"Every animal, part of whose flesh or intestines had been used as a medicine, laid claim to the invention of the science, and all of them, from the least to the greatest, held that they each had been used by man-doctors as universal panaceas. Would you believe it, these biped physicians dared to prescribe Tortoise broth for languor, and jelly of Viper for impurity of the blood!"

"Médor, you are wise, and if ever we add an Academy of Sciences to our journal, you shall belong to it."

"To the Academy, Prince?"

"No, to our journal; who do you take yourself for? Continue."

"You have not forgotten, gentlemen, that your humble servant objected chiefly to the diet, not to the science"——

"Is it much longer?" inquired the Fox.

"I must finish my narrative, sir; that is all I can conscientiously say."

"You are honest, but that is an useless quality nowadays."

"My brothers," continued Médor, "if we confine our attention to the remedies prescribed by men, we shall only foster sickness and hasten death. I once heard the remark made by a man, that the sublimest philosophy was that which stood the test of common sense. I am inclined to think that the sublime in the art of healing would be to return to and trust to instinct. These words are simple, but profound; think over them, although they will meet only with the world's scorn."

"Decidedly," said the Fox. "It is most unreasonable, when one wants to found a science, to begin with common sense; that is a vulgar natural gift which can only stand in the way of science."

"That is quite evident," murmured a Bear, who had come forward with a subscription.

Médor scratched his ear and proceeded in a lower tone. "My opinions were blamed, I was cursed, beaten, and treated as an incendiary. When I wished to raise my paws to heaven to protect my innocence, one of them was broken, and my colleagues ironically inquired what remedy instinct and common sense suggested to me under the circumstances, and if any to apply it. But as they had taken care to knock me on the head before asking the question, I was unable to reply, and so stood convicted of insanity."

"Herein is logic!" said the Fox.

"I was put to bed—on straw—and the chamber was soon filled by a Leech, a Crane, a heteroclitic animal, a Spanish Fly, and a dignified idler, who seated himself as soon as he arrived. The heteroclitic creature, a dry, cold, carefully-dressed personage, declared the *séance* open, the object of which was to effect my cure by purely scientific means. I thought I was dead, but a Sow who acted as my nurse reassured me by saying—

"'Do not be afraid; the good die, the bad remain.'

"'Old mother,' I replied, 'you were not placed here to poison my ear, on the contrary'—— and I turned on my miserable couch.

MEDICAL ANIMALS. 347

"The Leech then pronounced me delirious, and intimated his intention of sucking out the malady through a blood-vessel in my throat.

Happily the Spanish Fly noticed that my tongue protruded in token of exhaustion, and proposed to apply what he termed a counter-irritant

—that is, to set up a most painful competition between disease and remedy.

"'My dear sir,' said the Crane to the Fly, 'neither your treatment nor your opinion can have the least weight; it is a well-known fact that six thousand four hundred of you weigh only a miserable half-pound. Half a pound weight, think of that.'

"'What is your opinion, Mr. Idler?' inquired the Heteroclite.

"'I practise the leisurely science of meditating on the mysteries of life and death. We must consult together, and weigh the situation before we can hope to arrive at a just diagnosis of this important case. As a consulting physician, I'——

"'My opinion is,' gravely continued the first speaker, 'that the abnormal humidity of the feet, head, chest, and all the members, is one of the gravest symptoms of this case.'

"The Seal shrugged his shoulders.

"'Humidity I hold to be most dangerous, whether in the shape of rain, dew, or the saturation of a heated atmosphere. An umbrella or waterproof may ward off its influence, our patient is beyond that stage and requires more subtle remedies. As for myself, I am obliged to observe the greatest caution. I never travel without my carriage, and to walk over a cold flagstone without a carpet would be to court death. I have done: that being so, I make it a rule to inquire who is to pay me?'

"'And us,' cried a voice outside.

"'Who are you?'

"'We are the animal surgeons who alone can effect a cure; open, or we will cut our way through the door, just as we would to the heart of a disease.'

"The door was opened, and the Saw-fish entered, followed by its attendants. The operator showed his teeth, felt my pulse, and soon a circle formed round the couch. Under the circumstances it was natural to faint, and I did my best to do so; but as extremes sometimes meet, and there is but a step from fainting to delirium, I became mad. Dark scenes of dissecting-room practice passed before me. My name had changed from Médor to No. 33, just as if I had become a cab on a stand or a watchman. I was no longer a solitary invalid, but one of many stretched on beds in a long ward. My neighbour No. 32 had passed away, or rather his remains had been conveyed to a sort of dining-room at the end of the ward. The sole ornaments of this chamber were skeletons and bones. What had become of the flesh?"

"'My friend, these bones were doubtless fossils. You are slandering your fellow-citizens. But you are free, continue.'

"I wished to raise my voice against this profanation, this brutality, this sacrilege, but the Shark, biting my ear till it bled, advised me to be calm, resolute, and happy.

"'You must not puzzle your brain about the mysteries of clinical surgery,' said he.

"'I have already done that,' I replied.

"'Hush! I am about to describe your case to these gentlemen, who are only too anxious to see you on your legs again. It is necessary they should be made acquainted with the prognostics, diagnostics, the symptomatology, the dietetic and, shall we say, numismatic details, not one of which shall be overlooked. If you are not instantly cured, we will not waste precious time by following in the footsteps of physicians from whom we are separated by the *strictum* and the *laxum*, humours, mucous membranes, pores, not to name the 66,666 sorts of fever which specially attack the animal organisation. We will not occupy ourselves with Aristotle, Pliny, Ambrose Paré, a miserable idealist, who has said, "I dressed your wounds, but God healed them." No, that is not our business. Our patron, our hero, is Alexander; our practice, to tighten or relax the tissues—oh no! Alexander knew better than that, he cut them.'

"'Long live Alexander!' said the Vultures, Rats, and Crows of the audience.

"'You have understood me clearly,' said the speaker. 'I have now the honour to ask the opinion of the Saw-fish, my colleague, whose doctrines I hold in the highest esteem, although I have my own way of applying them; and now, gentlemen, we will proceed to incise the muscles, saw the bones, and in fact cure our patient.'

"They are bound to kill me, I thought; a thousand times death rather than vivisection."

"And you played the dead Dog?" said the Fox.

"Just so, and some good little fellow said that it would be unwise to operate owing to my weakness: it often happens that the most trifling incidents delay the greatest events."

"Say that again," said the Fox with a tinge of irony, "it seems good."

"Sometimes, sir, the smallest incidents delay the greatest events. It so happened that the orator fell not on the one who had interrupted him, but on his neighbour, whom he accused of lifting the hospital lint and bearing it off to line his nest.

"A large Vulture, a provincial student, as might easily be seen from his huge cloak and cap stuck on the back of his head, dared to remark that the profession of surgery was one of liberty, and that professors had no right to interfere in the private affairs of their pupils. In this way the question of the missing lint was satisfactorily disposed of, and the lecturer proceeded.

"'Gentlemen, as the operation must be postponed for to-day, permit me, in the interests of science, to make a few remarks on the subject of morals.'

"That was flattering you," remarked the Fox.

"Perhaps it was, at any rate, the little sermon which I here abridge was lost on me.

"'Dear pupils, the true student of science is to a certain extent invested with a God-like nature; our profession is a priesthood, for you know the healing art in ancient times was only exercised by the priests: it requires therefore more than talent, it demands virtue.'

"'Oh! oh!!' exclaimed several students of the same year.

"'Medicine will again become a priesthood, or, if you prefer it, a social function; doctors will preside over the public hygiéne. The fewer maladies there are, the more will medicine be honoured and recompensed. But in order to arrive at this desirable end it is necessary to raise the qualifications of the profession, and to exclude many aspirants, otherwise each family will have its physician. What, then, would become of us when there is a doctor to each floor and another to each attic? The study of our science is painful and costly. It must be rendered doubly so to check the influx of those who either by talent or morality are unfitted to enter our ranks.'

"'But, my master,' said the Vulture, 'you are not reasonable; what you dread is the ability of the young generation which threatens to eat up your sinecures. Your paternal solicitude is misplaced!'

"Another student objected to slandering misery and privation, the true attributes that alone by strengthening and purifying genius render it serviceable to the world.

"'Yes,' he continued, 'I myself have known that life is a hard, bitter struggle, but God is still all-powerful. The snow that covers every blade of grass and every seedling beneath its chill mantle, never caused me to doubt, even for an instant, that spring would come arrayed in its blossoms, or that autumn would again fill the storehouse with fruit and grain. I have known hunger, but never despair. What matters the numbers pressing forward to compete with us in allaying pain? There is room for all who honestly strive to make the world more joyous!'

"'Long live joy!' cried the Crow. 'Misery is the poetry of the cottage, just as the garret is the palace of students. If life becomes still harder, why, to-morrow we will move up a story higher nearer heaven—go to the roofs. Now, my friends, here is the whole truth in a nutshell, the houses of Paris must be viewed thus: our lofty attics contain the head, and therefore the brain, of this large city, something too of the heart. It is there one thinks, it is there one dreams, it is there one loves, while waiting to descend to the first floor, to meditate on ambition and riches. Our master may talk; for all that, he himself is a living proof of success—of the fact that very little merit indeed is frequently rewarded by much wealth and fame.'

"'Ah!' replied the Shark, 'you forget that one successful career is the product of a thousand failures. Only lofty qualities can bring the successful to the surface, while thousands sink into misery and obscurity. Some one said that the sun smiles on our successes, and the kindly earth throws her mantle over our failures. The truth is, the sun shines on a host of ungrateful convalescents, and the earth too soon receives our most astounding surgical cures!'

"The discussion was becoming too learned, I therefore slipped out by the foot of the bed—but not before they had resumed the discussion of my case—and left them in the thick of it to come here."

Saying this, the poor cripple made his bow and disappeared, totally regardless of the future of his important revelations.

We beg any one who may know the whereabouts of Médor to keep the secret to himself; being unable to help our fellow-creatures in distress, we wish them kept out of our way, or taken to our next-door neighbour, who has probably more time and money at his disposal.

THE GIRAFFE'S TABLETS.

JARDIN DES PLANTES.

LETTER TO HER LOVER IN THE DESERT.

PRAISED be the good spirits that protect Ants, Giraffes, and probably men! Before many days we shall meet, never to part.

The learned men of whom I shall presently speak, who in this land make the weather — bad weather, as a rule —have decreed in their wisdom that it is not good for Giraffes to be alone, as the social habits of our race can never be truly ascertained from the study of a single individual. How this happens I cannot explain. I have, however, put you in possession of the fact that you may know as much as I do myself.

Here I am transported to a land one finds it hard to get used to, a land where the sun is pale, the moon dim, the wind damp, the dust dry and dirty, and the air icy cold. Of the three hundred and sixty odd days which make up the year, it rains during three hundred and forty, when the roads become rivers unfit for the dainty foot of Giraffes. During winter the rain becomes white, and covers all things with one uniform dazzling carpet, which wounds the eye and saddens the heart. The water becomes solid, and misery waits upon birds and beasts, who perish on the banks of the streams without being able to quench their thirst.

The species of animal that rules in this region is the most ill-favoured of all God's creatures. His head, instead of conforming to our graceful model, is nearly round like a melon, and partly covered with short hair like hogs' bristles, only thicker, darker, and not so clean looking; his neck is almost hidden between his shoulders, and only develops by becoming thicker and shorter; his skin is of an earthy colour; and to complete this ridiculous picture, he has got into the stupid way of walking on his hind-legs, and swinging those in front to maintain his equilibrium. It is difficult to imagine any figure more vulgar or absurd. I am inclined to think that this poor animal is afflicted with a painful sense of his deformity, for he hides as much of his figure as possible. He uses for this purpose an artificial covering fabricated out of the bark of plants and skins of animals. This device does not mend matters, as it renders him an ugly piece of patchwork. The first sight of a man—that is the name by which this hideous animal is known—will cause you to be thankful you were born clothed by the Creator in matchless attire, and that you have never fallen into the hands of a Parisian tailor.

We express our sentiments and needs in simple sounds and looks; they, on the other hand—who appear formerly to have enjoyed the same privilege—carried away by a fatal instinct, or, if one must believe the wisest of them, subject to a destiny of incomparable punishment, supplanted nature's simple language by an almost continuous grumbling. They have invented sounds in abundance to signify what they don't want and can't get, and spend half their days in gabbling over the limited nature of their moral and physical appetites. These sounds sometimes express wishes, but more frequently what is called ideas. Ideas are in themselves nothing, although they are the key to all that is deficient, cross, and hostile in what these creatures call conversation. When two Men separate after conversing for hours, we may rest assured that the one ignores all that has been said by the other, and hates him more thoroughly than before.

It is also necessary for me to tell you that this animal is essentially ferocious, and feeds upon flesh and blood. This need not frighten you; either from his natural cowardice, or from a horrible refinement of ingratitude and cruelty, he only devours poor defenceless timid beasts, easy to surprise and kill, and who have often clothed him with their wool or enriched him with their service. Again, it is his custom to rear these victims in his own country. An animal from a strange land inspires a sort of religious respect, which is shown in the utmost care and homage. He lays out parks for the Gazelle, embellishes the Lion's den, and digs a pond for the Hippopotamus. As for myself, he had planted rows of trees with nourishing leaves; beneath my feet is a mossy sward and belt of fine sand, a miniature desert, while my dwelling is kept at a uniform temperature. His poor fellow-creatures would only be too delighted if he took the same care of them. He cares for them at a distance, and at times, without warning, breaks out into a frenzy and slaughters them right and left.

These massacres are said to be caused by some high-sounding nothing called a word or an idea. Men—being by nature harmless or unarmed—have invented destructive weapons of the most formidable kind. When they cannot agree about any given idea they bring out their weapons, and the side which works the greatest destruction of life and property is always right. Right is built upon the wreck of empires, so Men say, until some giant power proves right to be wrong and dethrones it, showing that right is a sort of weathercock that changes with every wind of government.

There are Men, and there are also extraordinary Men—that is, a class called Scholars. The grubs of these creatures are bred in books. Many of them die while yet buried in printed leaves, in the chrysalis state, from which they never emerge; but the Book-worm, after many days, ought, full fledged, to soar away into the light of science.

It is the duty of Scholars to pay more attention to the words in which ideas are expressed than to the ideas themselves, as well as to invent words, which few will understand, to denote the commonest things. When speaking, the Scholar is careful to use words so seldom pronounced, that it would be better if they were not pronounced at all.

Above all, the most interesting human type is Woman, a poor, soft,

ALL THE MEETINGS ARE MORE OR LESS ALIKE.

elegant, timid, delicate creature, who became the slave of Man. I do not know where or when, but he has trained her to submit to him like the Horse, either by force or cunning. I tell you she is by far the most graceful form in nature, yet Man spoils her appearance; she is seen to greater perfection without him. She has few sentiments save love; the need of loving some one or something shows itself early, and never leaves her. During her youth the hours are spent in conjuring up in her mind some ideal Man with whom she is to live a blissful life. She after a time becomes the wife of some one in whom she thinks she has found the lover of her dreams. Alas! too often the illusion soon passes away, and she learns that the fond image of her youth was a being of a higher sphere.

You will be surprised at my giving you so many details regarding this country and its animals, but as yet I have told you nothing about the way they govern themselves. Politics pure and simple is the science most talked about and least understood in France. If you listen to one person on the subject of politics, his ideas seem obscure; if to two, they are confused; if to three, they are chaotic. When the number of speakers increase to four or five, they are prepared to strangle each other. Judging from the universal favour in which I am held by all classes, it has once or twice crossed my mind that all their political sentiments had found a calm centre in myself, and that they would at last elect me their king. This seems all the more likely since Frenchmen are utterly unable to agree as to the exact moral and intellectual qualities which should adorn a prince, and it may be they have in a friendly way resolved to choose their masters according to height. By adopting this plan, party spirit would be demolished, and all questions settled by measurement.

Last week I resolved to be present at a meeting of deputies to be held nearer to the river than my abode. I accordingly bent my steps that way, and soon arrived at a sort of palace filled with a tumultuous throng.

The members of the Cabinet only differed from other men in characteristic ugliness, the result, it is said, of grave habits of thought, and of the manner in which they snatch their pleasures from the cares of office. What surprised me most was their activity, which never permitted them to rest for an instant in the same spot, for I was witnessing by chance one of the stormy meetings of the session. They tossed themselves about, jumped and mixed into a hundred confused

groups, apostrophising their adversaries with cries and menacing gestures, and showing their teeth with the most hideous grimaces. The object of most of them seemed to be to raise themselves above their fellows, and there were those who compassed this end by mounting on the heads and shoulders of their neighbours.

Unfortunately, though well pleased to witness the gambols of the assembly, owing to my superior stature I failed to catch a single word in the confusion of voices, and I retired sickened and deafened by the vociferation, grinding of teeth, whisking of tails, whistling and howling, without being able to form a conjecture as to the subject under discussion.

For all that, something was carried, and the speeches, it is said, appeared in the official organ next day in most harmonious prose. There are those who say that all the *séances* resemble this one in a greater or less degree, so I shall dispense with witnessing another.*

I had proposed to give you, before closing my letter, some specimens of the language now used in Paris. You will be able to form your own notions of it from the following sentences, which have just been exchanged between a young man with a Bison's beard, and a young woman with the eyes of a Gazelle, to whom he was trying to justify his long absence :—

"I was preoccupied, beautiful Isoline, with sublime ideas, of which your woman's heart has the noble intuition. Placed by the capacities which they have been willing to accord to me at the zenith of the adepts of perfectionabilisation, and long absorbed in philosophic, philanthropic, and humanitarian speculations, I was tracing the plan of a political encyclism which would moralise all peoples, harmonise all institutions, utilise all the faculties, and develop all the sciences ; but I was not the less drawn towards you by the most passionate attraction, and I "——

"Say no more," solemnly interrupted Isoline ; "do not think me a stranger to those lofty aspirations, and pray do not suspect my spirit capable of being charmed by the baits of a coarse nature. Proud of your destiny, dear Adhimar, in the sentiment which unites us I only see an elective affinity which the instinct of cohesion has confounded

---

* It is evident that the Giraffe falls into a mistake, which is scarcely an excusable one were she not quite innocent. Confined in the Jardin des Plantes, she could not visit the Chamber of Deputies, which she imagines she is describing. What she did see was the Monkeys' palace.—ED.

with a sympathetic individuality, or, to express myself more clearly, the fusion of these isolated idiosyncrasies which feel the need of becoming simultaneous."

Here the conversation was continued in a low voice, and I think I may suppose that it became more intelligible, for the young philosopher was beaming with pleasure when he left Isoline.

THE GIRAFFE.

THE CROAKINGS OF A CROW.

THE inferiority of man to the lower animals of the world does not admit of the faintest shadow of doubt, at least that is my belief, and in making it known, it must be understood that it is done honestly and without malice. I am one of the few creatures against whom man is powerless to do harm, happily considering me beneath his notice, as my flesh is too tough even to make soup for paupers. I am, in fact, a Crow, and consequently view the world and its inhabitants from a noble elevation.

Men themselves are conscious of their deplorable condition, and fully aware that their complex bodies are frequently impotent to respond to the wishes of their active brains. Poor architects are they who design impossible structures which no hands can build. Pitiable! pitiable!! Does any one believe that they are unconscious of their inferiority? If so, what can account for their eternal complaints, their incessant misunderstandings and litigations?

Mock, write, invent fables of moustached men. You shall never be able to render us animals ridiculous unless you first endow us with human vices, passions, and aspirations. You compel my pity, poor pariahs of the world; you who could not live for a day without us —without the wool of our friend the Sheep to make your attire, the silk of the Worm to line your coats or cover your umbrellas, for rain is often fatal to you, while the refreshing wind penetrates your thin pink skin and chills you to the heart. You doubtless wish you were a Crow like myself, to fly through the air in place of crawling along with your too solid bodies through slimy city streets. I dislike you least on horseback, and you yourselves are proud of borrowing a certain dignity from a brute; but the dignity belongs to the Horse, not to the rider, although the latter accounts it all his own, and, strange to say, thinks himself superior to the animal that carries him. Are you not weaker than the Ox or the Elephant? Does not the smallest insect become a burden to you? A Fly tickling your nose drives you mad, and in place of setting the misguided insect free, you take its life.

The sting of a Gnat swells and deforms your face, and spoils the image of the God that made you; while the bite of a reptile a hundred

times smaller than yourself proves fatal. Moreover, you cannot deny that you have spent whole nights in a bloodthirsty search for the Flea that has banished sleep from your pillow, and the little offender has after all evaded you. Tell me why do you grow pale before a caged Lion? It is, alas! his gentlest caress would break every bone in your frail body.

"Ah, well! We own our physical infirmity; it is of no consequence, as we are princes by our intelligence, and on that ground we defy you, Master Crow."

You flatter yourselves, gentlemen. Do you suppose for a moment you have more ingenuity, ability, and patience than the Spider, who unaided produces the silken material and weaves the most marvellous fabric in the world? You cannot even make lint compared to it, although the cotton is grown ready to your hand. Who, like the Spider, can prevail upon his food to come to his door, and secure it so cunningly? and who so deftly can escape danger? Again, are you more crafty than the Fox, more subtle than the Serpent? You boast of your heart, and yet when you want a symbol of tenderness or devotion it is among our ranks you look for it. Show me the human mother who, like the Pelican, would daily pierce her side, or, like the Kangaroo, bear the constant burden of her little ones. Talk as you like of your paternal kindness, and the sacrifices you make to bring up your children; in short, you parade everything that will in any way minister to your own vanity. You are careful to publish your good deeds with assumed humility, that the world may trumpet them abroad. But for constancy and unobserved devotedness to her offspring the meanest bird will put mankind to the blush. Show me the father who, while attending to the duties of his office, would prepare his children's food and rock them to sleep.

We, the birds and brutes of creation, do naturally what costs you an almost superhuman effort. We have no need of moral and religious institutions to teach us how dutifully to fill our allotted spheres. Natural instinct is our teacher, and we obey its faintest whisperings. We have no schools of music, the arts, or sciences; for all that, the Nightingale's notes are true and harmonious, and the comb of the Bee continues to be constructed with matchless beauty and precision.

You live in families, so do we; but supposing a human family were compelled to spend an entire winter, like the poor Marmots, shut up in one dark chamber, what would be the result? I fear some broken tempers and more fractured bones.

You are proud, so is the Peacock; but the latter lives on his pride, while you frequently die of it—it chokes you.

What can I say about human courage?—simply nothing. My own

good nature prompts me here to draw the veil, only adding a word on the subject of mendicity.

In our beastly kingdom mendicity is unknown. We would rather starve than mimic all the ills of life in order to gain a beggarly living.

When we have performed our allotted tasks in life, and are unable to provide for ourselves, we die. Not so with men; they are doomed to cling to the last shreds of life when all its joy and lustre have gone, and

live on as if overtaken by some fearful retribution. But here I touch upon a large and mysterious question, and being a modest Crow, I shall leave it, as I fold my wings to sleep, for the night is falling and the ink has dried on my quill. The twilight hour of love is passing, and the Nightingale is tuning his lute.—I have the honour to salute you.

Souvenirs of an Old Rook.

FRAGMENTS FROM AN ALBUM OF TRAVELS.

"Non animum mutant qui trans mare currunt."—HORACE, Epistles.

SUMMARY.

Why does one travel?—An old castle.—The Duke and Duchess.—The Terrace.—An old Falcon.—The hosts of the Terrace.—Make yourself a Grand Duke.—A magic Carp.—How an Owl dies of love.—How Madame Crow ends her story.

. . . . . To begin, why does one travel? Is not repose the greatest blessing in the world? Is it, after all, worth one's while going out of one's way to see or to avoid anything? Can one honestly say that any advantage is gained by travelling?

Some pursue happiness, and the pursuit invariably ends in the grave; others flee the evil which no one escapes. The Swallows follow the sun and flit with its beams, while Marmots close their eyes on all his wintry glory and court repose, having faith that nature will again awake at Phœbus's bidding. There are many creatures who leave their homes to face unknown dangers, but few return, for space is vast, and the insatiable ocean cries for ever, "Give! give!" Many more go to sleep and few awake, for sleepers are near to the death that broods over them. The Butterfly travels because he has wings. The Snail, rather than remain in one place, shoulders his house and moves along; the unknown is so attractive. Hunger wounds these, love woos those; for the former some happy region teems with food, for the latter with sentiment. Those alone who travel without aim are burdened with satiety. As for the Squirrel who turns in his cage, we may say, "S'agiter n'est pas avancer,"* Unfortunately, like him, many move, but few make progress. Thus it is said that the wise ones of the world prefer peaceful misery to active happiness; they are content to live on in the spot where they were born without troubling their heads about anything beyond the limits of their horizon, and they die, if not happy, at least tranquil. But it may be that this wisdom comes from the coldness of their hearts, and the weakness and powerlessness of their wings.

No one has answered the question, Why does one travel? better than a great writer of our sex, George Sand, who said, "One travels because no one is happy here below." It must be that motion is everywhere, nothing is perfect, therefore there is no repose. As for me, I have travelled not because I had a liking for motion, for I loved my nest and the short walks over the village green.

"What is the good of these interminable speculations and questions at the beginning of your tale?" said an old friend and neighbour, whose advice I sometimes ask, always reserving my right to do as I please. "It is not because you occupy yourself with philosophy, &c. &c., that you must bore your readers. You will be accounted a pedant. Are you going to favour us with the particulars of all you have seen and thought during the century you have been in the world? Do you intend, after the mistake of living so long, to add the folly of travelling interminably over paper? Believe me, if you really want to be thought a bold adventurous spirit, a travelling genius, write a book of travels. The century of Columbus has passed, one has no need to discover new lands, one may now set up as a traveller at less cost and no risk. Discover, if you will, the spot where you were born, your neighbours and your neighbours' affairs, yourself, or nothing, and write about them. Relate—what does it matter how you relate, so long

* S. La Valette, Fables.

as you do relate something? It is the time for stories. Imitate your contemporaries, those illustrious travellers, who, in the four corners of the globe, bravely write down their impressions while reclining on the straw or down of the paternal nest. Follow their example; I say, jot down everything about yourself, your friends, your servants; the time you dine, and all about your appetite. Detail the dishes you have, and those you have not, institute a comparison between the feathers of different birds, taking care never to dip beneath the surface, confine your descriptions to dress and manners. Whenever you come across an old tale, colour it freely and serve it up as new, and I shall promise you a great success. You will fall into many grave errors. What of that? they will never be discovered till after you are dead, when it may amuse your children to defend your reputation."

These reflections had a certain fascination for me, the advice might be good, or bad, it was at any rate easy to follow. But my conscience kept me out of harm's way, and I replied—

"One cannot always follow one's own inclination, as for me, I am an honourable Rook, and will do my best at all times. If what you have just said is intended for advice, it is so precious you ought to keep it to yourself."

"Be it so," he said, bowing gravely.

I returned the salute and again took up my pen. I am undoubtedly an old Rook. Old as I am I have no notion of concealing my age. I was once young, that I can well remember, young as the Starlings yonder, and less giddy, having a proper notion of the respect due to age. Old age, in spite of all its infirmities, would meet with greater marks of tenderness and reverence if we thought a little more of the silent grave, on whose brink the feeble steps are tottering.

As far as I can remember I was married then; yes, when I was young, that is true, it is some fifty years ago, and I seemed to grow old in a day when I lost my dear husband. How strangely the scene comes back to my poor old head. It was a dreadful day, the wind was moaning dismally through the crevices of the old tower, while the thunder, bursting in terrible peals from the dark sky, shook the foundations of the grim cathedral, making its grey stones tremble as if with fear. Chill rain fell in torrents, and for the first time menaced our nest, though it was well protected under one of the doorways of the Cathedral of Strasbourg. "I am dying!" said a feeble, yet resolute voice. That was my husband, poor dear; he made up his mind to die and he died. He was always a very determined bird. "Mind the

young ones, love!" These were his last words, and I did mind them, at least I tried to, but they, all of them, died within a week.

Worst of all, I could not die myself, and a sort of cousolation did steal into my widowed heart, that made me feel I would not be justified in dying.

"Travel," said an old Stork, who had nursed my husband. "You will start inconsolable, you will return calmed if not consoled. Many griefs have been starved out and left behind on the king's highways. This Stork was esteemed as a very sensible creature, but the world had hardened her heart : I would sooner kill my children than stifle grief! My children, alas! where are they? A number of friendly Crows, our neighbours, lent weight to the Stork's advice by urging me to leave the old scenes, and I did leave the place, although I almost felt certain that my husband and little ones would reappear some day.

Talk of travelling! why, I have travelled without halting almost for the last fifty years, but it did not take me a fiftieth part of that time to find out that the worldly old Stork was right.

From the moment of entering seriously on my journeys, I was reminded of this proverb by a celebrated moralist.—"One travels in order to relate one's travels." I determined to follow this maxim, and accordingly, armed with note book, set out to explore the world. As occasion presented itself, I related my adventures, and was fortunate in securing listeners who, however, were afraid to applaud what might prove unpopular. At last a bird (in truth no friend of mine), well-known in fashionable circles, hazarded his patronage, saying aloud with the most perfect assurance, that my tales were decidedly good. That made my fortune, not that my tales were improved by this notice, but they became sanctioned, so to speak. Soon my stories flew from beak to beak; I found them everywhere. However little one deserves praise, it is always flattering, I therefore continue.

AN OLD CASTLE.

There was once an old castle—I begin story-telling after the good old fashion, it somehow gives one a fair start, and it is expected—

There was once an old castle, the castle of . . . it neither matters what nor where.

At a time when France boasted almost impregnable castles, this one had often resisted the fiercest onslaughts, although it had been taken and retaken times without number, when the loves of valiant knights for maidens fair caused many bitter feuds. The castle during troublous times had been overthrown little by little, so that almost nothing remained of the original building.

It is sufficient to say, it was taken and pillaged during the Revolution of '93, which demolished many old strongholds; after that of 1815 it was about to be restored, and its fortune was visibly brightening when overtaken by the Revolution of 1830, so ably described by the Hare in the opening pages of this book.

The old fortress was then deprived of its rank and ancient aristocratic fame, and in its degradation, sold to a banker, an individual who, although rich, was ignorant of the archæological fitness of things. So it turned out that the purchaser while devoting wealth and ambition to his new property, gave it the final blow.

Masons were seen at work everywhere, filling up holes, plastering and whitewashing walls; just as if seeking to impart a delicate grace and refinement to a rugged old rock. A terrace was built (renaissance!), supposed to be in keeping with the old remaining parts of the castle, and the chapel became a billiard room. The old place was thoroughly rebuilt, and the new owner satisfied. There was a little of everything about it. Every style under heaven figured in the edifice, the heterogeneous mixture being hideous enough to disturb the reposing dust of ancient Byzantine architects. For all that, the restoration was much applauded by the courtiers of this king of bullion.

Some parts of the building were happily overlooked, or rather saved.

Thus it came about that the poor old castle was renewed, decked with a painted and plastered mask, as inferior to the genuine original as the mask of a harlequin to the face beneath.

As I have already said, I was born in Strasbourg Cathedral, that gem of Alsace, beneath the classic sculptured stone in the great porch. When one has had such a cradle, reared as I was to venerate antiquity and all its triumphs of art, it is natural to protest against the impunity of those who destroy the noble works of the ancients.

The restored portion was tenanted—the terrace, I mean—by barn and other Owls, comical creatures who gave themselves the airs of the first lords of the soil, dukes and duchesses forsooth.

One evening after a long day's flight I arrived at this castle, wearied and in the worst of tempers; out of tune with the world and myself. I was haunted by ennui, and one of those unskilful sportsmen who respect neither age nor species, and to whom nothing is sacred.

By chance I alighted on the balustrade of the terrace, from the midst of which a group of half-dead cypresses was waving as the hour of midnight sounded through the chill air. In romances this hour is never allowed to strike with impunity, but in the true tale I am relating, events must follow their natural course. The hour struck and nothing particular happened. It occurred to me to go to roost so as to be ready for a fresh start in the morning. I accordingly settled myself.

THE DUKE AND DUCHESS.

I was just going to sleep when the pale moonlight revealed an Owl sheltering with one wing an Owlet of rather striking appearance, while with the other he draped himself as would an operatic hero with his toga. I soon overheard them talking about the moon, the weather, &c., or rather singing sentiment to a very lame tune.

"Poor pale moon, if one only believed lovers, its light was made for them!"

I always shrank from intruding myself upon the hospitality of others, so I whispered to a passing Bat, "My dear, would you be so good as to tell your masters a centenarian Rook seeks shelter for the night."

"Who are you addressing?" replied the Bat; "I am neither nurse nor lackey. I am in the service of the Duchess, and have the honour of being her first maid-in-waiting. But who are you, Mrs. Rook of a hundred summers? Where do you hail from? How shall I announce you? What is your title?"

"My titles to consideration are my age and need of rest."

"What a silly old crone," said the stupid creature as she left me. "Nobles are never tired. Weariness is no title, it is the common attribute of the vulgar!"

Soon I came across the third maid-in-waiting, who proved herself two degrees less impertinent. "Do you know," she said, "the first maid has just been scolded on your account? The Duchess was just singing a nocturnal duet with my Lord, when she remarked, 'How dare you? I am invisible to the poor.' Besides, she only entertains titled persons, and it seems you have no title."

"What do you say? have I not eyes to see that your Grand Duke and Duchess are simply Owl and Owlet, on whom those airs sit badly ? "

" Hush ! " whispered the Bat, who was rather talkative. " Speak

A NOCTURNAL DUET.

lower. Were it known that I listened to you, I would be drawn away and perhaps eaten. Since leaving the place of their humble birth they only dream of grandeur, and hope one day to become real aristocrats in the midst of these old tokens of nobility. Bah! the cowl does not make the monk, any more than the castle does the prince. Fly over there, my old friend, to the right, and you will find a better shelter in the ruins of the castle."

"Show me them; lead me to the souvenirs of departed greatness, out of sight of this sickly, spurious, howling waste of plaster and paint, sham, and shoddy. Thank you, my dear, your mistress was only natural when she was rude."

Very little remained of the old castle, yet I would have given fifty restored ones for a single wall of the old pile.

Is there anything more touching in the world than ruins which bear witness, so eloquently, to the greatness of the past?

How can we hesitate between old and new? The great present is but the mimicry of the greater past.

AN OLD FALCON.

This venerable wall enclosed a court as old as itself, and decked on one side with the green shoots of a vine. Lilies and wild tulips were growing between the stones of a dilapidated flight of steps partly covered with ivy. Sweet-scented wall-flowers and a variety of weeds were disputing the spaces with mosses, lichens, grass, briars, and nettles.

Parsley, tufts of samphire and poppies, found a home among the debris, the bright flowers rivalling flames of consuming fire.

When the art of man has ceased to usurp the soil, nature slowly but surely demolishes his handiwork, and recovers her domain.

The court belonged to an old Falcon who was ruined by the revolutions. He was a most hospitable bird, who spent all his income in entertaining, thus the court was the resort of creatures of every fur and feather; resourceless Rats, Shrew-Mice, Mining-Moles, Crickets, and other musicians, some of whom had even taken up their permanent abode within its walls.

Alas, the chivalry and hospitality of the noble Falcon have vanished, and the old genuine sport in which he used to delight is mimicked by a troop of modern sportsmen whom the birds despise. They blaze away pompously with pellets and powder, secretly filling their bags at the nearest market-place.

During my stay at this ruin I had occasion to study the habits of a

Chameleon, whose character interested me greatly. I therefore hasten to publish my observations on this peculiar type of reptile.

WHAT ANIMATES THE HEART OF A CHAMELEON.

I.

In one of the most picturesque niches of the old wall dwelt a Chameleon, one of the handsomest, most distinguished, and most amiable creatures in the world. His figure was slight, his tail slender, his nails curved artistically, his teeth white and pearly, and his eyes quick and animated. His changing colours were all of them most agreeable to behold, indeed the whole aspect of this charming creature was delicate and bewitching.

When he ascended the wall, twisting his body into a thousand elegant forms, or when running through the flowering grass, one never tired of looking at him. Besides no one could be more simple or unaffected than this king of Lizards. He had no experience of the world, at least he only once had occasion to go into society, into the little world of Lizards, which is a hundred times less-corrupt than the world of Snakes, or of men. Yet he determined never to return to it, as the single day which he spent from home seemed to him a century. His contact with the world had left no taint, he lost nothing of that natural candour born of the freedom of the fields, where one sees the budding flowers opening to their fullest, to court the scrutiny of the midday light.

II.

In vain did a crested Jay assure him of his descent from the famous Crocodiles of the Nile, and that his ancestors were thirty-four feet in length. Finding himself so small, and feeling assured that the greatest of his ancestors had not been able to add a single line to his tail, he never troubled himself about his origin. It was sufficient for him to know that he had been brought into the world somehow, and to feel thankful for it. He was alike devoid of aristocratic weaknesses and vulgar vices. The most singular phase of his character was complete indifference to the sentiment of love. The most attractive female Lizards knowing this, had disposed of their hearts and affections to others.

III.

The truth was he had given his heart away, unknown to his friends. Love had stolen upon him without he himself knowing how—it is thus that the passion makes the heart captive. Love had so taken possession of him, that he could not get rid of it if he would. This is how one loves well and wisely.

He loved the sun. When it was out, he was in it, and could think of nothing else. He slept while yet awake, realising the sweetness of noonday dreams.

IV.

Our hero held that Lizard-love was a sentiment unknown, yet beneath the stone on which he sunned himself, a pair of bright eyes feasted upon his every look and action, and a little heart throbbed for him alone. This romantic worshipper feeling that she might just as well lavish her love upon a stone, that her adoration was unobserved, and her passion unrequited, sank into a state of despondency. Haunted by dark doubts, she at last thought of death as the end of her sorrows.

In her extremity, she inquired of an old Rat, whether it was better to live and suffer, or to die and be done with dreams and delusions?

"Die, of course," said the Rat, "if you cannot make yourself agreeable."

"I will die!" she exclaimed; "but he shall know the reason, he shall know all!"

Such is the force of a noble resolution, that the little Lizard who had never till now dared to look her loved one in the face, came forward. But her approaches were met by the gradual retreat of our hero, for he was naturally timid in the presence of females.

"Stay," cried the little one in a tone of despair. "I love you, and you do not even know that I exist. I must die."

"Don't die, my dear," he kindly replied; "that would be highly improper. What do you mean by saying you love me? I am a stranger to you, yet a joke comes well from those pretty lips."

He instantly perceived, for he was an honest fellow, that his cold doubts wounded her sensitive nature, and a light warmer and brighter than the sun flashed from her eyes and took possession of him. He was conquered—he proposed, and they were married.

It always happens so with bachelors. It is the last straw that breaks the camel's back, in love as in life.

Our hero still glories in the sunshine, and takes his ease stretched out before his own doorway.

HISTORY OF THE HOSTS OF THE TERRACE—*Continued.*

The Duchess was by nature a person born to be plump and healthy; to eat her food with the appetite of a country clown, and to enjoy drinking and dining with a savage relish. But she crushed and curbed these tendencies before the world, gratifying them only in secret. In token of her exalted station she professed sensitiveness and delicacy. She was frightened by the fall of a leaf, the flight of a bird or insect, and above all, by her own bulky shadow.

Before folk she uttered nothing but plaintive, feeble cries, reserving the full blast of her lungs for the ears of the Duke. The purest air was too heavy for this ethereal Owl, who detested the sun—the God of paupers, as she termed it—Her husband, astonished at the fine carriage, grace, and society-refinement of his poor barn-Owlet, exhausted his resources in efforts to keep pace with her. Alas! his highest flights left him far behind, so far, indeed, that his faithful spouse bemoaned and bescreeched her fate in being wedded to a person so hideously vulgar.

The Duchess eloped with a Kite, and no one pitied the Duke, for the fall brought by pride never begets pity.

As a finishing blow the lady left a perfumed note for her husband on the spot where they performed their moonlight duets on the terrace. It ran as follows:—

"THE DUKE,—It is part of my destiny to be misunderstood, I shall not therefore attempt to explain to you the motive for my departure,
"(Signed)   THE DUCHESS OF THE TERRACE."

The Duke stood petrified for some moments, after which, seized with a fit of despair, he rushed down to the edge of a dark pool, to ascertain whether the water would inspire him with courage to drown himself. First, he cautiously dipped his beak into the pool to feel its temperature, just as the moon stole out from behind a cloud, and he beheld his image on the surface. His mind at once grasped the frightful picture of his ruffled plumage, and he found sweet solace in arranging his toilet. The notion crossed his mind that the Duchess might repent, if she knew her Lord had died dressed in a style becoming his station.

Bracing his nerves for the fatal plunge, he bent over the pool at an unhappy moment, when it occurred to him, that birds about to die should think twice before they leap, and feel satisfied they have sufficient grounds for the sacrifice. Stepping backwards a few paces, he read his wife's letter for the hundredth and first time.

"What a fool I am!" he exclaimed, "it is possible after all, I am imputing a wrong motive to my wife. There is no knowing; she may have simply gone to the country for a week's repose, and will soon return." In his doubts he determined to consult a Carp, reputed for her knowledge of past, present, and future, and many things besides. The misery of the world is the making of these sorcerers. Approaching the river he cried out, "Tell me my fate old fish famed for finding out facts of the future." Slowly the Carp rose from the water—until her body was half way above the surface—and summoning a troop of piscine spirits, disposed them in a ring. Above floated circles of winged insects in the air, gleaming in the phosphorescent glow reflected from the scales of the water-witches. Dense clouds darkened the atmosphere, rendering the lurid light all the more intense; a profound stillness reigned, so hushed was the scene, that the Owl heard nothing, save the beating of his heart. The sorcerer placing herself in the centre of the ring, sent the spirits wheeling in a mad dance. After the third round, the Carp dived and brought up this reply,

"Your beloved wife is not dead!"

That said, she bent herself like a bow, kissed her tail, and bounding into the air, disappeared.

"She is not dead," repeated the chorus. "Owl, it is said you must die!"

"She is not dead!" repeated the Owl.

"She must be!"——

"Well, never mind. To sacrifice a life so valuable as my own would not mend matters," so he consigned the Carp and her oracle to the —— water.

I have been told that soon after these events, this rich, but weak-minded Owl poisoned himself with a Frog. That is how an Owl dies of love.

My tale ends here. I have plucked and used my last quill, and nothing remains but the stump. Age is telling on me, the effort to write seems too great. I must, therefore, see my physician.

Last Chapter.

In which it will be shown that with beasts, as with men, one revolution follows another, and that they are all more or less alike in fair promises, and failures to fulfil them.

THE Animals were once more assembled, and the tumult of voices worse than ever. Each and all of them were clamouring for reform.

"Of what do you complain?" cried the Fox, addressing the crowd.

"If we only knew our grievances," they replied, "we should not complain."

"We do not know," said a voice, "but if we examine we shall find out."

"Examine them, by all means," cried the Fox.

"What good have you done," shouted the voice, "by compiling a one-sided history? Too much here, and too little there. Let us fight. A revolution will purge the kingdom."

"That is all very well, my friend," replied the orator, "but reason is better than haphazard revolution. You must have learned that by experience."

"Gentlemen," said the Weasel, coming to the aid of his accomplice, the Fox, "it is by practising deceit, we become perfect. Let us begin again."

"I could have said so," cried the Mocking-bird, "ink, ink, always

THE LAST CHAPTER.

ink; it blots out a multitude of sins where good actions would prove of no avail."

"Bravo!" from all sides. "Down with the editors!"
There was only one ink-pot in the room, and it was smashed.
"It is not good for us to be here," said the Weasel to the Fox; "people invariably stone their prophets. Let us go hence!"

THE LAST CHAPTER.

The volume was closed, the animals dispersed, for the keeper appeared on the scene to lock the door.

The Ringdoves mounted to their clouds; the Bear departed with his cubs; the Doves ascended heavenward; while Tortoises, Beetles, Bats, Shrimps, and Apes danced round a bonfire of rejected manuscripts.

THE END.

www.ingramcontent.com/pod-product-compliance
Lightning Source LLC
Chambersburg PA
CBHW032014220426
43664CB00006B/238